RELIGIOUS
SIGNING

RELIGIOUS SIGNING

A Comprehensive Guide for All Faiths

ELAINE COSTELLO, Ph.D.

ILLUSTRATED BY LOIS LEHMAN

BANTAM BOOKS TRADE PAPERBACKS
NEW YORK

A Bantam Books Trade Paperback Original

Copyright © 1986, 2009 by Elaine Costello

Published in the United States by Bantam Books, an imprint of
The Random House Publishing Group, a division of
Random House, Inc., New York.

BANTAM BOOKS and the rooster colophon are registered
trademarks of Random House, Inc.

A previous edition was published in the United States
by Bantam Books, an imprint of The Random House Publishing Group,
a division of Random House, Inc., in 1986.

Library of Congress Cataloging-in-Publication Data
Costello, Elaine.
Religious signing : a comprehensive guide for all faiths /
Elaine Costello ; illustrated by Lois Lehman.
[Updated & completely rev. ed.].
p.   cm.
ISBN 978-0-553-38619-6
1. American sign language—dictionaries.   2. Christianity—Terminology.
3. Church work with the deaf.   4. Judaism—Terminology.   I. Title.
HV2475.C67 2009
419'703—dc22   2009027674

Printed in the United States of America

www.bantamdell.com

6 8 9 7 5

Book design by Jo Anne Metsch

To my wonderful parents,

Rev. Alvin A. Walter and Ella Schiebel Walter,

this book is most lovingly dedicated as a

token of my esteem and love.

CONTENTS

ACKNOWLEDGMENTS

Collecting religious signs to represent different denominations involved the cooperation and expertise of many people. The selflessness of those who contributed signs and gave of their time is hereby noted, as a small recognition of their efforts. It is hoped that in return for their help they find this volume exactly what they hoped it would be and what they need to assist them in their important work with Deaf people.

Rev. Barbara A. Allen *(Episcopal)*
Bader Alomary *(Muslim)*
Gina Bearden *(Baptist)*
Rev. Ray C. Bearden *(Baptist)*
Rev. Clifford Bruffey *(Baptist)*
Father Thomas Coughlin
  (Roman Catholic)
Rev. Don Chevalley *(Baptist)*
Rev. Jay L. Croft *(Episcopal)*
Alexander Fleischman *(Jewish)*
Rev. Ronald E. Friedrich *(Lutheran)*
Cynthia Gilmore
  (Assemblies of God)

Rev. Thomas J. Gilmore
  (Assemblies of God)
Nancy Grandel *(Lutheran)*
Sister Mary Ann Phelan, S. P.
  (Roman Catholic)
Rev. George Natonick *(Lutheran)*
Rev. Daniel Pokorny *(Lutheran)*
Rev. LeRoy E. Schauer
  (Methodist)
Dorothy J. Steffanic
  (Roman Catholic)
Patricia Stevens *(Jewish)*

I would like to express my deepest appreciation to LuAnn Walther, the editor of the first edition of this book, who believed in me and encouraged me to go beyond what I felt confident in doing. Without her encouragement I would not have undertaken the creation of this book. Her sensitivity to the integrity of American Sign Language gave me the courage to compile this text regardless of the magnitude of the task.

    I want to express special thanks to Gabriel Fontana and Miriam Hernandez, who helped me with the research and assembly of this book. Their support and assistance buoyed me when I thought collecting signs and compiling sign illustrations into a usable and comprehensive text was more than I could handle.

Most particularly I am grateful to Lois Lehman, who has incredible skill in rendering drawings of signs from her native language. She consistently exhibits the highest level of professionalism in photographing the models/informants and recording them with lifelike faithfulness and clarity.

INTRODUCTION

Since its early use in Spanish monasteries where silence was prescribed for the monks but manual communication was permitted, to the ever-increasing number of churches, synagogues, and mosques that are providing services to Deaf people today, sign language has played a major role in religious settings. It is thought that more hearing people develop a desire to learn sign language because of contact with Deaf people or interpreters in religious services than as a result of any other influence. The large number of sign language classes conducted in religious buildings is partial evidence of this phenomenon.

The signs presented in this book have been collected from various denominations working with Deaf people. The book does not purport to document all the variations of the signs used to convey religious concepts. It is, however, an earnest attempt to compile those signs that are commonly used, along with an indication of their appropriate application.

Although this book may be used by both beginning and advanced signers, it does not contain signs used in secular life. In order to converse in general terms with Deaf people, it will be necessary to supplement the religious sign vocabulary with signs presented in my companion book, *Signing: How to Speak with Your Hands*. Incorporating the grammatical structure of American Sign Language with the sign vocabulary will result in mastering sign language as it is used by Deaf people.

The Influence of the Church in Deaf Education

Ancient texts indicate that among the Egyptians, the Greeks, and, later on, the Romans, Deaf people were denied the rights of inheritance, marriage, education, and even salvation. The exclusion of Deaf people from religious rituals was more a result of ignorance than it was discrimination.

The first recorded use of sign language was not among Deaf people, but among hearing people. Monks, under vows of silence, used sign language in Cistercian monasteries as early as 328 A.D. and are still using it today, although the practice of silence has become somewhat relaxed. The number of signs used by the monks in the ancient Spanish monasteries seemed to vary from order to order, but by the eleventh century, sign lists from different monasteries averaged about four hundred signs. The more signs recorded on a list from a monastery, the stricter the code of silence. These signs and their system of use differ greatly from the sign language used by Deaf people. Nevertheless, it is certain that the monastic use of sign language had great influence on early attempts to teach Deaf children through the ages.

A Spanish nobleman placed his two Deaf sons in one of these Cistercian monasteries in 1545, presumably to prevent them from procreating and to put them out of sight. But there, one of the Benedictine monks, Pablo Ponce de León, began to teach the children about the doctrines of Christianity, thereby establishing the first school for the deaf. Little is known of Ponce de León's method, but it is said that he primarily used reading and writing to teach speech. It is also thought that he used a manual alphabet and signs, both drawn from the monastic environment. One of the boys died young, but the other learned to speak and sign in the monastery choir. As a result, other Deaf children of Spanish nobility were also sent to Ponce de León for instruction.

About thirty years after the death of Ponce de León, Juan Pablo Bonet, another Spanish priest, published a book about teaching the Deaf. In that book Bonet presented a system of training the Deaf by means of a one-handed manual alphabet. There is enough historical evidence to suggest that it was the same alphabet used by Ponce de León, and it is essentially the same manual alphabet used in the United States today.

The work among Deaf children in Spain influenced the establishment of educational work among the Deaf in France, although it lagged behind the Spanish work by about two hundred years. Jacob Rodrigues Péreire, the first teacher of the Deaf in France, was a Spanish native who migrated to France to escape religious persecution. Péreire began first by teaching his own Deaf sister, but after his reputation spread, he took on other pupils whom he taught to read, talk, lip-read, and use the manual alphabet.

The second leader in establishing educational practices in France was a Catholic monk. Abbé Charles Michel de l'Épée, who in the eighteenth century undertook the religious instruction of the two Deaf daughters of one of his parishioners. Espousing the concept that sign language was the natural language of the Deaf, Épée attempted to adapt the signs he found used by the Deaf community in Paris to French syntax and morphology, not unlike the manual English systems used in the United States today. He also used the manual alphabet from Bonet's book and the articulation techniques that had been published in a Dutch text. Épée's techniques were so successful that his fame spread to other European countries, who sent educators to him for training so they could begin schools for the deaf in their own countries.

Épée's work was carried on by another French priest, Abbé Sicard, who moved educational practices toward a more natural use of sign language and its grammar. It was Sicard who taught the French techniques to the American clergyman Thomas Hopkins Gallaudet, who had been traveling throughout Europe seeking methods of instruction to use with the Deaf in the United States. This French influence is evident in the structure of American Sign Language today.

When Reverend Gallaudet returned to the United States, he brought with him a Deaf French teacher, Laurent Clerc. The efforts of Gallaudet and Clerc resulted in the opening of the first permanent American school for the deaf, in Hartford, Connecticut. As in Europe, religion was an important influence in the founding of this school. Reverend Gallaudet, an Episcopal minister, recorded the following in his diary at the beginning of his work: "O Almighty God, Thou knowest my desire to be devoted to Thy service and to be made the instrument of training the deaf and dumb in heaven."

In the fifty years following the opening of Gallaudet's school in 1817, eighteen schools for the deaf were founded and funded by state legislatures. Of these eighteen schools, eight were begun under the leadership of a minister and two under sons of ministers.

Ministry to the Deaf People in the United States

Deaf ministry among different religious denominations has taken on a number of forms. In most instances churches and synagogues provide sign language interpreters to sign church services and other religious ceremonies. Often the interpreters are volunteers or children of Deaf parents. Generally such congregations have predominately hearing members, and the interpreter provides a vital link between the clergy and the few Deaf parishioners. Although this is an efficient way to reach both Deaf and hearing members simultaneously, Deaf people tend not to participate in other functions outside the regularly scheduled services since they cannot freely communicate with the other members. Some problems may also arise from issues of confidentiality in counseling sessions when an interpreter is used to assist the exchange between the clergy and the Deaf person.

To facilitate direct communication with their Deaf members, many ministers and rabbis learn sign language themselves. In some denominations special training programs are available in seminaries for students interested in future ministry to the Deaf. More often clergy take sign language instruction after being assigned to a congregation with a few Deaf members. As an even more effective measure to ready Deaf people, Deaf clergy have been ordained into almost every denomination. The Episcopal Church and the Methodist Church have particularly espoused this practice through the years, supporting their contention that a Deaf minister is more capable of ministering to Deaf people than a hearing minister because of a deeper understanding and rapport with his Deaf parishioners.

The following sections trace the history of religious ministry to Deaf people in the United States among those denominations whose early efforts have developed into fairly extensive ministries. In addition to denominations covered in depth, some notice should be given to other denominations with smaller, yet notable, ministries to Deaf people. The Mennonite Church began its ministry to the Deaf in 1911 and has concentrated its efforts in Pennsylvania and several northern states. The Church of Jesus Christ of Latter-Day Saints began its activities by teaching Deaf children in 1896, later merging their educational program into the Utah State School for the Deaf. The church's present efforts now reach nineteen communities served by fifty-eight missionaries, half of whom are deaf themselves. The Assemblies of God church established its first church for deaf members in 1929 in Los Angeles. Their evangelistic work has expanded tremendously among the Deaf during the past eighty years. Presently the church supports eight ministers to the Deaf and a large number of interpreters who serve in 340 churches across the country. The Church of Christ began its ministry to the Deaf in Texas in 1935 and now has about one hundred interpreters. The independent Christian Church began its ministry to the Deaf in Idaho in 1957, presently serving approximately eight congregations with ordained ministers and interpreters. Notably the Christian Church supports Deaf Missions in Council Bluffs, Iowa, whose goal is to prepare and distribute visual and printed materials for use in deaf ministries. Deaf Missions is involved in the ambitious Omega Project, an effort to record the Bible in American Sign Language on videotape/DVDs. The Presbyterian Church has been active in deaf ministry in a limited way since 1930, and in 1982 began formally to involve Deaf people in church decisions that affect them.

Episcopal. The Episcopal Church was the first denomination to meet the religious needs of Deaf people in the United States. The first known church services for the Deaf were held in 1846 by the Protestant Episcopal Church in Philadelphia in what now is known as All Souls Church. Shortly after that, Reverend Thomas

Hopkins Gallaudet's eldest son, Thomas Gallaudet, began conducting services in sign language in New York City in what is now Saint Ann's Church for the Deaf. These two churches were the beginning of any extensive ministry of the Episcopal Church among Deaf people.

The Episcopal Church has taken the leadership in installing Deaf priests to the ministry. The first Deaf man ever ordained to the ministry was Henry Winter Syle, who was admitted as a candidate for Holy Orders in 1875 amid considerable opposition from the bishops and priests of the church. He advanced to the priesthood in 1883 and spent the next seven years, before his premature death, establishing many new programs and services for the Episcopal Church in Pennsylvania. Through the years approximately forty-five Deaf men have been ordained to the priesthood of the Episcopal Church.

In 1972 the Episcopal Church established an umbrella organization for ministry to the Deaf nationwide. That organization, now known as the Episcopal Conference of the Deaf, provides financial support to establish new programs within the church.

Roman Catholic. The Roman Catholic Church was the second religious body to administer specially to the needs of Deaf people in the United States. Laurent Clerc, the Deaf teacher who Thomas Hopkins Gallaudet brought back from Europe with him to teach in the first school for the deaf, was a Roman Catholic. However, shortly after arriving in the United States, Clerc left the Catholic faith, and Catholic clergy were not permitted to enter the school for the next eighty years.

The first Catholic school for the deaf was founded in 1839 by two Sisters of Saint Joseph from Lyons, France, who began the school in a convent in St. Louis, Missouri. That school continues to this day, more than 150 years later. The opening of the Saint Joseph's Institute for the Deaf was followed twenty years later by the opening of Saint Mary's School for the Deaf in Buffalo, New York, and ten more schools have been established since that time. The Roman Catholic Church has taken the leadership in establishing parochial schools for the deaf, including setting up special classrooms for Deaf children in their existing day schools since the early 1950s.

In terms of pastoral care, the Roman Catholic Church presently has more than one hundred full-time salaried ministers and approximately fifty part-time salaried ministers for the Deaf, assisted by another four hundred lay workers. More than half of the dioceses have salaried personnel to minister to their Deaf parishioners. At the present time three Deaf men have been ordained as priests in this faith, the first of whom, Father Thomas Coughlin, is a model for sign illustrations in this book.

Lutheran. The Lutheran Church–Missouri Synod (LC–MS) was the third denomination to take an active interest in the spiritual needs of Deaf people. Its work began quite by accident when Deaf children came for religious instruction to what was intended to be a new orphanage in Detroit, Michigan. Instead, the institution opened in 1874 as a school for the deaf. It was by special request of one of the graduates of this school that church services for Deaf people were begun in 1894 at what is now Bethlehem Lutheran Church in Chicago, Illinois. August P. Reinke was the first pastor to that congregation; as his reputation for being able to conduct church services in sign language spread, he was called upon to establish a regular circuit of preaching in various Midwestern cities. Soon thereafter, LC–MS officially recognized the mission work among the Deaf and established a Deaf Mission Commission. Within the next five years the number of pastors serving Deaf people grew to seven, and by the time LC–MS celebrated its fiftieth anniversary of working with the Deaf, there were twenty pastors conducting church services in approximately 275 cities across the United States.

The Lutheran Church–Missouri Synod has special training programs in both of its seminaries for students wishing to study for the deaf ministry. At the present time there are approximately fifty full-time LC–MS pastors working with Deaf people, a few of whom are deaf themselves. The pastors are organized for the purpose of mutual support and continued education into the Ephphatha Conference, which was founded in 1903 and continues to meet annually. The International Deaf Association was organized to assist the LC–MS deaf ministry throughout the world. LC–MS supports one school for the deaf. The original one in Detroit has changed focus to serving multihandicapped children. The new school for the deaf, Mill Neck Manor, opened in Long Island, New York, in 1951, and continues with state and private support to serve Deaf students from preschool through high school.

A second Lutheran synod, the Lutheran Church in America (LCA) merged with a third Lutheran synod, the American Lutheran Church (ALC) to form the Evangelical Lutheran Church in America (ELCA) in 1987. The LCA had begun its deaf ministry in 1889 at what is now the Mount Airy School for the Deaf in Pennsylvania, where an LCA pastor began giving religious instruction to the students. The work of LCA among the Deaf has largely concentrated in the state of Pennsylvania over the years. The deaf ministry of ALC began with religious instruction of Deaf children at the Minnesota State School for the Deaf at Faribault, Minnesota, in 1898. Similar to the growth of LC–MS, ALC pastors began conducting services on an itinerant basis across the upper Midwest. The pastors were organized under the Ephphatha Missions to the Deaf and Blind giving synodical support. The first ALC church especially for Deaf members was the Bread of Life Lutheran Church for the Deaf, founded in 1950 in Minneapolis. ELCA moved ministries serving Deaf people to their disability ministry which served various disabilities, including developmentally disabled people. In 2001, in re-sponse to many requests from Deaf people, a director was hired to serve deaf ministry exclusively, thus separating it from disability ministries.

Methodist. The fourth religious body to begin work among Deaf people was the Methodist Church. Beginning in 1890, Philip J. Hasenstab, a Deaf teacher from the Illinois School for the Deaf in Jacksonville, Illinois, made monthly trips to Chicago to conduct services for the Deaf community. Three years later he left teaching and became a full-time pastor of the Chicago Mission for the Deaf. Hasenstab was the first of a large number of Deaf men who have been ordained into the Methodist ministry through the years, supporting the church's contention that a Deaf minister has a deeper understanding of the problems and needs of Deaf people.

Shortly after the founding of the Chicago mission, three more Methodist missions were started, in Baltimore, Cincinnati, and Florida. At the present time, the United Methodist Church has more than fifteen organized ministries especially for Deaf people and many more interpreted services for Deaf people who attend churches whose members are predominantly hearing.

In 1977 the United Methodist Congress of the Deaf was organized with the primary purpose of building support systems for hearing impaired Methodist members. It also develops religious curriculum materials and advances an awareness among hearing churches regarding ministry to Deaf people.

Baptist. After the turn of the century, the most active Baptist fellowship working among the Deaf began conducting religious services for the Deaf. The work began under the leadership of a Deaf man, John Michaels, principal of the Arkansas School for the Deaf, who traveled from city to city organizing Sunday School classes for Deaf people. His work and that of a Deaf woman who went to Cuba in 1902 to provide religious instruction were the first two missionary activities of the Southern Baptist Convention under its Home Mission Board. From these beginnings the work of the Southern Baptist Convention has grown to thirty-eight churches especially for Deaf people and about eight hundred other churches with special arrangements for Deaf people to participate in their services and programs. The most common arrangement is to have lay workers assist the minister in providing Sunday School classes or special Bible study groups. More than one thousand interpreters are in their employment to assist Deaf people in participating in the activities of hearing members of the congregation.

There are a number of Baptist fellowships actively involved in work with Deaf parishioners. One group, the Independent Baptist Church, has a sizable number of hearing and Deaf ministers, lay ministers, and interpreters. It supports a school for Deaf children, a high school, and even a college-degree program. One of its largest programs is a camp founded in 1950 by Dr. and Mrs. Bill Rich in Murfreesboro, Tennessee, for the purpose of providing spiritual training for Deaf people. As a result of programs for more than one thousand campers annually, more than eight hundred Sunday School classes for Deaf children have been begun, both in the United States and abroad.

Jewish. Around the turn of the 20th century, more than two million Eastern European Jews moved to the United States for religious freedom. Deaf Jews organized themselves into Hebrew associations to provide a place for members to meet for social and religious activities. New York City, the port of arrival for many Jewish immigrants, was the primary headquarters for such associations. The Hebrew Association of the Deaf, and what was later known as the New York Society of the Deaf, founded in 1907 and 1911 respectively, were two of the earliest associations and they are still active. They were followed by similar associations in Philadelphia, Baltimore, Cleveland, and Los Angeles.

During World War II, Nazi policy was to declare Deaf people "genetically diseased." Deaf people were denied marriage licenses, over 15,000 were sterilized, some experimented on, and many were murdered. Among the millions of victims of Nazi terror were thousands of Deaf Jews.

The National Congress of Jewish Deaf was established in 1956 and served as a clearinghouse of information about religion, education, and culture for approximately 170,000 hearing-impaired Jews in all branches of Judaism. Alexander Fleischman, who served as a sign model for this book, was the executive director of the congress for more than sixteen years.

A major concern in the Jewish faith, just as in other religions, is to encourage rabbis to work with Deaf people and for rabbinical seminaries to admit Deaf candidates. With increased numbers of men and women becoming ordained into the rabbinate for work with the Deaf, Deaf people now have the opportunity to participate in Jewish religious observances in most major cities. Only recently, the first Deaf rabbi, Rabbi Fred Friedman—a sign language model in this book—was ordained in 1985, in Baltimore. He is one of six regional representatives across the nation for Our Way, the outreach program for Jewish Deaf of all ages of the National Conference of Synagogue Youth.

Islam. At present there is no documented history of ministry to Deaf Muslims in the United States or even in the world. Deaf Muslims have largely been denied an Islamic education because there are so few teachers who can teach them about Islam, and how to give proper submission to Allah. Without having enough Islamic instruction, Deaf Muslims are left without any support to help them do what is right under their religion, and they often fall under peer pressure and do things that are contrary to the teachings of Islam. Many Deaf Muslims go to the mosque to observe Friday prayers, and after sitting for the duration of the sermon, they return home without having processed anything that the imam said.

There are a few Deaf people who are literate and have been able to read English versions of the Holy Qur'an on their own, but they are far outnumbered by those who cannot read it. Many of them only know what little their parents have taught them or what they have seen. Some people mistakenly assume that because Deaf Muslims cannot hear, the concept of Islam and the teaching of the Holy Qur'an in Arabic are too difficult for them. The Holy Qur'an makes it clear that the search and learning of knowledge is compulsory for all Muslims, including the Deaf.

Since June 2007, Friday prayers or *Khubah* are being interpreted into American Sign Language for Deaf Muslims in Northern Virginia's Dar Al-Hijrah Islamic Center. Since providing an interpreter, the attendance of Deaf Muslims has increased from two or three attendees to about thirty. It is not known if interpreters are assisting Deaf Muslims elsewhere in the United States.

As awareness spreads about the challenges Deaf Muslims face, a growing number of initiatives are beginning in the Muslim world. Groups like the U.S.-based Global Deaf Muslims are working to establish universal signs for Islamic words and concepts. This group, with headquarters at Gallaudet University in Washington, D.C., assisted in identifying signs related to the Islamic religion to include in this book. The Canadian Association of Muslims with Disabilities wants to improve access for people with disabilities by providing texts, classes, and services.

Even Deaf Muslims from Islamic countries and Europe lack confidence when asked about Islam. In Egypt, a new group called *Sarkha* (Cry) provides interpreters for mosque services for Cairo's Deaf community. In Lebanon, the Al-Hadi Institute for the Deaf and Blind has provided opportunities for young, Deaf Muslims to express themselves artistically. In the United Kingdom, the Muslim Youth Helpline has held the first ever Muslim Deaf Awareness day. A few mosques are beginning to cater to Deaf congregants with the help of the Muslim Deaf Group (MDG). The MDG hosts an Internet forum as well as monthly talks at mosques in London, Manchester, and Leeds. The Muslim Deaf Sisters Project has been working to translate the Qur'an into British Sign Language. In Holland, a Dutch organization that assists Deaf children developed 163 Islam-related signs so parents could communicate with their children. Endeavors such as these are helping promote an awareness and understanding of hearing-impairment issues that are often lacking in Muslim societies.

Signing in Religious Settings

Signs used for religious services and ceremonies are closely aligned with the particular doctrines of the faith represented. One must be very careful in choosing a particular sign or variation for an English gloss. In fact, it may often be better to use a string of signs to explain the sign's meaning rather than choose one sign, thus assuring that the concept is clearly and conceptually presented. This cautionary note is not meant to deter the beginner from learning religious signs, but rather to exercise somewhat more sensitivity in the selection of signs than one normally would with secular signs with generic references.

Religious signs are usually formed larger and more dramatically than when used in a personal conversation. Signs that traditionally may be formed with one hand are often rendered with two hands—CELEBRATE and HONOR, for example. One of the reasons for these enlarged movements is for clarity when leading a congregation. The exaggerated signs, when performed smoothly, are especially beautiful in the "singing" of hymns.

Many religious signs are iconic, that is, they resemble some aspect or character of the object they represent. For example, the sign CROWN looks very much like the hands are holding a crown and placing it on the head. In this book, the text accompanying each drawing brings these mnemonic clues to the reader's attention to help recall the sign. The text may also indicate the appropriate usage of that sign in a religious setting.

Many religious signs are also initialized, that is, the hands are formed like the fingerspelled first letter of the English gloss for that sign. Initialized signs are often used to differentiate between the literal meanings of a sign that may have originally had several English glosses. LAW, COMMANDMENT, HALACHA, and TESTAMENT, for example, have some similarities in meaning, but the initialized handshapes distinguish them from one another for precision in communication. In this book, signs that are formed in a similar manner but with different initialized handshapes are cross-referenced next to the drawings. Learning these similarly formed signs together sometimes helps in remembering them.

The signs in this book are more nationally representative than the models' current home addresses might indicate. Because ministers, priests, and rabbis tend to travel from region to region to attend conferences and are often reassigned to different parishes or communities, the signs in this book are, for the most part, being used nationally.

It is hoped that this volume will help the process of identifying those signs that fledgling congregations and others serving in a ministry to Deaf people find most applicable for their use. One must keep in mind that Deaf people themselves do not necessarily know or use all the religious signs contained in this book any more than a hearing person automatically knows or uses all of the words in a dictionary.

The Signs in This Book

The signs in this book were collected from interviews with Deaf and hearing ministers, priests, rabbis, laypeople, and interpreters who shared their expertise with a common sense of dedication and cooperation. In each case, the interviewed person seemed to be cognizant of the book's goal: to present widely accepted signs that appropriately represent each denomination's doctrines. In the case of minor variations of the signs suggested by different informants, this book illustrates the most common sign and notes the variation in the text under the drawing. If sign variations seemed quite diverse but widely used, they were included in the book as alternates.

Sign variations are probably more prevalent in the use of religious signs than with a more general vocabulary. The reason for these variations is that each religious denomination has terminology unique to the doctrines taught within that church. The doctrines must often be understood before the concepts can be transliterated into sign language. Prior to the publication of the first edition of this book, there were no comprehensive books of religious signs. Interpreters unfamiliar with the terminology and doctrines often had difficulty selecting appropriate strings of signs or equivalent signs for the concepts in the sermons, liturgies, religious ceremonies, and hymns. As a result the interpreters developed "impromptu" signs to facilitate expressing often repeated terms. After frequent use the impromptu signs are often adopted by the members of that congregation and after time may have spread within the region or denomination.

You will note that the "gloss" or English word equivalent written in this book, as is true in most sign language books, is written in all capital letters (e.g., COMMUNION). The reason that this linguistic notation is used is to emphasize that signs really communicate concepts, not English words. You may also notice that the word "deaf" is capitalized when referring to Deaf people or Deaf culture, although it begins with a small letter when referring to the disability of being deaf (e.g., school for the deaf).

Most of the illustrations in this book are presented from the front view of the signer. This means that the illustrations show a right-handed signer, and the descriptions are written for persons with a right-handed dominance. Left-handed signers should reverse the signs.

Lois Lehman's sign illustrations in this book have multiple images using arrows to describe the sign formation and movement as accurately as possible. The written explanation specifies the following: 1) the handshape of each hand; 2) the starting and ending location of each sign; 3) the palm orientation of each hand (e.g., the direction each palm is facing); and 4) the movement of one or both hands. The handshape is generally described as letters from the Manual Alphabet shown on page xxiv or one of the handshapes or numbers shown in the following charts. Grammatical forms used in religious settings are given for some signs, as well as other "synonyms" for signs used outside a religious setting.

HANDSHAPES USED IN THIS BOOK

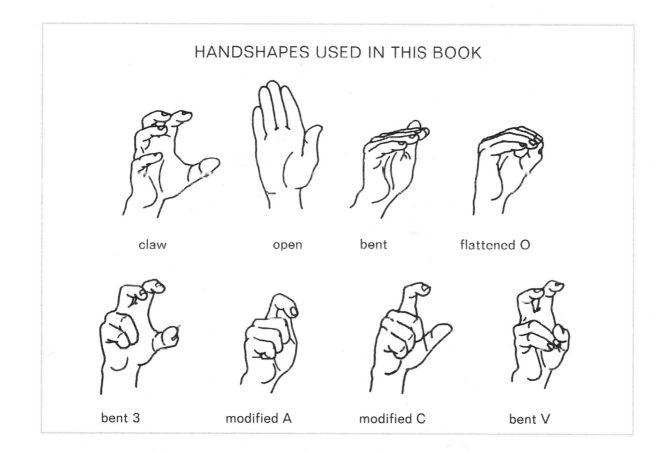

claw   open   bent   flattened O

bent 3   modified A   modified C   bent V

NUMBER HANDSHAPES USED IN THIS BOOK

one

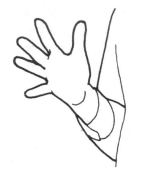

five

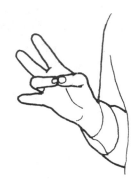

seven

ten

fourteen

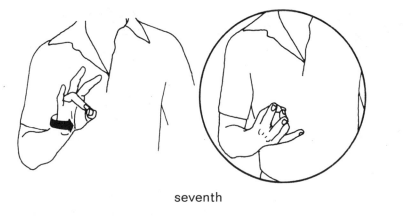

seventh

You will note that many signs (e.g., RE-DEEMER, SAVIOR, etc.) include the notation "Add the person marker." The marker is formed by bringing both flat hands, palms facing each other and fingers pointing forward, down along the side of the body. This marker is often used to designate an occupation, such as PREACHER, or nationality, such as AMERICAN.

Good luck with your signing. You will find Deaf people to be patient and willing to assist you in your efforts. Use every opportunity to practice your skills with Deaf people and observe firsthand the richness of this unique language, which uses space and movement for the purpose of communication.

THE PERSON MARKER

THE MANUAL ALPHABET

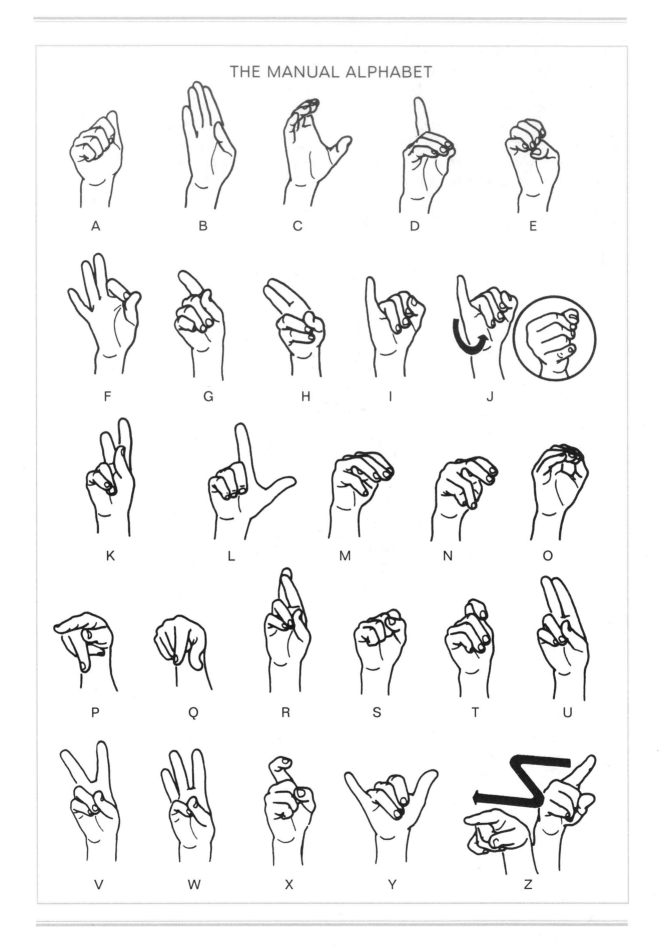

RELIGIOUS
SIGNING

SIGN ENTRIES

ABIDE (A)

This sign indicates a place where one is to remain or stay for a period of time.

Formation: Move the right *Y hand,* palm facing down, downward in front of the right side of the body with a deliberate movement.

Same sign for STAY

ABIDE (B) See LIVE

ABOVE, OVER

The hand moves to a position above the other hand and symbolizes the area on high from where God rules the world.

Formation: Starting with the palm of the right *open hand* lying on the back of the left *open hand,* elbows out and palms facing down, bring the right hand upward in a spiraling movement.

ABRAHAM, IBRAHIM *(Hebrew)*

The formation of this sign represents God staying Abraham's arm as he raised the knife to slay his son Isaac.

Formation: The right *A hand,* palm facing left, is brought deliberately down at a forward angle from in front of the right shoulder. The left *C hand,* palm up, moves upward to clasp the right forearm and stop it abruptly as it descends.

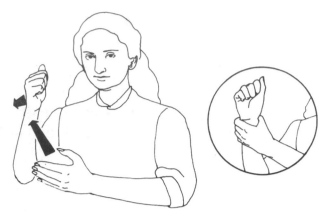

ABSOLUTION (A)

This sign is a combination of ANNOUNCE and FORGIVE signifying the declaratory statement that sins are forgiven after confession or penance.

Formation: Start with both extended index fingers touching each side of the mouth, palms facing in. Twist the wrists to bring the fingers outward past the shoulders, palms facing forward and fingers pointing upward at an angle. Then brush the fingers of the right *open hand* across the palm of the left *open hand* from heel to the fingers with a repeated movement.

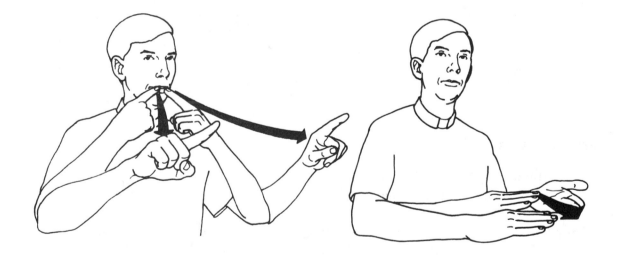

ABSOLUTION (B) See BLESS (A)(B), FORGIVE

ABSTAIN See FAST (A)

ABUNDANT (A), BOUNTY, PLENTY

The hands indicate a cup that is full and over-flowing.

Formation: Push the palm of the right *open hand,* palm down and fingers pointing forward, across the thumb side of the left *S hand,* palm right, curving the hand downward as it goes over the left index finger.

Related forms: ABUNDANCE, ABUN-DANTLY, BOUNTIFUL, PLENTIFUL

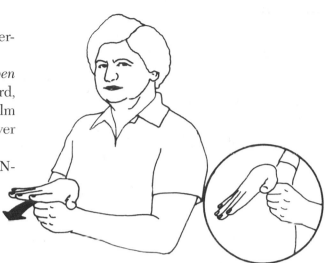

ABUNDANT (B), BOUNTIFUL

The hands in this sign seem to hold a large quantity.

Formation: Beginning with the fingertips of both *curved hands* touching in front of the body, palms facing each other, bring the hands outward to in front of each side of the chest.

Related form: ABUNDANCE

Same sign for A LOT

ACCOMPLISH See FULFILL

ACCUSE, AT FAULT, BLAME

This is a directional sign that seems to push re-sponsibility or blame at whomever it is directed.

Formation: Move the right *A hand,* palm left and thumb extended upward, in a downward arc toward the referent across the back of the left *open hand,* palm down.

Note: If you are the one being accused, direct the right thumb back toward oneself. The left hand may be an *S hand* instead of an *open hand.*

ACKNOWLEDGE See CONFESS (A)

ACQUIRE See OBTAIN

ADAM (A)

This is an initialized sign in the masculine position and signifies Adam's position as the first man.

Formation: Touch the right temple with the thumb of the *right hand,* palm facing forward.

ADAM (B)

This is the Islamic sign for Adam, the father of humankind and God's first prophet. In Islam, Adam is considered God's vice-regent (*caliph*) on earth.

Formation: Move the right *B hand,* palm facing left and fingers pointing up, upward in front of the right shoulder.

ADMIT See CONFESS

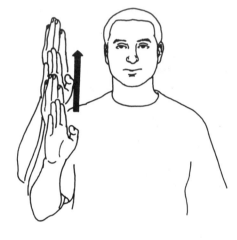

ADMONISH, WARN

The sign represents a slap on the wrist as a warning.

Formation: Slap the back of the left *open hand* with the fingers of the right *open hand,* both palms facing down.

Related forms: ADMONITION, WARNING

ADORE See WORSHIP

ADULTERY (A)

This is an initialized sign and the movement indicates the alternating attention that an unfaithful married person gives his or her spouse and then another person outside the marriage

Formation: Tap the heel of the right *A hand,* palm facing forward, alternating on each finger of the left *V hand* held in front of the chest, palm facing in and fingers pointing up.

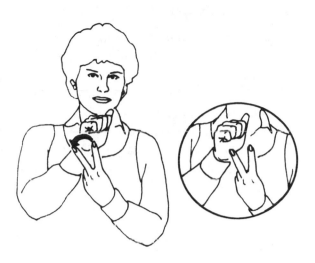

ADULTERY (B)

The sign seems to show someone slipping around the corner or behind someone's back for an affair.

Formation: Move the palm side of the right *open hand,* palm facing right and fingers pointing forward, around the little-finger side of the left *open hand,* palm facing right and fingers pointing up.

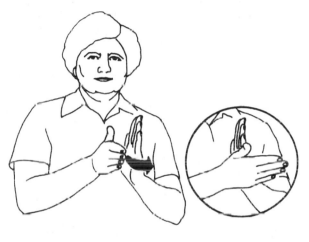

ADVENT, COMING

This is a directional form of COME and signifies the birth of Christ and the preparation period of four weeks before His Coming at Christmas.

Formation: Beginning with both extended index fingers pointing up in front of the head, palms facing in, bring both hands down simultaneously.

ADVERSARY See ENEMY

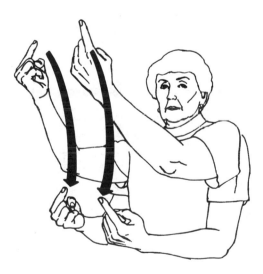

ADVOCATE, FOUNDATION, SUPPORT

The action of the right hand pushing the left hand upward shows active support for a cause.

Formation: Bring the knuckles of the right *S hand* upward under the little-finger side of the left *S hand,* both palms facing in, pushing it upward in front of the chest.

Same sign for ADVOCACY, IN FAVOR OF

See also HELP and VICAR for signs formed in a similar manner.

AFFILIATE See UNITE

AFFLICTION, PATIENT, SUFFER

The movement of the hand in this sign indicates a person keeping quiet or without complaint while enduring suffering.

Formation: Move the thumb of the right *A hand,* palm facing left, downward from the mouth to the chin.

Same sign for BEAR, ENDURE, TOLERATE

AFRAID See FEAR (A)(B)(C)

AGAPE

This sign is a combination of GOD and LOVE signifying the Greek word meaning "selfless love."

Formation: Move the right *B hand,* palm left, from above the front of the head downward in an arc toward the forehead and down in front of the face. Then with both palms facing the body, hold the right *S hand* across the left *S hand,* which is held on the chest over the heart.

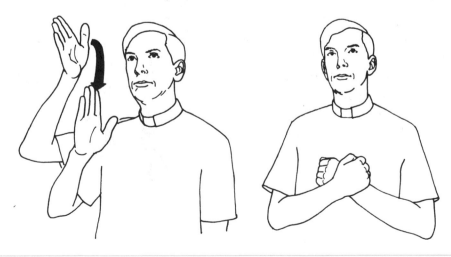

AGONY See SUFFER (B)

AISLE, WAY

The hands outline a passageway, such as between rows of seats in a church.

Formation: Move both *open hands* forward simultaneously, palms facing each other and fingers pointing forward and held several inches apart in front of the waist.

Same sign for PATH, ROAD

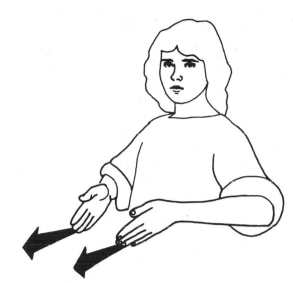

ALIVE See LIVE

ALLAH, GOD

This is the foremost name for the supreme being according to Islamic belief. Humans are called to worship and devote their faith only to him; hence he is the object of *Islam* ("submission").

Formation: Move the extended right index finger, palm facing left and finger pointing up, upward in front of the right shoulder.

ALLELUIA, HALLELUJAH

As an expression of praise of thanksgiving to God, this sign is a combination of PRAISE and CELEBRATION.

Formation: Bring both *open hands,* palms facing each other and fingers pointing up, together in front of the chest. Then raise both *modified A hands* near each shoulder, moving them in small circles outward.

ALMIGHTY (A), OMNIPOTENT

This sign is a combination of ALL and POWER, an attribute referring to God's unlimited universal power.

Formation: With the right *open hand,* palm facing forward, near the left shoulder, make a large loop to the right ending in the upturned palm of the left *open hand.* Then move both *S hands,* palms facing in, from near each side of the chest forward with a deliberate movement, ending abruptly.

See also POWER and MIGHTY for alternate signs.

ALMIGHTY (B) See POWER (A)(B)

ALONE

The single finger moving in a circle is an emphatic form of the sign ONE.

Formation: With the right extended index finger pointing up, palm facing in, rotate the arm and hand in a counterclockwise circle.

ALTAR

The sign is an initialized form of TABLE. The hands outline the shape of the altar, the structure before which the divine offices are recited and upon which the Eucharist is celebrated.

Formation: With the thumbs of both *A hands* touching each other in front of the chest, palms facing forward, move the hands apart to about shoulder width and then downward a short distance without changing orientation.

ALWAYS, CONSTANTLY, EVER

The circular motion of this sign shows something never ending.

Formation: Move the extended right index finger, palm angled up, in small clockwise circles near the right shoulder.

See also ETERNAL for an alternate sign.

AMAZE See ASTONISH

AMEN See PRAY

AMISH See MENNONITE

ANGEL, CHERUB, SERAPH

The hands represent the movement of wings traditionally attributed to angels, the immortal spiritual beings attending to God's will.

Formation: Touch the fingertips of both *bent hands* to the shoulders, palms facing down and elbows close at the sides. Turn the wrists outward and bend the hands up and down.

Same sign for WINGS

ANGER, FURY, RAGE, WRATH

The tense fingers represent angry emotions rased up in the body.

Formation: Bring both *claw hands,* palms facing in and fingers pointing toward each other, upward from near each other at the waist and out toward each shoulder.

ANGLICAN CHURCH, THE CHURCH OF ENGLAND

This sign is a combination of ANOINT (A) and CHURCH and refers to the form of Christianity that was shaped when, during the reign of Henry the VIII, England broke away from the Catholic Church by dissolving allegiance to the Pope.

Formation: Draw the thumbnail of the right *A hand,* palm down, first downward on the forehead a short distance and then from left to right. Then tap the thumb side of the right *C hand* on the back of the left *open hand,* palm facing down.

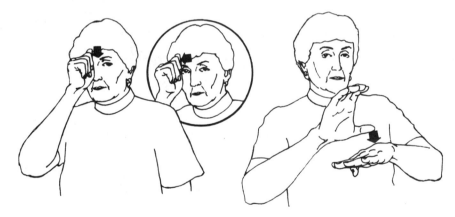

ANNOUNCE, ANNUNCIATION, CONFESS (FAITH), DECLARE, EVANGELISM, NOEL, PROCLAIM

The fingers indicate taking words from the mouth and declaring them broadly.

Formation: Start with both extended index fingers touching each side of the mouth, palms facing in. Twist the wrists to bring the fingers outward past the shoulders, palms facing forward and fingers pointing upward at an angle.

Related form: ANNOUNCEMENT

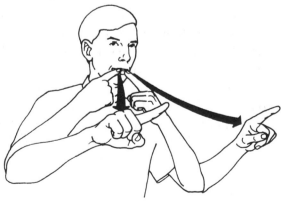

ANNUL See CONDEMN (A)

ANNUNCIATION (A)

This sign is a combination of ANNOUNCE and MARY and refers to the angel's announcement to the Virgin Mary that she would bear a son, Jesus.

Formation: Start with both extended index fingers touching each side of the mouth, palms facing in. Twist the wrists to bring the fingers outward past the shoulders, palms facing forward and fingers pointing upward at an angle. Then bring the right *M hand,* palm down, in an arc following the shape of the head from the top of the left side of the head to the right shoulder.

ANNUNCIATION (B) See ANNOUNCE

ANOINT (A), LENT

The sign symbolizes how a priest anoints a person's forehead with oil as a sign of consecration in a religious ceremony.

Formation: Draw the thumbnail of the right *A hand,* palm down, first downward on the forehead a short distance and then from left to right.

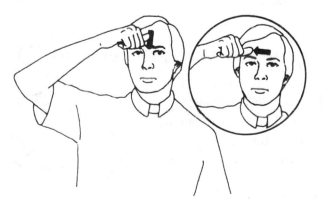

ANOINT (B), ATONE, OIL

The hand seems to pour oil over another as is done as a sign of consecration in a religious ceremony.

Formation: Move the thumb of the right *A hand* over the back of the left *A hand,* both palms facing down.

Related form: ATONEMENT

ANOINTING THE SICK

This sign is a combination of ANOINT and SICK. It is used in the Roman Catholic Church to indicate the sacrament formerly known as Last Rites, which is administered to terminally ill people.

Formation: Draw the thumbnail of the right *A hand,* palm down, first downward on the forehead a short distance and then from left to right. Then touch the bent middle finger of the right *5 hand* to the forehead while touching the bent middle finger of the left *5 hand* to the stomach, both palms facing in.

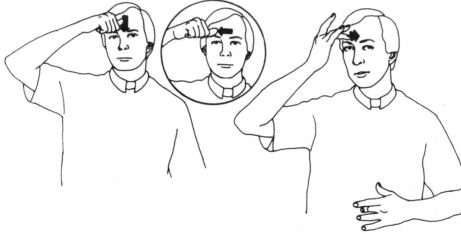

ANSWER, REPLY, RESPOND

The sign shows words directed from the mouth in reply.

Formation: Beginning with the right extended index finger in front of the mouth and the left extended index finger somewhat lower and forward, bring both fingers downward simultaneously by bending the wrists forward.

Note: RESPOND and REPLY are often initialized with *R hands*.

Related form: RESPONSE

See also COMMAND (A) for a related sign formed in a similar manner.

ANTHEM See HYMN

ANTICHRIST

This sign is a combination of OPPOSITE and CHRIST and refers to an enemy of Christ who usurps Christ's name and rights.

Formation: Beginning with the fingertips of both extended index fingers pointing toward each other in front of the body, palms facing in, pull the hands apart sharply. Then touch the index-finger side of the right *C hand,* palm left, first to near the left shoulder and then to near the right hip.

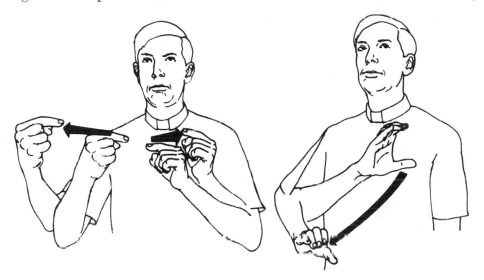

APOLOGETICS

This sign is a combination of PROVE and TRUE and refers to the defense of a faith based on intellectual grounds. The word comes from a Greek term meaning "defense."

Formation: Move the fingertips of the right *open hand,* palm facing in, from in front of the mouth downward, ending with the back of the right hand on the palm of the left *open hand,* both palms facing up in front of the chest. Then bring the right extended index finger, palm facing left and finger pointing up, forward from in front of the mouth

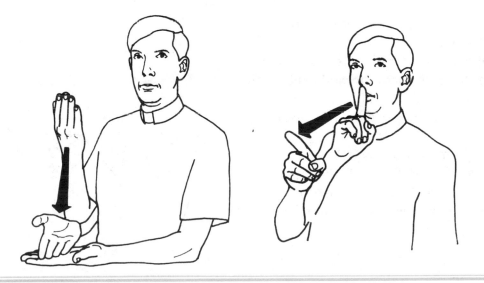

APOSTASY See BACKSLIDE, STRAY (A)

APOSTLE See DISCIPLE (B)

APOSTOLIC

This sign is a combination of SINCE and FOLLOW, indicating Christians follow the faith, teachings, and practices of the apostles.

    Formation: Begin with both extended index fingers touching near the right shoulder. Move the fingers forward in an arc, ending with the fingers pointing forward and palms facing up. Then with the right *A hand* behind the left *A hand,* palms facing each other, move both hands forward.

APPEAR

The right index finger popping up through the left hand indicates a sudden coming into view.

    Formation: Push the right extended index finger, palm facing forward, upward deliberately between the index and middle fingers of the left *open hand* held in front of the chest, palm facing down.

    Related form: APPEARANCE
    Same sign for SHOW UP, POP UP
    See also PRESENCE for the sign to use if referring to an appearance that is less sudden.

APPEARANCE See PRESENCE

APPOINT (A), CHOSEN, ELECT, SELECT

The fingers seem to select one out of available options.

   Formation: Bring the bent thumb and index finger of the outstretched right *5 hand* back toward the right shoulder while closing the thumb to the index finger.

   Same sign for PICK, CHOOSE

APPOINT (B), CHOSEN, ELECT, SELECT

The fingers seem to pick one out of many.

   Formation: Bring the bent thumb and index finger of the right *5 hand* from touching the palm of the left *open hand* back toward the right shoulder while closing the thumb to the index finger.

ARCHANGEL, SERAPHIM

This sign is a combination of CHIEF and ANGEL and refers to the powerful ranks of angels numbering either four or seven who stand before God and are concerned with human affairs.

   Formation: Move the thumb of the right *10 hand,* palm facing in, upward a short distance in front of the right shoulder. Then touch the fingertips of both *bent hands* to the shoulders, palms facing down and elbows close at the sides. Turn the wrists outward and bend the hands up and down.

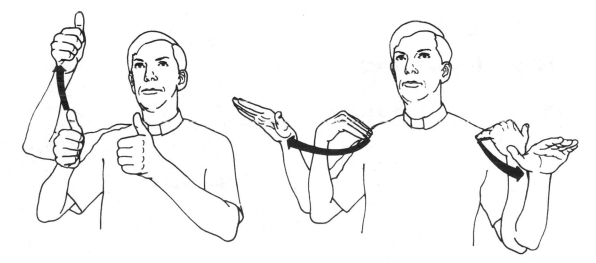

ARCHBISHOP

The sign is a combination of EXALT (B) and BISHOP and indicates the highest-ranking bishop who heads an archdiocese.

Formation: Beginning with both *bent hands* near each shoulder, palms facing down, move the hands upward simultaneously, stopping abruptly about eye level. Then press the base of the ring finger of the loosely closed right hand to the lips.

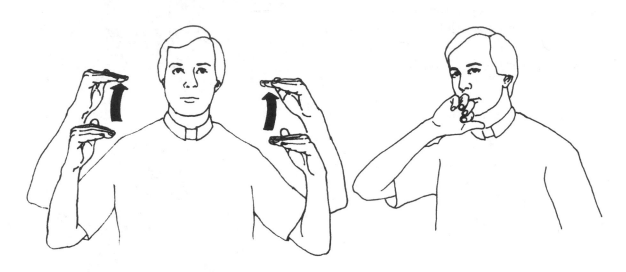

ARCHDIOCESE

This sign is a combination of EXALT (B) and DIOCESE and indicates the district under the jurisdiction of an archbishop.

Formation: Beginning with both *bent hands* near each shoulder, palms facing down, move the hands upward simultaneously, stopping abruptly about eye level. Then with the fingertips of both *D hands* touching in front of the chest, move the hands forward in a small circle until the little fingers touch and the palms face the body.

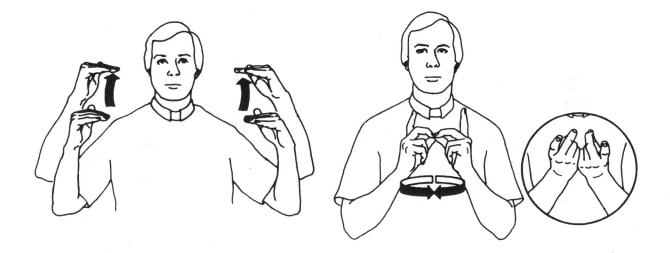

ARISE See RESURRECTION

ARK

The hands in this sign show the shape of a boat's hull and the boat moving across the water.

Formation: With the little-finger sides of both *curved hands* together, palms facing up, move the hands forward in a bouncing double arc.

Same sign for BOAT, SAIL, SHIP

ASCENSION

The fingers represent a person standing on the ground and then ascending, as in the ascension of Christ into heaven, which is celebrated on the fortieth day after Easter.

Formation: Starting with the fingertips of the inverted right *V hand* touching the palm of the upturned left *open hand,* move the right hand upward a short distance.

Related form: ASCEND

ASH WEDNESDAY

This sign is a combination of ANOINT and WEDNESDAY and indicates the custom of placing ashes on the forehead as a token of penitence on the first day of Lent, the seventh Wednesday before Easter.

Formation: Draw the thumbnail of the right *A hand*, palm down, first downward on the forehead a short distance and then from left to right. Then move the right *W hand*, in a small circle in front of the chest, palm facing in.

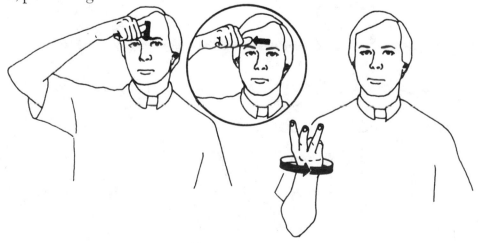

ASK, PETITION, REQUEST

This sign is a natural gesture used when requesting something. It is used only in the verb form.

   Formation: Beginning with both *open hands* apart in front of the waist, palms facing each other and fingers pointing forward, bring the hands back toward the chest while closing the palms together, ending with the fingers pointing up.

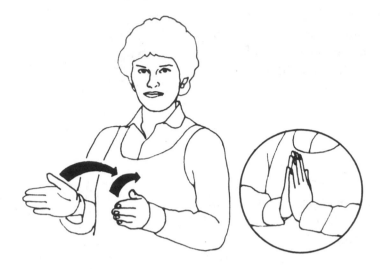

ASPERGILLUM See HYSSOP

ASR *(Arabic)*, SALAT-UL-ASR *(Arabic)*

This is the third of the ritual prayers offered in the middle of the day by Muslim worshippers every day. The sign is a combination of TIME and FOUR and refers to its four *rakas* (units).

   Formation: Tap the index finger of the right *X hand* on the back of the left *S hand*, both palms facing down. Then hold up the right *4 hand* in front of the right shoulder, palm facing forward and fingers pointing up.

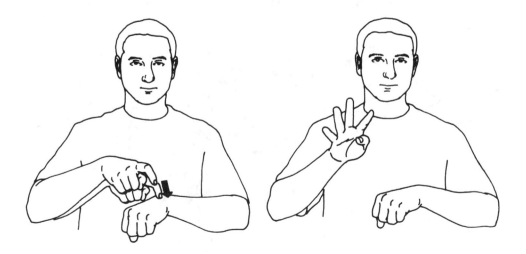

ASSEMBLE, CONGREGATE, GATHER

In the first part of the sign, the fingers represent people flocking to a central location, such as a church or synagogue. The second part is the sign for TOGETHER.

Formation: Bring both loose *5 hands* from in front of each side of the chest, palms facing down, toward each other until the fingertips touch. Then move both hands to *A hands,* knuckles and palms touching each other, in a flat circle in front of the chest.

See also MEETING for the noun form of this sign.

ASSEMBLIES OF GOD

This initialized sign combined with GOD refers to the largest of the Pentecostal sects, which was formed in 1914 and whose chief work is evangelistic and missionary.

Formation: Bring the thumb side of the right *A hand* to the forehead in a small downward arc. Then bring the right *B hand*, palm facing left and fingers angled upward, in an arc toward the forehead and down in front of the face.

Note: The second part of the sign can be made with an *open hand* or a *G hand* instead of a *B hand.*

ASSEMBLY See MEETING

ASSOCIATION See CONGREGATION

ASSUMPTION

The right hand represents the power of God taking the Virgin Mary, as represented by the left hand, bodily into heaven after her death.

Formation: Starting with the fingertips of the inverted *V hand* in the palm of the upturned right *open hand,* push the left hand upward by raising the right hand in front of the chest.

ASTONISH, AMAZE

The sign depicts the eyes opening wide in great surprise.

Formation: With the extended thumb and index finger of each hand pinched together near the outside corner of each eye, palms facing each other, flick the thumbs and index fingers apart simultaneously, ending with the index fingers pointing up and the thumbs pointing toward each cheek.

Related forms: ASTONISHMENT, AMAZEMENT

Same sign for SURPRISE, SURPRISED

ASTRAY see BACKSLIDE

AT FAULT See ACCUSE

ATHEIST See DOUBT (A)

ATONE (A), VICARIOUS

This sign indicates one thing changing places with another and symbolizes Jesus's role in taking man's punishment for sin upon himself in order to reconcile God and mankind.

Formation: With both *F hands* apart in front of the body, palms facing each other and the right hand somewhat forward of the left hand, bring the right hand in a circle toward the body over the left hand while moving the left hand down to circle around the right hand, exchanging places.

See also COVENANT, PROPITIATION, and RECONCILIATION for related signs.

ATONE (B), VICARIOUS

This sign is a combination of JESUS, PAY, and SIN and signifies that when Jesus died sacrificially, it reestablished the relationship between God and man by eradicating man's sins in the eyes of God.

Formation: Touch the bent middle finger of the right 5 *hand* to the center of the palm of the left *open hand*. Reverse the action by touching the bent middle finger of the left 5 *hand* to the palm of the right *open hand*. Then move the right index finger across the palm of the left *open hand* from the heel to the fingers. Then, beginning with both *X hands* in front of each side of the body, both palms facing up, move the hands in repeated upward circular movements.

See also PROPITIATION for a sign with a similar meaning.

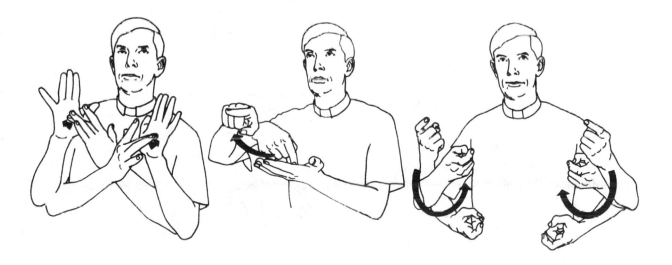

ATONE (C) See ANOINT (B)

ATONEMENT, CONTRITION, PENITENT, REGRET, REPENT, SORROW, SORRY

The movement of this sign indicates rubbing away pressure from the heart as an act of contrition.

Formation: Rub the palm side of the right *A hand* over the heart in a repeated circular movement.

Same sign for APOLOGIZE

See also MOURN and SUFFER for signs with a related meaning.

ATTAIN See TRIUMPH (A)

ATTEND

This is the sign for GO TO formed with a double movement indicating regularity.

Formation: With both *D hands* in front of the chest, palms facing forward and the right hand held somewhat closer to the body than the left hand, direct both extended index fingers forward and downward in a deliberate double movement.

Related form: ATTENDANCE

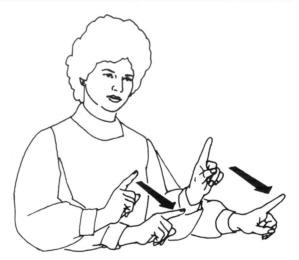

ATTRIBUTE

The hand in this sign encircles the heart, the location of one's nature. This sign is used to refer to the attributes of God.

Formation: Move the right *C hand,* palm facing left, in a small circle and then back against the left side of the chest.

Same sign for CHARACTER

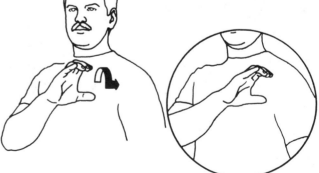

AUTHORITY See MIGHTY (B)

AWARD See GIFT, GIVE

AWE, FEAR OF GOD

This sign is a natural gesture indicating surprise, wonder, amazement, etc.

Formation: Limply swing the right 5 *hand,* palm facing in and fingers pointing left, down in front of the right side of the body.

Note: This sign can be made with both hands swinging downward with a limp movement.

Same sign for WOW

BACKSLIDE, APOSTASY, ASTRAY, STRAY

The sign represents someone or something falling back, as when a person reverts from former religious practices to sinful ones.

Formation: Beginning with both A *hands,* palms facing each other and knuckles touching, pull the right hand in toward the body with a wavy movement.

Same sign for BACK, BEHIND

See also STRAY for an alternate sign.

BAD, EVIL, WICKED

The hand seems to take something distasteful from the mouth and throw it away.

Formation: Starting with the fingertips of the right *open hand* on the lips, palm facing in, turn the wrist and move the hand forward and down away from the mouth.

See also WICKED (A) for an alternate sign.

BAPTIST

The hands in this sign mime dunking a person's head under water and refers to a Protestant denomination characterized by adult baptism, congregational independence, and advocacy of religious freedom and separation of church and state. The Baptist movement began in England in the early 1600s in a congregation of Puritan Separatists led by John Smyth.

Formation: Starting with both *A hands* several inches apart in front of the body, palms facing each other, dip the hands to the left with a double movement, turning the left palm up and the right palm down each time.

BAPTIZE (A), IMMERSION

The sign is a combination of WATER and a gesture showing the dunking of a person's head under water.

Formation: Tap the index-finger side of the right *W hand,* palm facing left, on the chin. Then starting with both *A hands* several inches apart in front of the body, palms facing each other, dip the hands to the left with a double movement, turning the left palm up and the right palm down each time.

Related form: BAPTISM

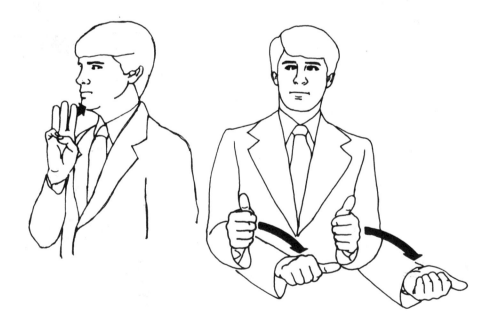

BAPTIZE (B), CHRISTEN

This sign is a combination of WATER and a gesture that indicates pouring water over the head of the person being baptized.

Formation: Tap the index-finger side of the right *W hand*, palm facing left, on the chin. Then tip the right *C hand*, palm facing left, over the top of the head, ending with the palm facing up.

Related forms: BAPTISM, CHRISTENING

BAPTIZE (C), CHRISTEN

This sign is a combination of WATER and a gesture showing the sprinkling of water, which is used by some Christian churches during baptism, a sacrament in which the recipient is cleaned of Original Sin.

Formation: Tap the index-finger side of the right *W hand*, palm facing left, on the chin. Then, holding the right *O hand* above the right side of the head, flick the fingers open.

Related forms: BAPTISM, CHRISTENING

BAPTIZE (D), CHRISTEN

This sign is a combination of BABY and a gesture miming the sprinkling of water and signifies the spiritual regeneration of an infant through baptism.

Formation: Place the back of the right *open hand,* palm up, in the crook of the left arm. Then rock the arms back and forth. Then flick the right *O hand* open over the bent left arm held across the body, palm up.

Related forms: BAPTISM, CHRISTENING

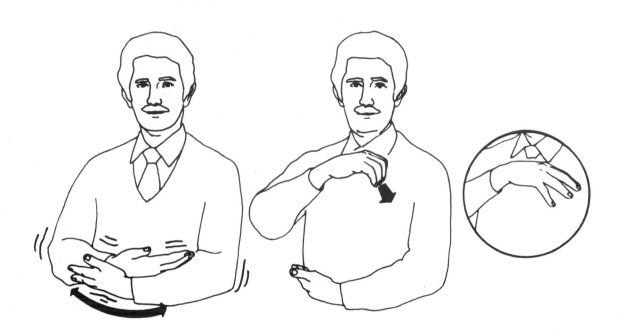

BAR MITZVAH (*Hebrew*), PHYLACTERIES, TEFILLIN (*Hebrew*)

This sign mimes wrapping a leather phylactery strap around the bare arm, a ritual taught a Jewish boy preparing for his bar mitzvah, the ceremony following the successful completion of a course of Jewish studies. This ritual is performed by the man throughout his life.

Formation: Move the palm side of the right *modified A hand* around the left forearm extended across the body.

See also BAT MITZVAH and MITZVAH for related signs.

BAT MITZVAH *(Hebrew)*

This sign is a combination of GIRL and MITZVAH, referring to the ceremony following a girl's successful completion of a course of Jewish studies.

Formation: Drag the thumb of the right *A hand*, palm left, down the cheek along the jaw. Then move both *M hands*, palms down, back and forth in front of the waist.

See also BAR MITZVAH and MITZVAH for signs with related meanings.

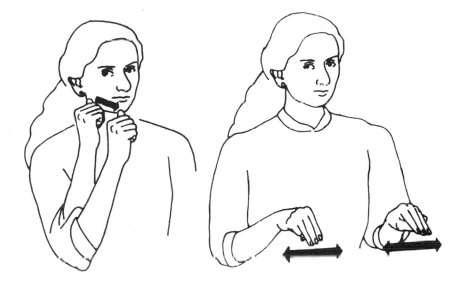

BEAR See OBLIGATION, SUFFER (A)

BEFORE See PRESCENCE

BEG, ENTREAT, INTERCEDE, PLEAD, SUPPLICATION

This is the natural motion used by some beggars wanting coins.

Formation: Hold the extended left index finger under the wrist of the right *claw hand*, palm facing up. Constrict the right fingers toward the palm with repeated movements.

Note: The left hand may be an *S hand*, palm down, or may hold the right wrist instead.

See also ASK for a sign with a related meaning.

BEGINNING, INSTITUTED

The action of the hands demonstrates turning a key in the ignition to start a car.

Formation: Twist the right extended index finger, palm down, between the index and middle fingers of the left 5 *hand,* palm right, until the right palm is facing upward.

Same sign for BEGIN, START, INITIATE

See also FOUND for a sign with a related meaning.

BEHOLD (A), WATCH, WITNESS

The extended fingers represent the gaze of the eyes.

Formation: Jab the fingers of both V *hands* forward in a double movement with the right hand a little closer to the chest than the left hand.

Same sign for LOOK, OBSERVE

See also PROPHECY and WITNESS (A) for signs with similar meanings.

BEHOLD (B), WITNESS

This sign is a combination of SEE and LOOK and signifies the practice of seeing something and observing it for a period of time.

Formation: Beginning with the fingertips of the right V *hand,* palm down, pointing at the eyes, twist the right wrist to point the fingers forward near the left V *hand,* fingers pointing forward and both palms facing down.

BELIEVE, CONVICTION, CREED

This sign is a combination of THINK and a movement indicating taking a thought and holding it.

Formation: Move the extended right index finger smoothly down from the right temple, palm facing in, to clasp the left hand held in front of the body, palms facing each other.

Related form: BELIEF

BELIEVER

This sign is a combination of BELIEVE and the person marker and refers to Christians who have faith that Christ's sacrifice atoned for mankind's sins.

Formation: Move the extended right index finger smoothly down from the right temple, palm facing in, to clasp the left hand held in front of the body, palms facing each other. Add the person marker.

See also UNBELIEVER for a sign with an opposite meaning.

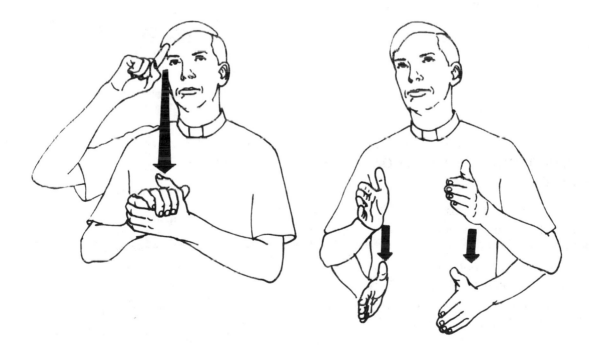

BELL (A)

The hand mimes the action of the clapper striking inside a bell.

Formation: Swing the right *A hand*, palm down, from right to left, striking the right thumb against the left palm held in front of the body, palm right and fingers pointing up.

BELL (B)

The hand mimes the action of the clapper striking inside a bell.

Formation: Strike the thumb side of the right *A hand*, palm down, against the left palm held in front of the body, palm right and fingers pointing up. Then bounce the right hand to the right with a wavy movement.

BELONG See UNITE

BELOVED, CHARITY, DEVOTION, LOVE, REVERE

The hands seem to clasp something near the heart and indicate someone or something held with great affection.

Formation: With both palms facing the body, hold the left *open hand* across the right *open hand*, which is held on the chest over the heart.

See also LOVE for an alternate sign.

BELOW

The hands demonstrate that something is below another thing.

Formation: Starting with the right *open hand* under the palm of the left *open hand,* both palms facing down, bring the right downward in a spiraling movement.

BENEDICTION See BLESS (A)(B)

BENEVOLENT See GRACIOUS

BENTSH LICHT *(Hebrew)*

The hands mime the natural gesture of striking a match and refers to the kindling of the Sabbath lights.

Formation: Strike the thumb of the right *A hand* on the thumbnail of the left *A hand,* both palms facing down, bringing the right hand forward to the right with a flick of the wrist.

BESTOW See GIFT, GIVE

BETHLEHEM

This sign is a combination of the initial *B* and TOWN, referring to the town in Israel where David lived and Jesus was born.

Formation: Move the right *B hand,* palm facing forward, slightly upward near the right shoulder. Then tap the fingertips of both *open hands,* palms angled toward each other, first in front of the left side of the chest and then again in front of the right side of the chest.

BETRAY See MOCK

BETROTHED

This sign shows the location of an engagement ring, although it is doubtful that betrothed couples during biblical times wore engagement rings.

Formation: Beginning with the right *E hand* over the left *open hand,* both palms facing down, move the right hand in a small circle and then straight down to land on the ring finger of the left hand.

Same sign for ENGAGED

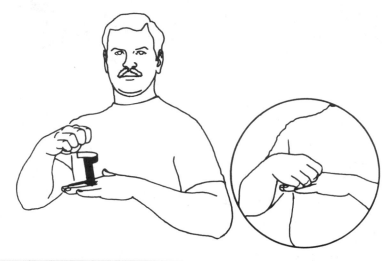

BIBLE (A)

This sign is a combination of JESUS and BOOK and refers to the sacred book of Christianity including the books of both the Old Testament and the New Testament.

Formation: Touch the bent middle finger of the right *5 hand* to the center of the palm of the left *open hand.* Reverse the action by touching the bent middle finger of the left *5 hand* to the palm of the right *open hand.* Then, starting the palms of both *open hands* together in front of the chest, move the hands apart at the top, keeping the little fingers together.

BIBLE (B)

This sign is formed like BOOK and refers to God's word coming down from heaven.

Formation: Beginning with the palms of both *open hands* together above the head, fingers pointing up, bring the hands downward to in front of the chest, ending with palms of both *open hands* facing upward, keeping the little fingers together.

BIBLE (C), HOLY SCRIPTURE, TANACH *(Hebrew)*

This sign is a combination of GOD and BOOK, referring to the sacred book for those of Jewish faith.

Formation: Move the right *B hand*, palm left, from above the front of the head downward in an arc toward the forehead and down in front of the face. Then, starting the palms of both *open hands* together in front of the chest, move the hands apart at the top, keeping the little fingers together.

35

BIBLE (D), HOLY SCRIPTURE, TANACH *(Hebrew)*

This sign is a combination of HOLY and BOOK, referring to the sacred book for those of Jewish faith.

Formation: Form an *H* with the right hand above the left *open hand*, palm up. Then move the right *H fingers* across the left palm from its base to off the fingertips. Then, starting the palms of both *open hands* together in front of the chest, move the hands apart at the top, keeping the little fingers together.

BIRTH, CONCEPTION, NATIVITY

The right hand seems to bring the baby forth from the womb and presents it for view.

Formation: Bring the palm of the right *open hand* from the stomach forward, landing the back of the right hand on the palm of the left *open hand,* palm up.

Related form: BORN

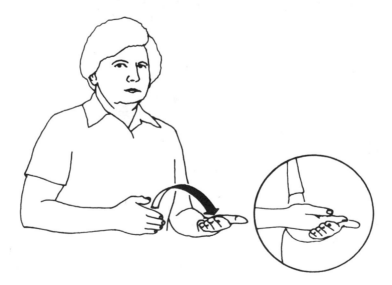

BISHOP (A)

This sign is a combination of CATHOLIC and a gesture symbolizing the custom of kissing the bishop's ring in the Roman Catholic Church.

Formation: Draw the fingers of the right *H hand* first downward and then from left to right on the forehead, fingers pointing up. Then, with the palm facing forward, press the base of the right ring finger to the lips.

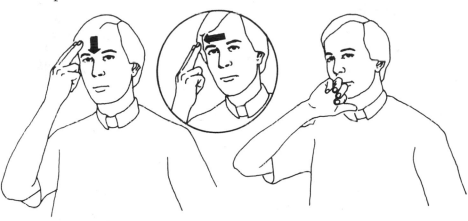

BISHOP (B), MITER

The hands follow the shape of an imaginary miter worn by a bishop, a high ranking Christian clergyman.

Formation: With the palms of both *open hands* held near each side of the head, move the hands upward at an angle until the fingers touch above the head.

See also POPE for a sign formed in a similar manner.

BLAME See ACCUSE

BLAMELESS See INNOCENT

BLASPHEMY (A), CURSE, SWEAR

The hands show taking words from the mouth and shoving them outward angrily as an act of dishonor for the being or work of God.

Formation: Beginning with the thumb of the left *C hand,* palm left, near the mouth, move the hand abruptly outward while closing to an *S hand.*

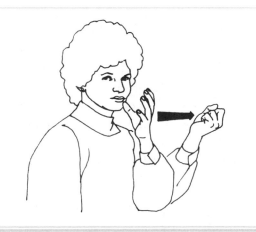

BLASPHEMY (B), CURSE, SWEAR

The hands show taking words from the mouth and shoving them angrily toward the location of hell.

Formation: Beginning with the thumb of the right *C hand,* palm left, near the mouth, move the hand abruptly downward while closing to an *S hand.*

BLEED, SHED

This sign has a movement that symbolizes blood trickling from a wound.

Formation: With the left 5 *hand* in front of the chest, palm in and fingers pointing right, bring the right 5 *hand* downward past the left hand with a repeated movement.

See also BLOOD for the noun form.

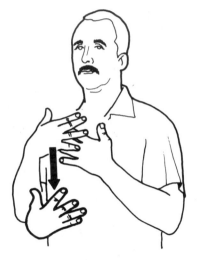

BLESS (A), ABSOLUTION, BENEDICTION

The hands symbolize taking prayer from the mouth and placing it over the thing or person being blessed with natural gesture.

Formation: Beginning with the thumbnail of the right *A hand* near the mouth and the left *A hand* somewhat forward of the right hand, palms facing in opposite directions, move the hands downward and outward, while opening into 5 *hands,* palms down.

Related form: BLESSING

BLESS (B), ABSOLUTION, BENEDICTION

The hands seem to take words of blessing from the mouth and spread them over the thing or person being blessed with natural gesture.

Formation: Beginning with the fingertips of both *bent hands* touching in front of the mouth, palms facing down, move the hands downward and outward, while opening into 5 *hands,* palms facing down.

Related form: BLESSING

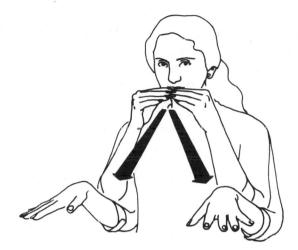

BLESS (C)

The hands show taking a prayer from the mind and spreading it out over the thing or person being blessed.

Formation: Place the thumbnails of both *A hands* on the forehead, palms facing down. Then move the hands downward and outward while opening into 5 *hands* as they move, palms facing down.

Related form: BLESSING

BLOOD

This sign is a combination of RED and a movement that symbolizes blood trickling from a wound.

Formation: With the left 5 *hand* in front of the chest, palm in and fingers pointing right, bring the right *1 hand* from near the lips downward past the left hand while changing to a 5 *hand,* wiggling the right fingers as the hand moves.

See also BLEED for the verb form.

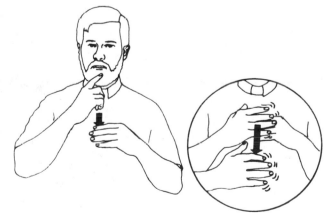

BOARD

This initialized sign is formed like MEMBER and refers to an organized decision-making group.

Formation: Touch the thumb side of the right *B hand*, palm left, first near the left shoulder and then near the right shoulder.

See also BOARD OF DEACONS, DEACON (B), and MEMBER (A) for other initialized signs formed in a similar manner.

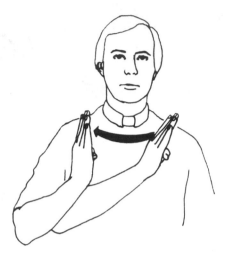

BOARD OF DEACONS

This initialized sign is formed like MEMBER and refers to an organized group of leaders in some denominations.

Formation: Touch the thumb side of the right *B hand*, palm left, near the left shoulder. Then, while moving the hand across the chest, change to a *D hand* touching it near the right shoulder.

See also BOARD, DEACON (B), and MEMBER (A) for other initialized signs formed in a similar manner.

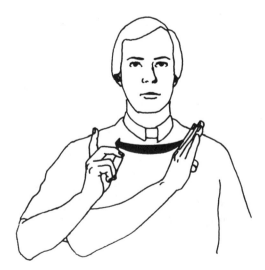

BODY, FLESH

The hands in this sign pat the body, indicating the body as distinguished from the mind or soul of man.

Formation: With the fingers of both *open hands* on each side of the chest, palms facing in and fingers pointing toward each other, move the hands down to touch again on each side of the body.

BONDAGE See SLAVERY

BORN AGAIN (A), REGENERATION

This sign is a combination of BIRTH and AGAIN and refers to Christians who have a confirmatory experience of knowing Jesus and sensing the Spirit.

Formation: Bring the palm of the right *open hand* from the stomach forward, landing the back of the right hand on the palm of the left *open hand,* palm up. Then move the right *bent hand* from beside the left *open hand* up in a circular movement, ending with the right fingers in the palm of the left hand.

See also REINCARNATION for a sign formed in a similar manner.

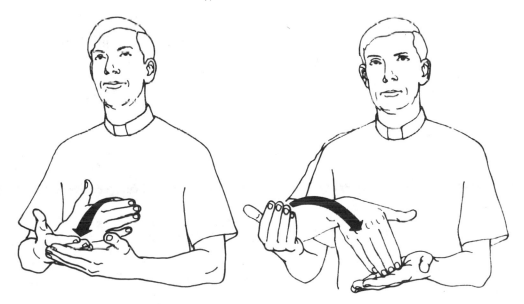

BORN AGAIN (B), REGENERATION

This sign is a combination of NEW and BIRTH, signifying the new life and putting off of the old self experienced by born-again Christians.

Formation: Sweep the back of the right *curved hand,* palm facing up across the palm of the left *open hand,* held in front of the body, palm facing up. Then bring the palm of the right *open hand* from the stomach forward, landing the back of the right hand on the palm of the left *open hand,* palm up.

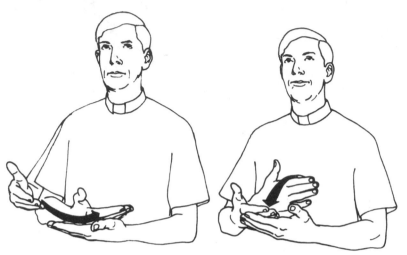

BOUNTY See ABUNDANT

BOW, BOW DOWN

The right hand in this sign represents bowing one's head as one does in reverence to God.

Formation: Beginning with the forearm of the right *S hand,* palm facing forward, against the thumb side of the left *B hand,* palm facing down and fingers pointing right, bend the right arm downward while bending the body forward.

Same sign for BEND, NOD

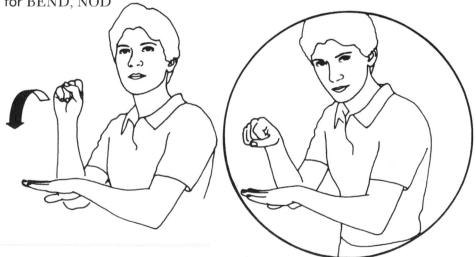

BOW DOWN See BOW

BREAD, HOST

The hands mime cutting slices of bread from a loaf. The sign refers to the unleavened bread used in religious rites.

Formation: Roll the little-finger edge of the right *bent hand* down over the back of the left *bent hand* several times, both palms facing in.

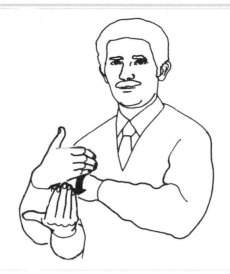

BRIGHT See LIGHT (A)

BRIS MILAH *(Hebrew)* See CIRCUMCISION (C)

BROTHER, CHRISTIAN BROTHER

The fingers follow the shape of the stole worn by the clergy.

Formation: Move the thumb and index finger-tips of both *modified C hands*, palms facing in, downward simultaneously on each side of the chest a short distance.

See also TALLITH for a Jewish sign formed in a similar manner.

BROTHERHOOD OF BELIEVERS See FELLOWSHIP OF BELIEVERS

BUDDHA See BUDDHIST

BUDDHISM

This sign refers to the religious tradition that traces its origin to Siddhartha Gautama who, after performing generosity and self-sacrifice in a succession of previous lives, established the principles of nirvana and reincarnation that define the religion.

Formation: Beginning with the extended right index finger held up in front of the chest, palm facing forward, move the finger forward striking the thumb and middle finger of the left *8 hand*, palm facing right.

Related forms: BUDDHA, BUDDHIST

BURNT OFFERING

This sign is a combination of SACRIFICE and FIRE and refers to the ancient ritual of sacrificing an animal as an offering to God to restore the relationship with God or to atone for a sin.

Formation: Beginning with both *S hands*, palms facing up, in front of each side of the waist, move the hands upward and forward while opening into 5 *hands*, palms facing up. Then, while wiggling the fingers of both 5 *hands*, palms facing in and fingers pointing up, move the hands in upward.

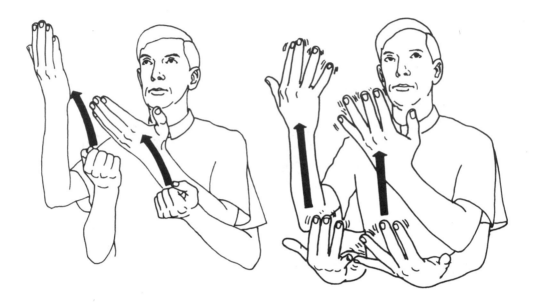

BURQA, NIQAB *(Arabic)*, FACE VEIL

This sign shows the slot of vision through which a Muslim woman wearing a burqa can see.

Formation: Beginning with the fingers of the right *G hand,* palm facing left, in front of the right eye, move the hand to the right.

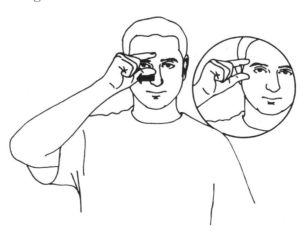

BURY, GRAVE

The hands show the shape of the mound of dirt covering a grave.

Formation: Move both *curved hands*, palms facing down and fingers pointing forward, back toward the body simultaneously in an arc.

Note: The hands may begin as *A hands* and change to *curved hands* as they move back toward the body.

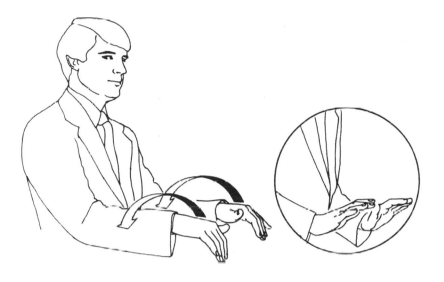

CALL (A), VOCATION

This is a directional variation of the sign normally used for CALL or SUMMON. The direction of the movement indicates a calling from God, representing the predisposition or desire to undertake a religious career.

Formation: With the right *bent hand* forward of the left hand, palm facing down and fingers pointing toward the chest, slap the back of the left *open hand*, palm down, pulling the right hand forward quickly.

Related form: CALLED

See also VOCATION (A)(B) for alternate signs.

CALL (B), INVITE, SALUTATION

The hand makes a natural welcoming motion to bring another in close to oneself, similar to God's invitation to mankind to become His children.

Formation: Swing the right *curved hand* from in front of the body, palm up, in toward the body in an arc.

Related forms: CALLED, INVITATION

Same used sign for GREET, INVITE, HIRE, WELCOME

CALL TO PRAYER

This sign refers to the five-times-a-day ritual of a Muslim being called to pray to Allah. In areas where mosques are nearby, an appointed person or a recording calls out "Hasten to prayer." The Muslim, when praying, usually kneels on a prayer rug facing in the direction of Mecca.

Formation: Beginning with the extended right finger pointing up near the right side of the head, bring the hand down to the right ear.

See also FAJR, ZUHR, ASR, MAGHRIB, and ISHA'A for the five required prayers.

CALVARY

This sign is a combination of MOUNTAIN and CROSS and represents the hill outside ancient Jerusalem where Jesus was crucified.

Formation: Tap the knuckles of the right *S hand* on the back of the left *S hand,* both palms down. Then move both *open hands* upward to the left with a wavy movement, left hand higher than the right hand. The move the right *C hand,* palm facing forward, first downward from above the right side of the head and then from left to right in front of the right shoulder.

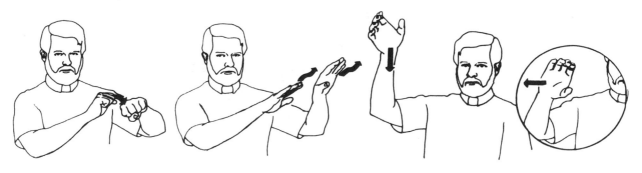

CANDLE

The wiggling fingers indicate the movement of flickering candlelight.

Formation: While holding the right extended index finger, palm in, at the wrist of the left 5 *hand,* palm facing forward, wiggle the left fingers.

CANON LAW

This sign is a combination of CHURCH and LAW and represents the ecclesiastical code of laws established by a church council.

Formation: Tap the thumb side of the right *C hand,* palm forward, on the back of the left *S hand,* palm down. Then strike the palm side of the right *L hand* first on the fingers and then on the palm of the left *open hand.*

CANONIZE

This sign is a combination of NAME and SAINT and refers to the practice in the Roman Catholic Church of declaring a deceased person to be a saint and entitled to be fully honored as such.

Formation: Tap the middle-finger side of the right *H hand* on the index-finger side of the left *H hand* held perpendicular to each other. Then drag the palm side of the right *S hand* across the palm of the left *open hand* from the base to the fingertips and outward.

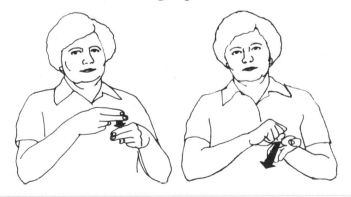

CANTOR

This sign is a combination of an initialized form of MUSIC and the person marker. The sign is used to designate the chief singer of the liturgy in a synagogue.

Formation: Swing the right *C hand*, palm left, back and forth in a large arc over the extended left arm. Add the person marker.

See also CHOIR (A), HYMN, and PSALM for other signs formed in a similar manner.

CAPTIVITY See SLAVERY

CARDINAL (A)

This sign is a combination of RED and BISHOP and refers to the highest-ranking position in the Roman Catholic Church. The sign refers to the vivid red cassock worn by cardinals, who are appointed by the Pope.

Formation: Stroke the extended right index finger downward on the lips. Then, with the palm facing forward, press the base of the right ring finger to the lips.

CARDINAL (B)

This is an old sign still used in certain cities, such as Baltimore, New York City, and Buffalo.

Formation: Tap the inside edge of the extended little finger of the right *I hand*, palm left, against the middle of the chin in a short double movement.

CARE See TROUBLE

CATECHESIS, DOGMATICS

This sign is a combination of RELIGION and TEACH and refers to oral religious instruction before baptism or confirmation and the study of religious doctrines in the Christian church.

Formation: Bring the fingertips of the right *R hand* from the left side of the chest downward and forward, ending with the palm facing down and the fingers pointing forward. Then, with both *flattened O hands* in front of the head, palms down, move the hands forward with a short double movement.

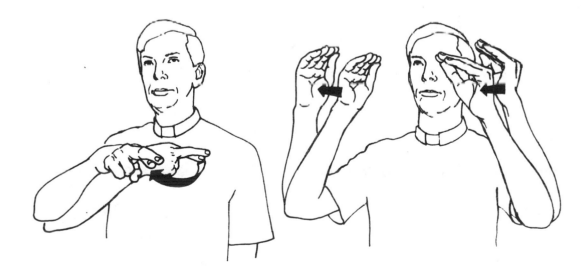

CATECHISM

This sign is a combination of RELIGION, BOOK, and TEACH and indicates the book that presents a brief summary, in question-and-answer form, of the basic principles or beliefs of any given religion.

Formation: Bring the fingertips of the right *R hand* from the left side of the chest downward and forward, ending with the palm facing down and the fingers pointing forward. Then, starting the palms of both *open hands* together in front of the chest, move the hands apart at the top, keeping the little fingers together. Then, with both *flattened O hands* in front of the chest, palms down, move the hands forward with a short double movement.

CATHEDRAL (A)

This initialized sign is formed similar to CHURCH with a gesture that indicates that it is higher, signifying a large or important church.

Formation: Move the right *C hand* from touching the back of the left *S hand,* palm facing down, upward in an arc to the right.

See also SYNAGOGUE for an initialized sign formed in a similar manner.

CATHEDRAL (B)

This initialized sign follows the shape of a cathedral's dome.

Formation: Move the right *C hand,* palm facing left, from near the left shoulder to near the top of the head and then down to near the right shoulder.

50

CATHOLIC (A), ROMAN CATHOLIC

This is the traditional sign of the cross made on the forehead, representing the Christian church that is characterized by leadership by apostolic succession with the Pope as its head.

Formation: Bring the fingertips of the right *H hand* downward in front of the forehead, palm facing in and fingers pointing up. Then move the fingers from left to right in front of the forehead.

See also ANOINT for a sign formed in a similar manner.

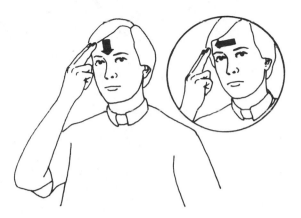

CATHOLIC (B) See UNITY

CELEBRATE, FESTIVAL, REJOICE, TRIUMPH, VICTORY

The hands seem to be waving small flags in celebration.

Formation: Make small circles near each shoulder with both *modified A hands*, palms facing each other.

Related form: CELEBRATION

Note: This sign may be formed with only one hand.

See also EASTER and VICTORY for signs formed in a similar manner.

CELESTIAL See HEAVEN (A)(B)

CELIBACY

This initialized sign is formed like BACHELOR and signifies the practice among Roman Catholic clergy to never marry.

Formation: Move the right *C hand*, palm left, downward a short distance first at the left side of the chin and then again at the right side of the chin.

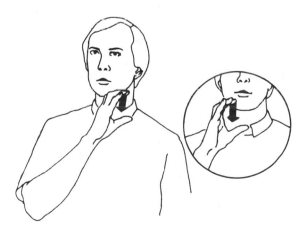

CENSER See INCENSE

CENTURION

This is the sign for ARMY and the person marker and refers to an officer in the Roman army in command of one hundred soldiers.

Formation: With both *10 hands* on the right side of the chest, the right hand above the left hand and palms facing in, with a double movement, pat the hands against the chest. Add the person marker.

Same sign for MILITARY, SOLDIER

CEPHEUS See PETER

CHALICE, CUP

The right hand follows the shape of a chalice, the cup used for the consecrated wine of the Eucharist.

Formation: Move the right *C hand,* palm facing left, upward a few inches from the palm of the left *open hand,* palm facing up.

Same sign for GLASS

CHANGE See CONVERT

CHANUKAH, FESTIVAL OF LIGHTS, HANUKKAH, MENORAH

The hands form the shape of a menorah, a nine-branched candelabrum used during Chanukah, which commemorates the victory of the Maccabees over the Syrians in 165 B.C. and the rededication of the temple in Jerusalem.

Formation: Beginning with both *4 hands* near each other in front of the chest, palms facing in and fingers pointing up, move the hands outward away from each other while spreading the fingers apart slightly.

CHAPEL See CHURCH

CHAPTER

This initialized sign seems to outline a column of words in a passage of text, such as in the Scriptures.

Formation: With the left *open hand* held in front of the body, palm facing right and fingers pointing forward, move the fingertips of the right *C hand* downward across the left palm.

CHARISMATIC (A)

This initialized sign indicates speaking in tongues, the basis of the charismatic belief.

Formation: Beginning with the thumb of the right *C hand* near the mouth, palm facing left, move it forward in small double arcs.

CHARISMATIC (B)

This initialized sign is formed like PENTE-COST, the festival sometimes known as the start of speaking in tongues, which is part of the charismatic belief.

Formation: Tap the right *C hand*, palm facing forward, downward once in front of the body and again slightly to the right.

See also PENTECOST and TONGUE for other signs with related meanings.

CHARITY See BELOVED, ZAKAT *(Arabic)*

CHASSIDIC See HASIDIC

CHERUB See ANGEL

CHIEF See RECTOR

CHOIR (A)

This is an initialized form of MUSIC. The movement shows the rhythmic sway of music.

Formation: Swing the palm side of the right *C hand* back and forth in an arc over the extended left forearm.

See also CANTOR, HYMN, and PSALM for other signs formed in a similar manner.

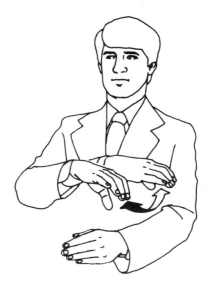

CHOIR (B)

This is a combination of MUSIC and GROUP and designates an organized company of church singers.

Formation: Swing the right *open hand* back and forth in a large arc over the extended left forearm. Then, beginning with both *C hands*, palms facing each other, near each other in front of the chest, move the hands in a circle outward and then together until the little fingers meet.

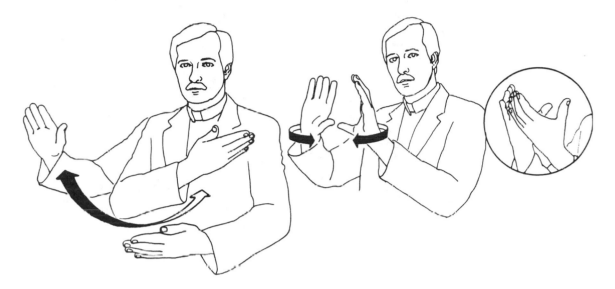

CHOSEN See APPOINT (A)(B)

CHRIST

This is an initialized sign showing the sash worn by royalty. The sign refers to the Messiah, as foretold by the prophets of the Old Testament.

Formation: Touch the index-finger side of the right *C hand*, palm facing left, first to near the left shoulder and then to near the right hip.

See also DAVID, KING, LORD (A), and MESSIAH for other initialized signs formed in a similar manner.

CHRISTEN See BAPTIZE (B)(C)(D)

CHRISTIAN (A)

This sign is a combination of CHRIST and the person marker and refers to persons who follow the religion based on Jesus Christ's teachings.

   Formation: Touch the index-finger side of the right *C hand*, palm facing left, first to near the left shoulder and then to near the right hip. Add the person marker.

CHRISTIAN (B)

This sign is a combination of JESUS and the person marker and refers to persons who follow Jesus Christ and His teachings.

   Formation: Touch the bent middle finger of the right *5 hand* to the center of the palm of the left *open hand*. Reverse the action by touching the bent middle finger of the left *5 hand* to the palm of the right *open hand*. Add the person marker.

CHRISTIAN (C), CROSS

This sign, forming a cross, is the sign Muslims use when referring to a Christian.

Formation: Place the extended index fingers of both hands perpendicular to each other in front of the chest.

CHRISTIAN BROTHER See BROTHER

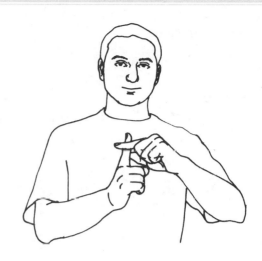

CHRISTLIKE

This sign is a combination of CHRIST and SAME indicating that a person's actions reflect what Christ would do under similar circumstances.

Formation: Touch the index-finger side of the right *C hand*, palm facing left, first to near the left shoulder and then to near the right hip. Then move the right *Y hand*, palm facing down, back and forth with a repeated movement.

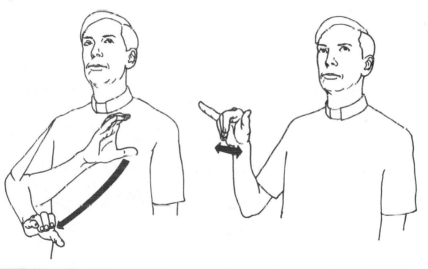

CHRISTMAS

The hand of this initialized sign mimes opening a present and refers to the holiday on December 25 celebrating the birth of Jesus.

Formation: Move the right *C hand*, palm facing down, from near the left shoulder to the right in a large arc.

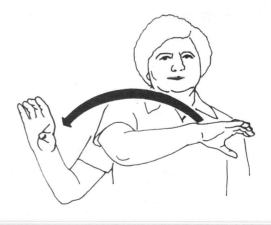

CHUPPAH (Hebrew)

The hands outline the shape of a chuppah, the wedding tent used in Jewish weddings.

Formation: Bring both *B hands*, palms facing down, from near each other in front of the forehead, outward and upward in a slight arc. Then change to both *S hands*, bringing them from above each shoulder straight downward, palms facing each other.

CHURCH, CHAPEL, DENOMINATION, ECCLESIASTICAL

This is an initialized sign formed similar to the sign for ROCK, symbolizing the rock of faith upon which the church was founded as described in the New Testament.

Formation: Tap the thumb side of the right *C hand* on the back of the left *S hand,* palm facing down.

See also PETER, LUTHERAN (B), PARISH, and TEMPLE for other initialized signs formed in a similar manner.

CHURCH OF CHRIST (A)

This sign is a combination of CHURCH and CHRIST.

   Formation: Tap the thumb side of the right *C hand* on the back of the left *S hand*, palm facing down. Then touch the index-finger side of the right *C hand*, palm facing left, first to near the left shoulder and then to near the right hip.

CHURCH OF CHRIST (B)

This is an initialized sign.

   Formation: Bounce the right *C hand*, palm facing left, first in front of the center of the chest and then in front of the right side of the chest.

CHURCH OF ENGLAND, THE See ANGLI-CAN CHURCH

CHURCH OF GOD

The sign is a combination of CHURCH and GOD.

Formation: Tap the thumb side of the right *C hand* on the back of the left *S hand*, palm facing down. Then move the right *B hand*, palm facing left, from above the front of the head downward in an arc toward the forehead and down in front of the face.

CIRCUMCISION (A)

The fingers mime the surgical removal of the male prepuce and refers to the Jewish religious ceremony in which a person is circumcised and thereby spiritually purified.

Formation: Move the extended thumb of the right *10 hand* in a circle around the extended thumb of the left *10 hand*, both palms facing down.

CIRCUMCISION (B)

This sign mimes the act of circumcision, which, when performed as a religious rite, cleanses the participants from sin.

Formation: Move the extended thumb of the right *10 hand*, palm facing down, in a circle around the extended left index finger, palm facing in.

CIRCUMCISION (C), BRIS MILAH
(Hebrew)

The hand mimes cutting away the male prepuce with scissors, a Jewish religious rite performed on a male child on the eighth day after his birth.

Formation: Abruptly close the fingers of the right *V hand*, palm facing left and fingers pointing forward, at the tip of the left extended index finger, while moving the right hand forward a short distance.

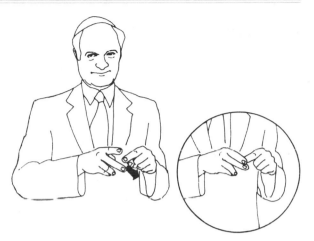

CLEANSE, WASH

The movement of this sign shows scrubbing something until it is clean. In a religious sense it means to free a person from sin through Christ's atonement.

Formation: Rub the palm side of the right *A hand* back and forth on the palm side of the left *A hand*.

COLLECT See PRAY

COLLECTION, OFFERING

This sign is a combination of COLLECT and MONEY and refers to the process of collecting money during a church service as an offering to God.

Formation: Bring the right *curved hand* from the right side of the body in an arc to the left, moving the little-finger side of the right hand across the palm of the left *open hand*, closing the right fingers to an *S hand* as it moves. Then tap the back of the right *flattened O hand* in the palm of the left *open hand* with a double movement, both palms facing up.

COLUMN See PILLAR

COME BEFORE See PRESENCE

COMFORT, SOOTHE

This sign shows stroking the hands in a smooth, comforting manner.

Formation: Bring the palm side of the right *curved hand* across the back to the fingers of the left *curved hand,* both palms facing down. Repeat with the left hand over the right hand.

    Related form: COMFORTABLE

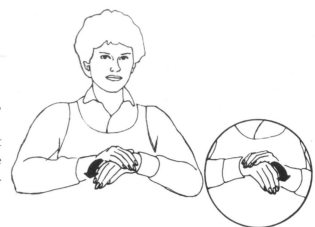

COMFORTER

This sign is a combination of COMFORT and the person marker and usually is used to refer to the Holy Spirit's attributes as an advocate, counselor, and helper.

Formation: Wipe the palm of the right *curved hand* down the fingers of the left *curved hand,* and then repeat with the palm of the left *curved hand* on the back of the right *curved hand,* both palms facing down. Add the person marker.

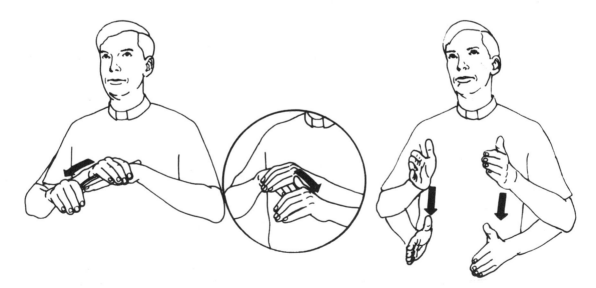

COMING See ADVENT

COMMAND (A), ORDER

The hand represents words being directed deliberately from the mouth.

Formation: Beginning with the extended right index finger pointing up at the mouth, bring the right hand forward and downward in a deliberate movement, ending with the finger pointing forward, palm facing down.

Note: This sign may be formed with two hands.

See also ANSWER for a related sign formed in a similar manner.

COMMAND (B), DEMAND, REQUIRE

The finger seems to hook into something that it requires and bring it to the body. The sign refers to God's commandments to mankind.

Formation: Strike the fingertip of the right *X hand* against the palm of the left *open hand* and bring both hands back toward the body.

COMMANDMENTS

This is an initialized sign formed like LAW. The Ten Commandments constitute the laws of God given to man; the left hand may symbolize the stone tablet on which the commandments were written.

Formation: Move the index-finger side of the right *C hand* down the palm of the left *open hand,* touching first the fingertips and then the heel of the left hand.

See also HALACHA (B), LAW (B), MOSES, and TESTAMENT for other initialized signs formed in a similar manner.

COMMUNION (A), EUCHARIST, HOLY COMMUNION

This sign is a combination of WINE and BREAD, the consecrated elements used in this sacrament.

Formation: Stroke the index-finger side of the right *W hand* in small circles on the right cheek. Then roll the little-finger edge of the right *bent hand* down over the back of the left *bent hand* several times, both palms facing in.

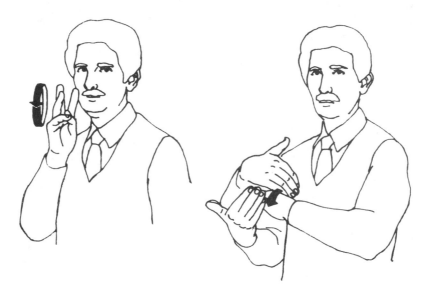

COMMUNION (B), EUCHARIST, HOLY COMMUNION, HOST

The fingertips move an imaginary Host in the shape of a cross in front of the lips.

Formation: Move the fingertips of the right *F hand* first downward and then from left to right in front of the lips.

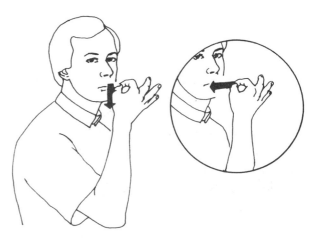

COMMUNION (C), LORD'S SUPPER

This sign is a combination of LORD and EAT and signifies the Last Supper eaten by Christ with his disciples on the night before his Crucifixion.

Formation: Touch the thumb of the right *L hand,* palm facing down, first to near the left shoulder and then to near the right hip. Then tap the fingertips of the right *flattened O hand,* palm facing down, to the lips with a short repeated movement.

COMMUNION OF SAINTS (A)

This sign is a combination of UNITY and SAINT (A), referring to the common religious faith that unites Christians.

Formation: With the thumb and index finger of each hand touching and intersecting with the other hand, palms facing each other, move the hands in a flat circle in front of the body. Then slide the palm side of the right *S hand* across the palm of the left *open hand* from its base to the fingertips and outward.

See also RECONCILIATION and UNITY for signs formed in a similar manner.

COMMUNION OF SAINTS (B)

This sign is a combination of UNIVERSE, HOLY, and PEOPLE and refers to the whole body of Christians, both living and dead, who are united through a common faith.

Formation: Bring the right *U hand* in a circle over and around the left *U hand*, palms facing in opposite directions and fingers angled up. Then slide the little-finger side of the right *H hand* across the palm of the left *open hand* from its base to the fingertips and outward. Then make large outward circles with both *P hands*, palms facing each other, in front of each side of the body.

COMMUNION OF SAINTS (C) See UNITY

COMPASSION See MERCY (A)

COMPLETE See FULFILL

CONCEIVE (A)

This sign refers to Mary's conception occurring from the Holy Spirit.

Formation: Beginning with both *flattened O hands* in front of the body, right hand over the left hand and palms facing each other, move the hands toward each other while opening into *5 hands*.

CONCEIVE (B)

This sign is a directional form of RECEIVE and refers to the Virgin Mary's conception by the Holy Spirit.

Formation: With both *C hands* held over the head, right hand above the left and palms facing in opposite directions, bring the hands down to the chest while closing into *S hands*, ending with the little-finger side of the right hand on the index-finger side of the left hand.

See also OBTAIN for a sign formed in a similar manner.

CONCEIVE (C)

This is the sign for PREGNANT and refers to the Virgin Mary becoming pregnant by the Holy Spirit.

Formation: With the fingers of both *5 hands* entwined in front of the stomach, move the hands forward a short distance.

CONCEIVE (D)

This is the sign for PREGNANT. The hands show the growing belly of a pregnant woman who has conceived a child.

Formation: Move the right *5 hand,* palm facing in and fingers pointing down, from the middle of the body outward a short distance.

Same sign for PREGNANT

CONCEPTION See BIRTH

CONDEMN (A), ANNUL, JUDGMENT

The finger crosses out something as a declaration or judgment against it.

Formation: With the extended right index finger draw a large *X* across the palm of the left *open hand*.

Note: When referring to the Last Judgment, the movement should be large and deliberate.

Related form: ANNULMENT

Same sign for CANCEL, CORRECT, CRITICIZE, REVOKE

See also JUDGMENT for an alternate sign.

CONDEMN (B) See JUDGMENT (A)

CONFERENCE See MEETING

CONFESS (A), ACKNOWLEDGE, ADMIT

This sign represents getting something off one's chest, as in the confession of sins.

Formation: Move both *5 hands* from touching the chest, palms facing in and fingers pointing toward each other, forward by twisting the wrists, ending with both palms facing up.

See also CONFESSION for the noun form of this sign.

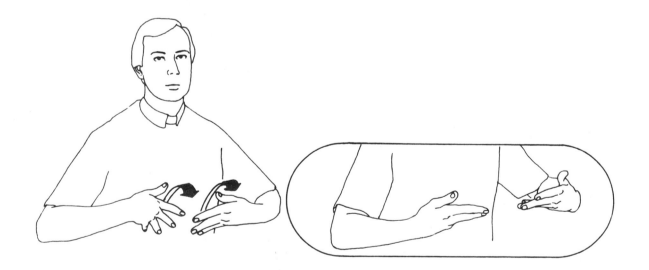

CONFESS (FAITH) (B) See ANNOUNCE

CONFESSION, PENANCE

This sign is a combination of CONFESS and a gesture showing the grating of a confessional stall through which a priest hears a person's confession of sins.

Formation: Move both *5 hands* from touching the chest, palms facing in and fingers pointing toward each other, forward by twisting the wrists, ending with both palms facing up. Then place the back of the right *4 hand* perpendicular across the palm of the left *4 hand*.

Related form: CONFESSIONAL

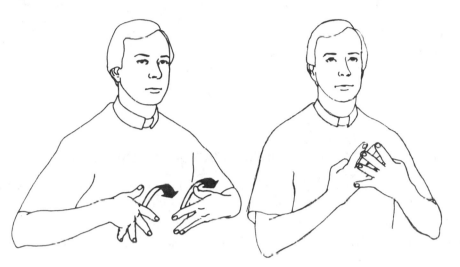

CONFIDENCE See TRUST (A)

CONFIRM See INSTALL

CONFIRMATION (A)

This sign shows the Roman Catholic custom of slapping and then blessing a confirmand with the sign of the cross on the forehead when being admitted to the church through this sacrament which renews the vows of baptism.

Formation: Pat the palm of the right *open hand* on the right cheek. Then draw the thumbnail of the right *A hand*, palm facing down, first downward on the forehead a short distance and then from left to right.

CONFIRMATION (B)

This sign shows blessing the imaginary head of the confirmand in front of the pastor or priest.

Formation: Bring the right *B hand* from near the right temple down to the back of the left *S hand* held in front of the body, both palms facing down.

CONGREGATE See ASSEMBLE

CONGREGATION, ASSOCIATION, ORGANIZATION, SOCIETY, SYNOD

This sign is a combination of BELIEVE and GROUP and refers to members of a specific religious group who regularly worship at a common church.

Formation: Move the extended right index finger smoothly down from the right temple, palm facing in, to clasp the left hand held in front of the body, palms facing each other. Then move both *C hands*, palms facing each other in front of the chest, in a outward circular movement, ending with the little fingers together.

Note: ASSOCIATION, ORGANIZATION, and SOCIETY are often formed with initialized handshapes.

See also DIOCESE, ERUV, and SOCIETY for other initialized signs with related meanings formed in a similar manner.

CONQUER, DEFEAT, OVERCOME, SUBDUE

This sign suggests forcing a person's head down in humbling defeat.

Formation: Move the right *S hand* forward and down with force over the back of the left *S hand* held in front of the body, ending with the right wrist resting on the back of the left hand and the right hand hanging down.

Same sign for BEAT

CONSCIENCE (A), CONVICTION, GUILT

This sign is a natural gesture for scolding directed at the heart, which traditionally governs a person's discrimination of right and wrong.

Formation: Tap the thumb side of the right *1 hand*, palm down and extended finger pointing left, on the left side of the chest with a repeated movement.

Related form: GUILTY

CONSCIENCE (B), CONVICTION, GUILT

This is an initialized sign for GUILT and is formed near the heart, signifying feeling responsibility for some reprehensible act.

Formation: Tap the index-finger side of the right *G hand* on the left side of the chest with a repeated movement.

Related form: GUILTY

CONSECRATE (A)

This sign is a combination of OFFER and HOLY and signifies the practice in some liturgical churches of transforming the elements of Communion into the body and blood of Christ.

Formation: Raise both *open hands,* palms facing up, from in front of the body upward and forward. Then slide the little-finger side of the right *H hand* across the palm of the left *open hand* from its base to the fingertips and outward.

Related form: CONSECRATION

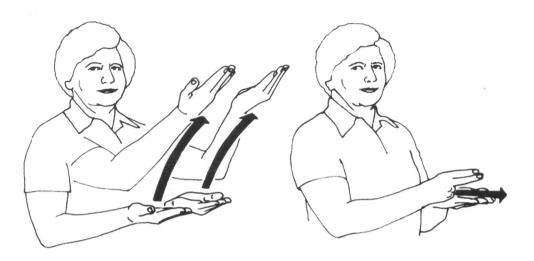

CONSECRATE (B) See SANCTIFY (B)

CONSERVATIVE

This is an initialized sign formed similar to CLEAN and signifies those Jews who do not accept liturgical and ritual changes in traditional Jewish laws. It also is used to refer to certain churches in some denominations that have traditional practices and do not embrace more liberal beliefs and practices.

Formation: Move the thumb side of the right *C hand* across the left *open hand* from its base to the fingertips and outward.

See also DIVINE, HOLY (B), ORTHODOX, RIGHTEOUS (A), and SAINT (A)

CONSTANTLY See ALWAYS

CONTEMPORARY

The hands in this sign show a place in front of the body that represents the present time and is used to describe music, services, or other religious activities that are of a modern era as contrasted with century-old religious activities.

 Formation: Bring a *bent hand,* palm facing up, downward in front of each side of the body.

 Note: This sign can be made with *Y hands* instead.

 Same sign for CURRENT, NOW, PRESENT

CONTRIBUTION See GIFT

CONTRITION See ATONEMENT

CONVENTION See MEETING

CONVERT, CHANGE, REFORM

The hands in this sign seem to turn into something else, similar to the change that occurs in a person upon adopting a religion.

 Formation: With the palm side of the right *A hand* on top of the palm side of the left *A hand,* twist the hands in opposite directions, ending with the hands in reverse positions.

 Related forms: CONVERSION, REFORMATION

 See also INTERPRET, REDEEMER, and TRANSLATE for initialized signs formed in a similar manner.

CONVOCATION See MEETING

CORNERSTONE

This sign is a combination of ROCK and SUPPORT and refers to the stone that is laid at the corner to bind two walls together and to strengthen them. The term is used as a symbol of strength and prominence in the Bible.

Formation: Tap the palm side of the right *S hand* on the back of the left *S hand*, palm facing down. Then bring the knuckles of the right *S hand* upward under the little-finger side of the left *S hand*, palm facing in, pushing it upward in front of the chest.

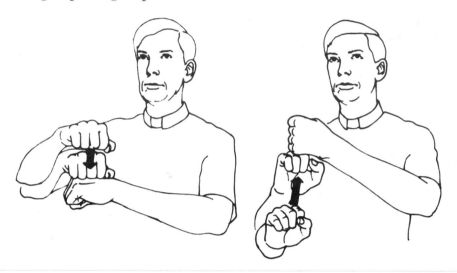

COUNSELOR

This sign is a combination of COUNSEL, a gesture indicating sending out advice, and the person marker.

Formation: Move the right *flattened O hand* forward across the back of the left *open hand*, both palms facing down, opening the right fingers into a 5 *hand* as the hand moves forward. Add the person marker.

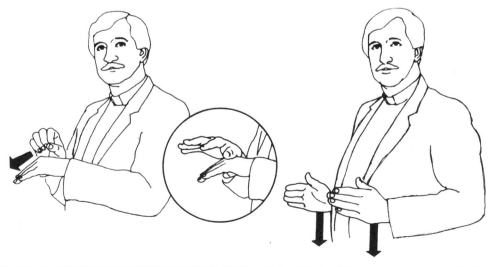

COUNTENANCE

The hand in this sign encircles the area of the face or countenance.

Formation: Move the extended right index finger, palm facing in, in a large circle in front of the face.

Same sign for APPEARANCE

COURAGE See MIGHTY (A)

COVENANT (A)

This sign seems to take an idea from the head and place it alongside another idea to indicate that they are the same as in a covenant.

Formation: Move the extended right index finger from pointing to the right side of the forehead, down and forward to beside the left extended index finger, ending with both fingers pointing forward and palms down in front of the body.

Same sign for AGREE

COVENANT (B)

This initialized sign indicates comparing one's ideas with another's and finding them to be in agreement.

Formation: Move the extended right index finger from pointing to the right side of the forehead, down and forward while changing to a *C hand,* ending with the right *C hand* beside the left *C hand,* palms down in front of the body.

COVENANT (C) See RECONCILIATION (A)

COVET (A), ENVY, JEALOUS

This sign is a natural gesture of biting one's nails out of jealousy.

Formation: Put the tip of the bent extended right index finger between the closed lips on the right side of the mouth.

Related form: JEALOUSY

See also DESIRE (A)(B) for an alternate sign and GREEDY for a sign with a related meaning.

COVET (B) See DESIRE (A)

CREATE, FORM, MAKE

The hands in this sign seem to be molding a form, symbolizing God's causing the world and all things in it to exist.

Formation: With the little-finger side of the right *S hand* on the index-finger side of the left *S hand,* palms facing in opposite directions, twist the wrists in opposite directions several times, touching the hands together after each twist.

CREATION

This sign is a combination of GOD, CREATE, and WORLD.

Formation: Move the right *B hand,* palm facing left, from above the front of the head downward in an arc toward the forehead and down in front of the face. Then, with the little-finger side of the right *S hand* on the index-finger side of the left *S hand,* palms facing in opposite directions, twist the wrists in opposite directions several times, touching the hands together after each twist. Then bring the right *W hand* in a circle over and around the left *W hand,* palms facing each other and fingers pointing forward.

CREATOR, MAKER

This sign is a combination of GOD, CREATE, and the person marker and refers to God's role in bringing the world and all things into existence.

Formation: Move the right *B hand,* palm facing left, from above the front of the head downward in an arc toward the forehead and down in front of the face. Then with the little-finger side of the right *S hand* on the index-finger side of the left *S hand,* palms facing in opposite directions, twist the wrists in opposite directions several times, touching the hands together after each twist. Add the person marker.

CREED See BELIEVE

CROSS (A), CRUCIFIX

The hand in this sign outlines the shape of the traditional cross upon which Jesus Christ was crucified.

Formation: Move the right *C hand,* palm facing forward, first down from near the right side of the head and then from left to right in front of the right shoulder.

See also EUCHARIST for an initialized sign formed in a similar manner.

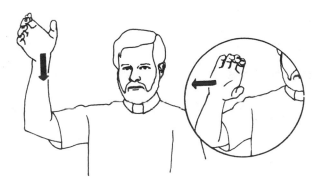

CROSS (B) See CHRISTIAN (C)

CROSS ONESELF

This sign demonstrates the act of crossing one-self as an act of respect when entering a sanctuary or approaching the altar or a sacred object.

Formation: Move the fingertips of the right *bent hand* from the forehead to the center of the body, and then from the right side of the chest to the left side.

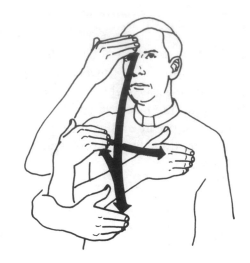

CROWD See MULTITUDE

CROWN, DIADEM

The fingers in this sign seem to be placing a crown on one's head.

Formation: Bring the curved thumb and middle fingers of both 5 *hands* down on top of each side of the head, palms facing each other.

CROWN OF THORNS

This sign demonstrates the placing of a crown on the head and then the piercing of thorns into the head, as done to Jesus prior to His Crucifixion.

Formation: Move both *bent 3 hands* downward on each side of the head. Then move the fingertips of both 4 *hands,* palms facing down, in against each side of the forward, while bending the fingers.

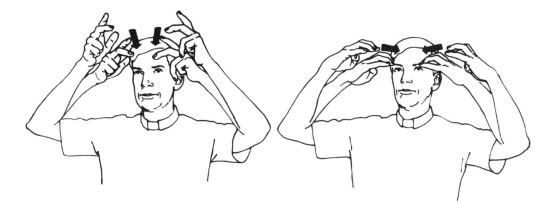

CRUCIFIX See CROSS (A)

CRUCIFY

The hands in this sign mime the nailing of Christ's hands to the cross on Calvary.

Formation: Strike the left *open hand* with the little-finger side of the right *S hand*. Then strike the right *open hand* with the little-finger side of the left *S hand*. Then hold out both *open hands*, palms facing forward, outside each side of the body.

Related form: CRUCIFIXION

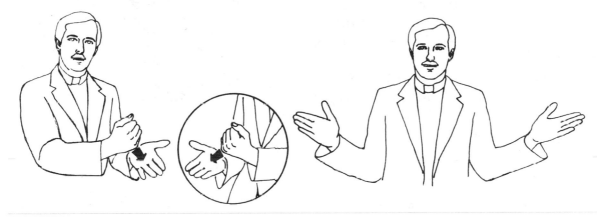

CULT (A)

This initialized sign is formed with a movement similar to FALSE and refers to a religious body sharing an esoteric interest.

Formation: Move the right *C hand*, palm facing left, from the right side of the chin in an arc to the left, ending with the palm facing down.

CULT (B)

This sign is a combination of FALSE and CHURCH and signifies a community of religious worship focusing upon a single ideal or principle.

Formation: Move the extended right index finger, palm left, from right to left across the nose, striking the nose as it passes. Then tap the thumb side of the right *C hand* on the back of the left *S hand*, palm facing down.

CUP See CHALICE

CURSE See BLASPHEMY (A)(B)

CURSILLO

This sign is formed similar to the sign for COURSE and signifies a short course reviewing doctrine or principles usually presented during a religious retreat.

Formation: Move the thumb side of the right *C hand,* palm facing forward, from the fingertips to the base of the palm of the left *open hand,* palm facing up.

CUSTOM (A)

The hands in this sign move downward, a movement in American Sign Language that signifies a continued pattern, such as the practices handed down in the Jewish religion.

Formation: With the heel of the right *S hand* on the back of the left *S hand,* palms facing down, move both hands slowly downward a short distance.

CUSTOM (B)

This is an initialized sign formed with a downward movement signifying continued activity.

Formation: With the heel of the right *C hand* on the back of the left *S hand,* palms facing down, move both hands slowly downward a short distance.

DAMN

This initialized sign is directed downward to the traditional location of hell.

Formation: Move the right *D hand* from the left side of the chest, palm facing left and extended index finger pointing up, downward, and outward with a deliberate movement to the right side of the waist, ending with the extended index finger pointing down.

Related forms: DAMNATION, DAMNED

See also HELL (B) for an initialized sign formed in a similar manner.

DANGER, PERIL

The right hand in this directional sign seems to threaten the body.

Formation: Brush the thumb of the right *A hand* with a repeated movement back toward the body across the back of the left *A hand,* both palms facing in.

Related form: DANGEROUS

DAVEN

This sign mimes the movements of a person davening, that is, reciting the prescribed prayers in the daily Jewish liturgies.

Formation: With the little-finger sides of both *curved hands* touching close to the chest, move the hands up and down slightly in rhythm with the head and shoulders bowing with them.

Related form: DAVENING

DAVID, KING DAVID

This initialized sign is formed similar to the sign for KING and refers to David's status as the second king of Judah and Israel, from 1013 to 973 B.C.E.

Formation: Move the right *D hand,* palm facing left, from near the left shoulder down to the right hip.

Note: This sign is identical to the sign for DEACON; the meaning that is intended should be determined from the context.

See also CHRIST, KING, LORD (A), and MESSIAH for other initialized signs with similar meanings and formed in a similar manner.

DAY OF ATONEMENT (A)(B) See YOM KIPPUR

DAY OF JUDGMENT See JUDGMENT DAY

DEACON (A)

This initialized sign is formed like the sign for DAVID and refers to lay assistants in the church.

Formation: Move the right *D hand,* palm facing left, from near the left shoulder down to the right hip.

Note: This sign is identical to the sign for DAVID; the meaning that is intended should be determined from the context.

See also CHRIST, KING, LORD (A), and MESSIAH for other initialized signs with similar meanings and formed in a similar manner.

DEACON (B)

This initialized sign is formed like the sign for MEMBER. The sign refers to those people in the church who are clergy just below the rank of pastor or priest.

Formation: Touch the fingertips of the right *D hand,* palm facing left, first near the left shoulder and then near the right shoulder.

See also BOARD, BOARD OF DEACONS, and MEMBER for other initialized signs with related meanings formed in a similar manner.

DEAD See DEATH

DEAR See LOVE (A)

DEATH, DEAD, DIE, PERISH

The movement of the hands in this sign refers to turning over and dying.

   Formation: Beginning with both *open hands* in front of the body, right palm facing down and left palm facing up and fingers pointing forward, flip the hands to the right so that the right palm faces up and the left palm faces down.

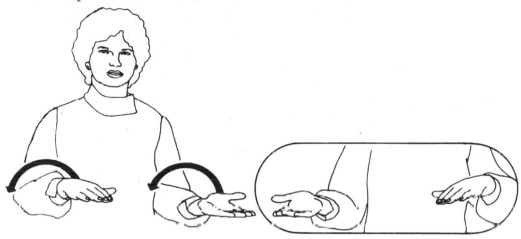

DECALOGUE, TEN COMMANDMENTS

This sign is a combination of TEN and COMMANDMENTS and refers to ten precepts given by God to Moses on Mount Sinai that define how God wants man to live in a covenant relationship with Him.

   Formation: Twist the thumb of the right *10 hand*, palm facing left, forward in front of the chest, ending with the palm facing forward and the thumb pointing up. Then move the index-finger side of the right *C hand* and down the palm of the left *open hand*, touching first the fingertips and the heel of the left hand.

   See also COMMANDMENTS for an alternate form of this sign.

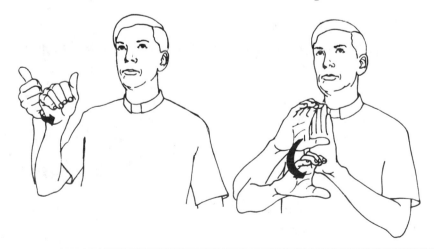

DECEIVE See MOCK

DECLARE See ANNOUNCE

DEDICATE

This initialized sign is formed similar to OFFER and is used to refer to something set apart for religious use.

Formation: Raise both *D hands,* palms facing up, from in front of the body upward and forward, while changing into *open hands*.

Related form: DEDICATION

See also OFFERING and SACRIFICE for signs formed in a similar manner.

DEEDS See WORKS

DEFEAT See CONQUER

DEFEND See PROTECT

DEFILED See IMPURE

DEJECTED See SORROWFUL

DELIVER (A)

This initialized sign is formed like SAVE and is used to designate man's release from the bondage of sin.

Formation: Bring both *D hands,* wrists crossed in front of the chest and palms facing outward in opposite directions, away from each other by twisting the wrists, ending with the palms facing forward in front of each side of the body.

Related form: DELIVERANCE

See also REDEEM, REFORM (B), and SALVATION for initialized signs with related meanings formed in a similar manner.

DELIVER (B) See SALVATION

DEMAND See COMMAND (B)

DEMON See DEVIL

DENOMINATION (A)

This initialized sign is formed similar to RELIGION and refers to a religious sect with specific beliefs, usually including many churches.

Formation: Bring the fingertips of the right *D hand* from the left side of the chest forward in a small arc, ending with the palm facing down and the index finger pointing forward.

See also RELIGION and THEOLOGY for signs formed in a similar manner.

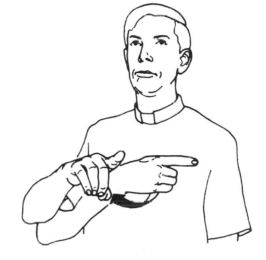

DENOMINATION (B) See CHURCH

DENY (A)

This is the sign for NOT formed with a repeated movement for emphasis and signifies that one believes something not to be true.

Formation: Bring the thumbs of the right *10 hand* and then the left *10 hand* forward from under the chin with an alternating movement.

Note: Both *10 hands* may move forward simultaneously from under the chin in a strong single movement.

Related form: DENIAL

See also UNBELIEF for a sign with a similar meaning.

DENY (B)

The hands in this sign seem to be pushing down inner desires.

Formation: Move both *10 hands,* thumbs pointing down, downward on each side of the chest.

Note: This sign may be formed with the right hand alone.

Related form: DENIAL

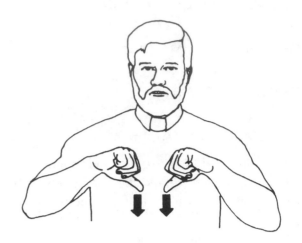

DENY (C), SELF-DENIAL

The hand in this sign seems to squelch a built-up desire.

Formation: Bring the right *C hand* from under the chin, palm facing up, downward in front of the chest while changing into an *S hand.*

DESCEND (A)

This sign mimes a descending action.

Formation: Beginning with the right extended index finger pointing down above the right shoulder, bring the hand down in front of the body in a large wavy movement, ending with the extended finger pointing down in front of the waist.

DESCEND (B)

The fingers in this sign represent a person's legs standing on ground and then descending as in the descension of Christ into hell after His death.

Formation: Beginning with the fingertips of the right *V hand*, fingers pointing down, in the palm of the left *open hand*, move the fingers off the palm downward a short distance.

DESERT See WILDERNESS

DESERVE (A), EARN, MERIT

The hand in this sign seems to be gathering earned money together and refers to the rewards one gets because of one's own efforts.

Formation: Bring the right *curved hand* from the right side of the body in an arc to the left, moving the little-finger side of the right hand across the palm of the left *open hand*, closing the right fingers to an *S hand* as it moves.

DESERVE (B) See WORTHY (A)

DESIRE (A), COVET, LONGING, WANT, (GOD'S) WILL

The hands in this sign seem to bring something to oneself that is wanted.

Formation: Beginning with both *open hands* in front of the body, palms facing up, bring the hands in toward the body while constricting the fingers into *claw hands*.

See also COVET (A) and WILL for alternate signs.

DESIRE (B), LONGING, WISH

This sign is an exaggeration of the sign for HUNGRY and indicates an intense desire for something.

Formation: Move the fingertips of the right *C hand,* palm facing in, from the throat downward on the chest.

See also COVET (A) for a sign with a related meaning.

DESPISE, DETEST, DISLIKE, HATE

The fingers flick away something from the body that is distasteful. This is a directional sign that is formed toward the disliked person or object.

Formation: Flick the middle fingers of both *8 hands,* palms facing each other, off the thumbs while moving the hands forward with a deliberate movement and opening into *5 hands.*

DETEST See DESPISE

DEVIL (A), DEMON, SATAN

This sign shows the traditional conception of the horned devil, the major spirit of evil, ruler of hell, and foe of God.

Formation: With the thumbs of both *3 hands* touching each side of the forehead, palms facing forward, bend the extended index and middle fingers with a double movement.

Note: This sign may be formed with one hand.

Same sign for MISCHIEF, MISCHIEVOUS

See also WICKED for a sign with a related meaning formed in a similar manner.

DEVIL (B) See SATAN (A)

DEVOTED (A)

This initialized sign is formed like GIFT and symbolizes the giving of oneself to a religious cause or use.

Formation: Move both *D hands,* palms facing each other, from near the chest forward in arcs.

Related form: DEVOTION

See also GENUFLECT for an alternate sign and GIFT for a sign formed in a similar manner.

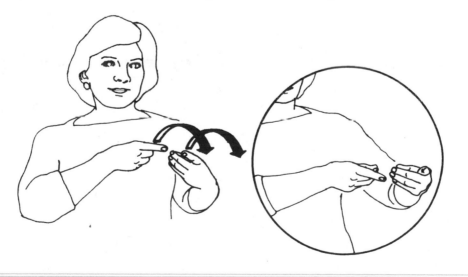

DEVOTED (B) See GENUFLECT

DEVOTION See BELOVED

DEVOUT See WORSHIP

DHUHR *(Arabic)* See ZUHR *(Arabic)*

DIADEM See CROWN

DIASPORA, DISPERSION, GALUT *(Hebrew)*

This sign is a combination of JEW and SPREAD and refers to the scattering of Jews from the land of Palestine into other parts of the world over several centuries.

Formation: With the right 5 *hand* near the chin, palm facing in and fingers pointing up, bring the fingertips downward from the chin with a double movement while closing the fingers to a *flattened O hand* each time. Then, beginning with the fingers of both *flattened O hands* together in front of the chest, both palms facing down, bring the hands forward and apart while opening into 5 *hands*.

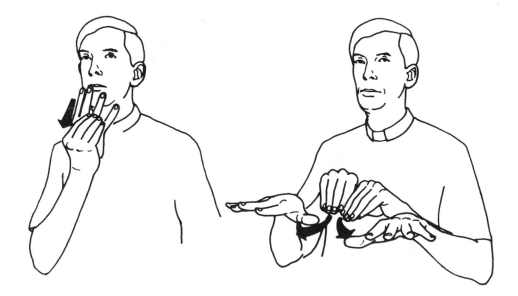

DIE See DEATH

DIOCESE

This initialized sign seems to encompass a defined area.

Formation: With the fingertips of both *D hands* touching in front of the chest, move the hands around in a small circle, ending with the little-finger side of both hands touching and palms facing in.

Same sign for DEPARTMENT

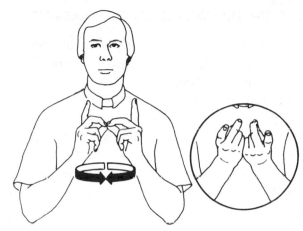

DIRECT See RULE

DIRTY See IMPURE

DISBELIEF See DOUBT (A), UNBELIEF

DISCIPLE (A)

This is an initialized sign formed like FOLLOW and indicates one of the twelve companions of Christ who followed His teachings.

Formation: With the left *D hand* in front of the right *D hand,* both palms facing forward, move the hands forward simultaneously in double arcs.

DISCIPLE (B), APOSTLE, FOLLOWER

This sign is a combination of FOLLOW and the person marker and signifies either the followers of Christ, the missionaries of the early Christian church, or the members of the Mormon administrative council.

Formation: With the right *A hand* near the heel of the left *A hand,* palms facing in opposite directions, move both hands forward simultaneously in front of the body. Add the person marker.

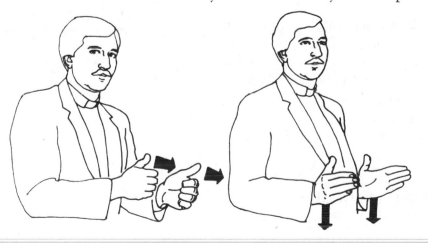

DISCIPLINE (A), PRACTICE, TRAINING

The movement in this sign signifies the repetitive nature of training that provides moral or mental improvement.

Formation: Rub the knuckles of the right *A hand,* palm facing down, on the extended left index finger, palm facing in, with a repeated movement.

See also PUNISH for the verb form of DISCIPLINE.

DISCIPLINE (B) See PUNISH

DISLIKE See DESPISE

DISOBEY (A), REBEL

This sign is a combination of THINK and a natural gesture for rebellion and signifies a disregard for God's commands.

Formation: Touch the extended right index finger to the forehead, palm facing in. Then with a deliberate movement, twist the wrist outward and upward to the right while changing into an *S hand,* palm facing forward.

Related forms: DISOBEDIENCE, REBELLIOUS

DISOBEY (B), REBEL

The hands in this sign move with a rebellious gesture.

Formation: Beginning with the thumbs of both *A hands* touching each side of the forehead, palms facing each other, move the hands deliberately upward and outward a short distance by twisting the wrists sharply, ending with the palms facing forward.

Related forms: DISOBEDIENCE, REBELLIOUS

DISPENSATION See FORGIVE

DISPERSION See DIASPORA

DISTRICT (A)

This initialized sign shows an area signifying a designated region established for administrative purposes.

Formation: Bring the right *D hand,* palm facing down, from the back of the left *S hand,* palm down, in a large forward circle, ending back where it began.

DISTRICT (B)

The hand in this sign encompasses a large area and signifies a jurisdiction designated for administrative purposes.

Formation: Beginning with the right *open hand,* palm facing down, in front of the left side of the body, bring the hand in a large arc back toward the left side of the body over the left *open hand,* palm facing down.

DIVINE (A)

This initialized sign is formed similar to the sign for CLEAN.

Formation: Move the palm side of the right *D hand* across the left *open hand* from its base to the fingertips and outward.

DIVINE (B) See HOLY (A)

DIVINE PROVIDENCE (A)

This sign is a combination of GOD and SUPERVISE and refers to divine direction or care provided by God.

Formation: Move the right *B hand,* palm forward left, from above the front of the head downward in an arc toward the forehead and down in front of the face. Then, with the little-finger side of the right *K hand* on the index-finger side of the left *K hand,* palms facing in opposite directions, move the hands in a outward circle in front of the body.

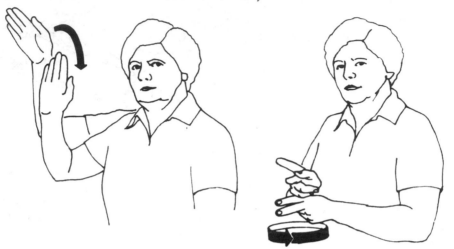

DIVINE PROVIDENCE (B) See PROVIDENCE

DIVORCE

This is an initialized sign showing an abrupt parting, such as on the occasion of the dissolution of a marriage.

Formation: Beginning with the fingertips of both *D hands* touching, palms facing each other, twist the wrists outward, pulling the hands apart, ending with the palms facing forward in front of each side of the body.

DO See WORKS

DOCTRINE, DOGMA

This is an initialized sign formed similar to the sign for TEACH and signifies religious principles that are taught.

Formation: Move both *D hands*, palms facing each other, a short distance forward from each side of the head with a double movement.

See TEACH for a sign formed in a similar manner.

DOGMA See DOCTRINE

DOGMATICS See CATECHESIS

DOUBT (A), ATHEIST, DISBELIEF

This sign begins similar to BLIND and signifies being blind to an idea.

Formation: Beginning with the fingers of the right *V hand* pointing at the eyes, bring the hand forward and down a short distance while bending the fingers as the hand moves.

DOUBT (B)

This alternating movement in American Sign Language is used for concepts that seem to weigh the possibility of a fact being true.

Formation: Move both *A hands*, palms facing down, up and down in alternating movements in front of each side of the body.

DOUBT (C) See UNBELIEF

DWELL See LIVE

DWELLING See TABERNACLE

EARTH, TERRESTRIAL

The movement of the hands in this sign represent the earth rotating on its axis.

Formation: While holding the back of the left *S hand,* palm down, with the bent thumb and middle finger of the right *5 hand,* rock the right hand with a small side-to-side repeated movement.

Related form: EARTHLY

EASTER, PASCHAL

This is an initialized sign formed similar to the sign for CELEBRATE and refers to the Christian festival commemorating Christ's resurrection.

Formation: Beginning with both *E hands* near each shoulder, palms facing back, twist the hands forward with a small repeated movement.

ECCLESIASTICAL See CHURCH

ECCLESIOLOGY

This sign is a combination of CHURCH and ORGANIZATION and refers to the study of church doctrine and church furnishings.

Formation: Tap the thumb side of the right *C hand* on the back of the left *S hand,* palm facing down. Then move both *O hands,* palms facing each other in front of the chest, in a outward circular movement, ending with the little fingers together.

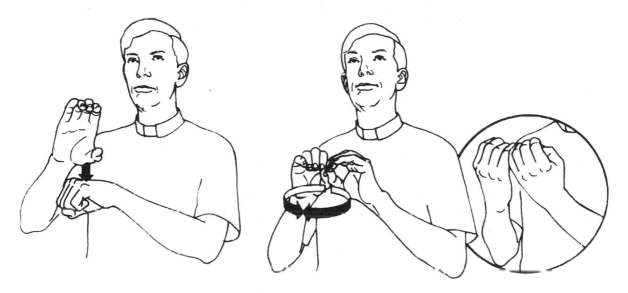

ECUMENICAL

This sign is a combination of CHURCH and UNITY and refers to the quest for Christian unity through dialogue and collaboration among diverse Christian groups.

Formation: Tap the thumb side of the right *C hand* on the back of the left *S hand,* palm facing down. Then, with the thumb and index finger of each hand touching and intersecting with the other hand, palms facing each other, move the hands in a flat circle in front of the body.

Related form: ECUMENISM

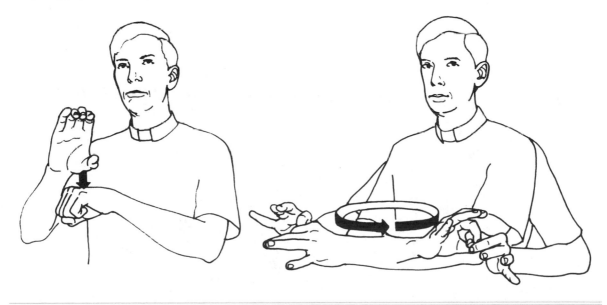

EDIFY See CHURCH

EGYPT

The bent finger in this sign represents the serpent on the front of the headdress of Egyptian pharaohs.

Formation: Bring the back of the right *X hand*, palm forward, against the center of the forehead.

EID *(Arabic)*

This sign refers to the three-day celebration that is held at the end of the fast of Ramadan. The word *eid* means "festival" in Arabic.

Formation: Beginning with the right *5 hand* on the chest, bring the hand forward while changing into a *10 hand*.

ELDER

This sign is a combination of CHIEF and the person marker and refers to one of the governing officers of a church often having pastoral or teaching functions.

Formation: With both *10 hands* in front of the chest, plams facing in and thumbs pointing up, move the right *10 hand* upward to near the right side of the head. Add the person marker.

ELECT See APPOINT (A)(B)

ELECTION See PREDESTINATION

EMMANUEL, IMMANUEL

This sign is a combination of GOD, WITH, and US, which is the translated meaning from the Hebrew. This is the name that the prophet Isaiah gave for the Messiah that was to come.

Formation: Move the right *B hand,* palm left, from above the front of the head downward in an arc toward the forehead and down in front of the face. Then bring the palm side of both *A hands* together in front of the body. Then touch the right *U hand,* palm facing left, first in front of the left side of the chest and then to the right side of the chest, turning the palm left as the hand moves.

ENDURE (A), PATIENCE

The thumb in this sign seems to silence a person to endure a burden.

Formation: Bring the thumbnail of the right *A hand,* palm facing left, down from the lips to the chin with a slow movement.

Related forms: ENDURANCE, PATIENT

ENDURE (B), LASTING, PERPETUAL, PRESERVE

The hands in this sign show moving something into the future with a continuing action.

Formation: With the thumb of the right *A hand* on the thumb of the left *A hand,* both palms facing down, move the hands forward in two small arcs.

Related form: ENDURANCE

Same sign for CONTINUE, KEEP ON, PERMANENT

See also PRESERVE for an alternate sign.

ENDURE (C) See SUFFER (A)

ENEMY, ADVERSARY, FOE

This sign is a combination of OPPOSITE and the person marker and indicates a person with opposing opinions.

Formation: Beginning with the fingertips of both extended index fingers touching in front of the body, palms facing in, pull the hands apart sharply. Add the person marker.

Note: This is a directional sign; change the orientation if you are the point of reference.

Same sign for OPPONENT, RIVAL

ENLIGHTEN See PREACH

ENTREAT See BEG

ENVY See COVET (A)

EPHPHATHA

The hands in this sign seem to remove a blockage from in front of the ears so one who is deaf may hear. Ephphatha is what Christ said as he caused a man who had been deaf from birth to hear again, and is translated as "Be opened."

Formation: Beginning with the back of both *B hands* held side by side by the right ear, fingers pointing up, swing the hands outward and apart in outward arcs, stopping with the palms facing each other about a foot apart.

EPIPHANY, LIGHT

The hand in this sign represents a light going on and its rays spread out. The sign is used to refer to the Christian festival held on January 6 to commemorate the manifestation of the divine nature of Christ to the Magi.

Formation: Beginning with the right *flattened O hand* held near the right side of the head, palm facing back, twist the wrist forward while opening the fingers into a *5 hand*, palm facing forward.

EPISCOPAL, PROTESTANT EPISCOPAL

The finger in this sign follows the outline of the sleeve of a priest's surplice, worn by the clergy of the Episcopal Church, which separated from the Church of England in 1789.

Formation: Move the extended right index finger from touching the wrist to touching the elbow of the bent left arm held across the chest.

Related form: EPISCOPALIAN

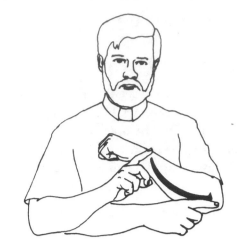

EPISTLE

This is the sign for LETTER and refers to the letters written by the Apostles to the ancient churches.

Formation: Bring the thumb of the right *10 hand,* palm facing down, from the mouth down to touch the thumb of the left *10 hand* held in front of the body, palm facing in.

ERROR See WRONG

ERUV (*Hebrew*)

This initialized sign is formed like AREA and symbolizes the boundary line that establishes community limits for Jewish activities on the Sabbath.

Formation: With the index-finger sides of both *E hands* touching in front of the chest, move the hands around in a small circle, ending with the little-finger side of both hands touching and palms facing in.

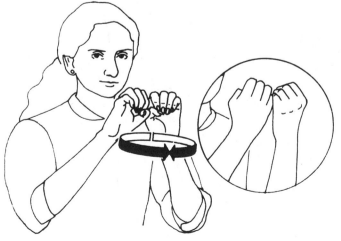

102

ESTABLISH See FOUND

ETERNAL, ETERNITY, EVER, EVERLAST-ING, FOREVER, IMMORTAL, INFINITE, PERPETUAL

This sign is a combination of ALWAYS and STILL and indicates something of eternal duration, such as the infinite attributes of God.

Formation: Move the extended right index finger, palm angled up, in a small clockwise circle near the right shoulder. Then move the right *Y hand*, palm down, forward and upward in an arc, ending with the palm facing forward.

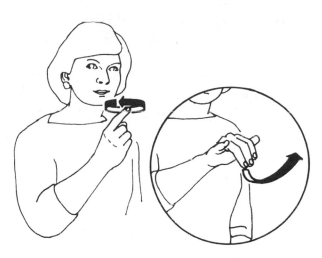

ETERNAL LIFE, IMMORTAL

This sign is a combination of LIFE and ETERNAL and refers to the quality of life including the promise of resurrection which God gives to those who believe in Christ.

Formation: Bring both *L hands,* palms facing in and index fingers pointing toward each other, upward from the waist to the chest. Move the extended right index finger, palm facing forward and finger pointing up, downward in an arc while changing into a *Y hand,* palm facing down, and moving forward in an arc.

Related form: IMMORTALITY

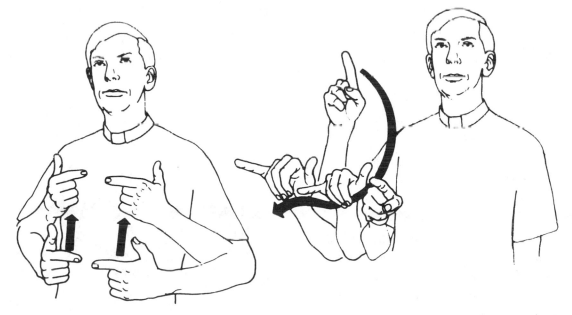

ETERNITY See ETERNAL

EUCHARIST (A)

This initialized sign is formed like the sign for CROSS and refers to the Christian sacrament commemorating the Last Supper.

Formation: Move the right *E hand*, palm facing forward, first down from near the right side of the head and then from left to right in front of the right shoulder.

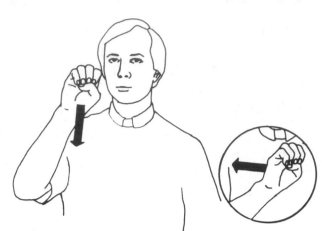

EUCHARIST (B) See COMMUNION (A)(B)

EVANGELISM (A)

This initialized sign is an abbreviation formed similar to the sign for PREACH and signifies the spreading of God's word through missionary efforts.

Formation: Beginning with a right *E hand*, palm facing forward, in front of the right shoulder, move the hand forward a short distance while opening into a *V hand*.

Related form: EVANGELICAL

See also PREACH for another sign formed in a similar manner.

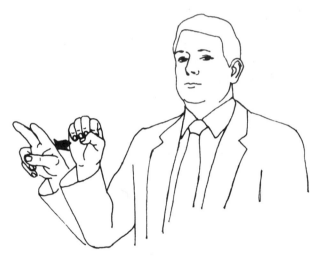

EVANGELISM (B)

This initialized sign is formed similar to the sign for PREACH and indicates zealous preaching of the Gospel.

Formation: Beginning with a right *E hand*, palm facing forward, in front of the right shoulder, move the hand forward a short distance.

Related form: EVANGELICAL

See also PREACH for another sign formed in a similar manner.

EVANGELISM (C) See ANNOUNCE

EVE

This initialized sign is formed at the lower part of the face, the location of female-designated signs. This is the name sign for Eve, the first woman and the wife of Adam.

Formation: Move the right *E hand*, palm facing left, in against the right side of the chin.

EVENING PRAYER See VESPERS

EVER See ALWAYS, ETERNAL

EVERLASTING See ETERNAL

EVIDENCE See PROOF

EVIL See BAD

EXALT (A), RAISE

This sign is a natural gesture that signifies elevating God to a level of highest honor.

Formation: Move both *open hands*, palms facing up, from in front of the body straight upward to in front of the face.

Related form: EXALTATION

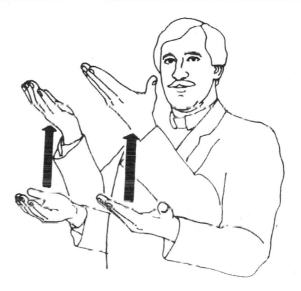

EXALT (B), HIGHER, RAISE, SUPERIOR, SUPREME

The hands in this sign indicate a position at a higher level.

Formation: Beginning with both *bent hands*, palms facing each other in front of each shoulder, move the hands upward in outward arcs simultaneously, stopping abruptly at about eye level.

Related form: EXALTATION

EXAMPLE See REVEAL

EXCOMMUNICATION See REJECT (A)(B)

EXIST See LIVE

EXODUS (A)

This sign is a combination of EGYPT and LEAVE and refers to the departure of the Israelites from Egypt after captivity.

Formation: Bring the back of the right *X hand,* palm forward, against the center of the forehead. Then beginning with both *5 hands,* palms facing down, in front the left side of the body, bring the hands to the right side of the body while closing the fingers forming *flattened O hands.*

EXODUS (B)

This sign is a combination of ESCAPE and FLEE and refers to the Israelites' escape from slavery in Egypt and journey toward the Promised Land under Moses.

Formation: Beginning with the extended right index finger pointing up between the index finger and middle finger of the left *open hand,* both palms facing down, move the right index finger deliberately to the right. Then, beginning with both *5 hands* in front of the chest, palms facing down and fingers pointing forward, move both hands forward while wiggling the fingers.

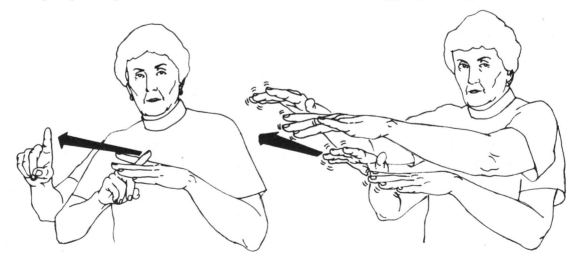

EXPECT See HOPE (B)

EXPIATION See PROPITIATION

EXPLAIN See INTERPRET (B)

FACE VEIL See BURQA

FAITH (A), TRUST

This sign is a combination of THINK and TRUST and indicates a conviction regarding religious doctrines without logical proof or material evidence.

Formation: Move the extended right index finger from touching the right side of the forehead down smoothly while changing into an *S hand*, ending with the little-finger side of the right *S hand* on the thumb side of the left *S hand* held in front of the body, palms facing in opposite directions.

FAITH (B)

This sign is a combination of THINK and an initialized sign formed like the sign for TRUST.

Formation: Move the extended right index finger from touching the right side of the forehead down smoothly while changing into an *F hand*, ending with the little-finger side of the right *F hand* on the thumb side of the left *F hand* held in front of the body, palms facing in opposite directions.

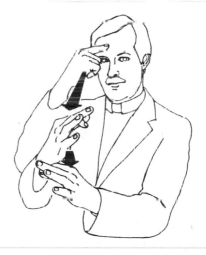

FAITHFUL, LOYAL

This is an initialized sign formed similar to REGULAR and indicates the practicing members of a religious faith.

Formation: Tap the little-finger side of the right *F hand* on the thumb side of the left *F hand* held in front of the body, palms facing in opposite directions.

Related form: LOYALTY

FAJR *(Arabic)*

This sign is a combination of FIRST and a movement showing the sun coming up and refers to the first of a Muslim's required five daily prayers. This prayer must be recited between the beginning of dawn and sunrise. The word *fajr* means "dawn" in the Arabic language.

Formation: Move the extended right index finger from in front of the right shoulder to the left to touch the extended thumb of the left *10 hand* held in front of the chest, palm facing in and thumb pointing up. Then, beginning with the right *O hand* in front of the right shoulder, palm facing up, move the hand upward while opening to a *curved hand*.

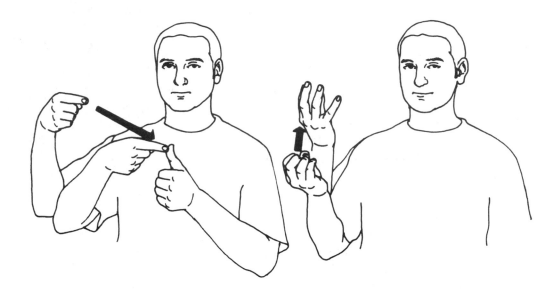

FALSE

The finger in this sign seems to push the truth aside.

Formation: Move the extended right index finger, palm facing left, in a downward arc from the right to left across the nose.

Same sign for ARTIFICIAL, COUNTER-FEIT, FAKE

See also HYPOCRITE for a sign with a similar meaning.

FALSEHOOD See LIE (A)(B)

FAMINE

The hand in this sign shows the passage to an empty stomach during a famine.

Formation: Beginning with the fingertips of the right *C hand* touching the center of the chest, palm facing in, move the hand downward a short distance.

Same sign for APPETITE, CRAVE, FAMISHED, HUNGER, RAVENOUS, STARVED, YEARN

FAST (A), ABSTAIN

This initialized sign seems to seal the lips in order to prevent eating, such as when abstaining from certain foods as a religious discipline.

Formation: Move the fingertips of the right *F hand*, palm left, from left to right across the lips.

Related forms: FASTING, ABSTINENCE
See also YOM KIPPUR for an alternate sign.

FAST (B), SAWN *(Arabic)*

The hand in this Muslim sign seems to wipe food from the mouth in order to fast.

Formation: Wipe the fingers of the right *open hand* from the left side of the mouth to the right.

Related form: FASTING

FATHER (A), HEAVENLY FATHER

This sign is a combination of the signs HEAVEN and FATHER and indicates the first person of the Trinity.

Formation: Beginning with both *open hands,* palms facing each other near each side of the head, move the hands toward each other while crossing the right hand in front of the left hand in front of the forehead, ending with the palms facing forward. Then, beginning with both *A hands* near the forehead, right palm facing forward and left palm facing in, move the hands upward to the left while opening into 5 *hands,* ending with both palms facing up.

FATHER (B), HEAVENLY FATHER

This is an exaggerated form of FATHER and refers to God the Father, the first person in the Trinity.

Formation: Beginning with both *A hands* near the forehead, right palm facing forward and left palm facing in, move the hands upward to the left while opening into 5 *hands,* ending with both palms facing up.

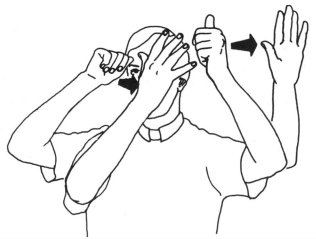

FATHER (C) See PRIEST (B)

FAULT See OBLIGATION

FEAR (A), AFRAID, FRIGHTENED

This a natural gesture protecting the body against something causing alarm or disquiet.

Formation: Beginning with both 5 *hands* in front of the body, right hand higher than the left hand, palms facing in and fingers pointing toward each other, move the hands toward each other with deliberate movements.

Same sign for SCARED, TERRIFIED, TERROR

FEAR (B), AFRAID, FRIGHTENED

The hands in this sign quiver in alarm from something frightening.

Formation: Beginning with both 5 *hands* in front of the body, right hand higher than the left hand, palms facing forward and fingers pointing up, move the hands downward with a wiggling movement.

Same sign for SCARED, TERRIFIED, TERROR

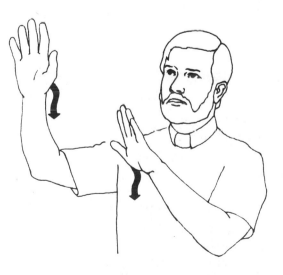

FEAR (C), AFRAID, FRIGHTENED

The hands in this sign are held up to protect the body against the unknown. This sign is used when referring to extreme reverence or awe of God.

Formation: Beginning both *5 hands* in front of the body, palms facing in and fingers pointing toward each other, move the hands toward each other with short movements while shaking the hands.

Same sign for SCARED, TERRIFIED, TERROR

FEAR OF GOD See AWE

FEAST

This is a sign formed similar to EAT but with an alternating movement used to indicate the feasts held during religious festivals in honor of God.

Formation: Move both *flattened O hands*, palms facing in, in toward the mouth with alternating movements.

Same sign for BANQUET, MEAL, CONSUME

FEAST OF TABERNACLES See SUKKOTH (*Hebrew*)

FEAST OF WEEKS See SHAVUOT (*Hebrew*)

FELLOWSHIP

The hands in this sign seem to show an interaction symbolizing the sharing of similar interest and beliefs among people of the same faith.

Formation: Circle the thumb of the right *10 hand* over the left *10 hand,* thumbs pointing toward each other and palms facing in opposite directions.

Same sign for ASSOCIATE, EACH OTHER, MINGLE, ONE ANOTHER, SOCIALIZE

FELLOWSHIP OF BELIEVERS, BROTHERHOOD OF BELIEVERS

This sign is a combination of SOCIETY, BELIEVE, and the person marker to refer to a partnership of people believing in Christ to support the Gospel and do charitable work for the church.

Formation: With the right *10 hand* over the left *10 hand,* thumbs pointing toward each other and palms facing in opposite directions, circle the thumbs of both *10 hands* around each other in opposite directions. Then move the extended right index finger smoothly down from the right temple, palm facing in, to clasp the left hand held in front of the body, palms facing each other. Add the person marker.

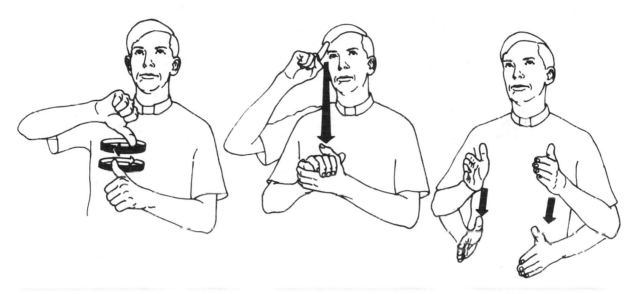

FESTIVAL See CELEBRATE

FESTIVAL OF LIGHTS See CHANUKAH *(Hebrew)*

FILLED WITH See INSPIRE

FILTHY See IMPURE

FINALLY See TRIUMPH (A)

FINISH See FULFILL

FIRMAMENT See HEAVEN (A)(B)

FIRSTBORN

This sign is a combination of FIRST and BIRTH. The Hebrew word refers chiefly to men, but it also may be used to refer to animals. Among the Israelites the firstborn son had special privileges.

Formation: Strike the thumb of the left *10 hand*, palm facing right, with the right extended index finger. Then bring the palm of the right *open hand* from the stomach forward, landing the back of the right hand on the palm of the left *open hand*, palm facing up.

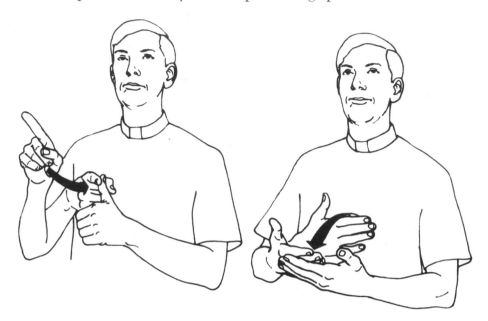

FIVE PILLARS See PILLARS OF ISLAM

FLESH (A), MEAT

The fingers in this sign grab a section of body tissue and symbolizes the meat of animals used in religious sacrifices.

Formation: With the bent index finger and thumb of the right *5 hand*, grasp the flesh at the base of the thumb of the left *open hand*, palm facing in and fingers pointing right, and shake both hands.

FLESH (B) See BODY

FLOOD

This sign is a combination of WATER and a gesture showing the water rising, as occurred during the universal deluge described in the Bible.

Formation: Touch the index finger of the right *W hand* to the mouth, palm facing left. Then raise both *open hands* from in front of the body upward simultaneously, palms down and fingers pointing forward.

Note: The fingers may wiggle as the *5 hands* are raised.

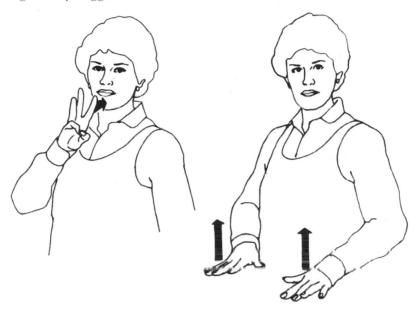

FOE See ENEMY

FOLLOWER See DISCIPLE (B)

FORBID

The finger in this sign strikes the other hand as a reprimand or warning against an undesired action.

Formation: Strike the side of the extended right index finger, palm facing down, against the palm of the left *open hand,* palm facing left.

   Related form: FORBIDDEN
   Same sign for BAN, PROHIBIT
   See also LAW (A) for a related sign formed in a similar manner.

FORETELL See PROPHECY

FORGIVE, ABSOLUTION, DISPENSATION, PARDON

The hand seems to brush away a fault or offense to free the offender from the consequences of it.

Formation: Brush the fingers of the right *open hand* across the palm of the left *open hand* from heel to the fingers with a repeated movement.

Related form: FORGIVENESS

Same sign for EXCUSE, PAROLE

See also ABSOLUTION for an alternate sign.

FORM See CREATE

FORSAKE

This sign is a combination of FORGET and LEAVE and signifies abandoning and renouncing previous habits.

Formation: Beginning with the fingers of the right *open hand,* fingers pointing left, on the left side of the forehead, bring the hand to the right while closing into an *A hand.* Then, beginning with both *A hands,* palms facing each other in front of the chest, bring the hands down to the left side of the body while opening the fingers into *5 hands,* palms facing down and fingers pointing forward.

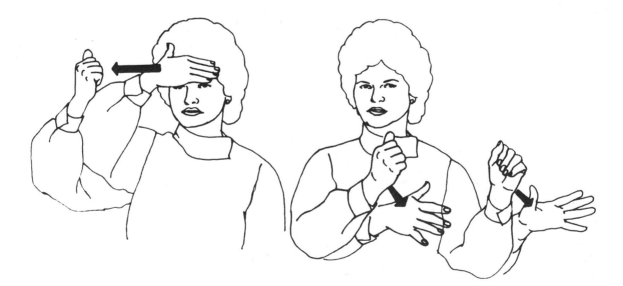

FOUND, ESTABLISH, INSTITUTE

The hand in this sign seems to take something and set it firmly in place such as establishing or setting up a practice.

Formation: Beginning with the right *A hand,* palm facing down, above the left *open hand,* palm facing down, twist the right wrist in an arc and land the little-finger side of the right hand on the back of the left hand.

Related forms: FOUNDED, INSTITUTED
Same sign for APPOINT, APPOINTMENT
See also BEGINNING for a sign with a related meaning.

FOUNDATION See ADVOCATE

FREE WILL (A)

This is a combination of FREE and WILL and signifies the idea that man has the power to make choices, which are not predetermined by God.

Formation: Bring both *F hands,* wrists crossed in front of the chest and palms facing outward in opposite directions, away from each other by twisting the wrists, ending with the palms facing forward in front of each side of the body. Then bring the index-finger side of the right *W hand,* palm facing forward, against the palm of the left *open hand,* palm facing right.

117

FREE WILL (B)

This sign is a combination of FREE and WANT and refers to the belief that man's choices in life are ultimately voluntary and not predetermined by God.

Formation: Bring both *F hands*, wrists crossed in front of the chest and palms facing outward in opposite directions, away from each other by twisting the wrists, ending with the palms facing forward in front of each side of the body. Then, beginning with both *open hands* in front of the body, palms facing up, bring the hands in toward the body while constricting the fingers into *claw hands*.

FRIDAY PRAYER See JUM'AH *(Arabic)*

FRIEND (A), QUAKERS

The fingers of this sign intertwine, symbolizing the close relationship between companions.

Formation: Hook the bent index finger of the right *X hand,* palm facing down, down over the bent index finger of the left *X hand,* palm facing up. Turn the hands to repeat the action in reverse.

See also QUAKERS and DISCIPLE for alternate signs.

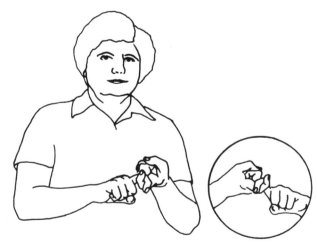

FRIENDS (B) See QUAKERS (A)(B)

FRIGHTENED See FEAR (A)(B)(C)

FRUM (*Hebrew*), OBSERVANT, RELIGIOUS

The hand in this sign beats on the chest slowly as a sign of piety and refers to those Jews who observe the 613 commandments.

Formation: Tap the palm side of the right *S hand* against the left side of the chest with a small, slow, repeated movement.

See also YOM KIPPUR for a sign formed in a similar manner but with a quicker movement.

FULFILL, ACCOMPLISH, COMPLETE, FINISH

This sign is a combination of FINISH and AGREE and refers to the accomplishment of a prophecy as it was foretold.

Formation: Beginning with both *5 hands* in front of the chest, palms facing in and fingers pointing up, twist the wrists sharply downward and outward, ending with the palms facing down and fingers pointing forward. Then, beginning with the extended right index finger touching the right side of the forehead, palm facing down, and the left *1 hand* in front of the left side of the chest, palm facing right, bring the right hand smoothly down while twisting both wrists, ending with both hands side by side in front of the body, palms facing down and fingers pointing forward.

FUNDAMENTAL

This is an initialized sign formed similar to the sign for FOUNDATION and signifies the belief in the Bible as factual, historical record and incontrovertible prophecy.

Formation: Make a circle with the right *F hand,* palm facing left, under the palm of the left *open hand* held in front of the chest, palm facing down.

Related form: FUNDAMENTALIST

FUNERAL

The hands in this sign seem to portray a procession to the burial ceremony of the dead.

Formation: With both *V hands* in front of the body, right hand closer to the body than the left hand, both palms facing forward and fingers pointing up, move the hands forward in short double arcs.

FURY See ANGER

GALUT *(Hebrew)* See DIASPORA

GARMENT

This sign shows the shape of the front of a robe worn by Israelites.

Formation: Bring the thumbs of both *A hands* from near each shoulder, palms facing in, downward and toward each other, ending near the waist.

Same sign for COAT, JACKET

GATHER See ASSEMBLE

GATHERING See MEETING

GENESIS

This sign is formed similar to the sign WORD and refers to the first book of the Bible.

Formation: Move the right *G hand*, palm facing left, to the left in front of the chest to touch the extended left index finger, palm facing right and finger pointing up.

GENTILE

This sign is a combination of NOT and JEW and was used in ancient times to refer to those people who were not part of God's chosen family at birth and thus can be considered "pagans."

Formation: Bring the thumb of the right *10 hand* forward from under the chin. Then, with the right *bent hand* near the chin, palm facing in and fingers pointing up, bring the fingertips downward from the chin with a double movement while closing the fingers to a *flattened O hand* each time.

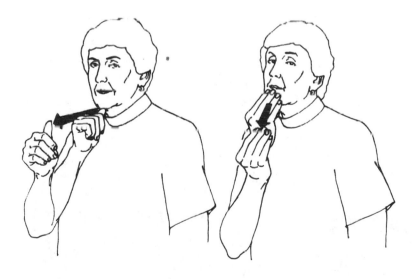

GENUFLECT, DEVOTED

The fingers represent knees that are bending as in the custom, particularly in the Roman Catholic Church, of bending the knee in respect.

Formation: Beginning with the fingertips of the right *V hand,* palm facing in and fingers pointing down, touching the palm of the left *open hand,* palm facing up, bend the fingers downward at the knuckles.

Related form: DEVOTION

See also DEVOTED for an alternate sign and KNEEL for a sign with a related meaning formed in a similar manner.

GET See OBTAIN

GIFT, AWARD *(noun),* CONTRIBUTION, PRESENT *(noun)*

The hands seem to take something and present it to another person. This sign may refer to either a present or to a natural talent or aptitude. This sign is used for the noun form only.

Formation: Move both *modified A hands,* palms facing each other, forward in deliberate arcs.

See also GIVE for the verb form of the sign and DEVOTED for an initialized sign formed in a similar manner.

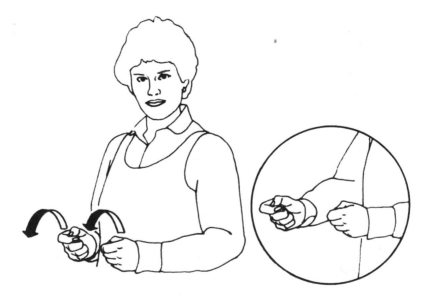

GIVE, AWARD *(verb)*, BESTOW, CONTRIBUTE, PRESENT *(verb)*

The hands in this sign seem to take something and present it to another.

Formation: Beginning with both *flattened O hands,* palms facing up, in front of the body, move the hands forward in an arc while opening into 5 *hands.*

Note: This is a directional sign formed toward whomever is the recipient of the gift. The beginning position may have the palms facing up or down. This sign may be formed with only the right hand.

See also GIFT for the noun form of this sign.

GLORY, MAJESTY

The hand in this sign represents the rays that reflect from something of splendor. This sign refers to exalted honor as well as to the bliss of heaven.

Formation: Beginning with the palms of both *open hands* together in front of the body, bring the right hand upward toward the right shoulder while opening into a 5 *hand* and wiggling the fingers.

Related forms: GLORIFY, GLORIOUS

GOD (A), LORD, HASHAYM *(Hebrew)*

This sign is formed with a similar movement as in HONOR and RESPECT, indicating God's position as the originator and ruler of the universe.

Formation: Move the right *B hand,* palm facing left, from above the front of the head downward in an arc toward the forehead and down in front of the face.

Note: This sign may be made with an *open hand* or a *G hand* instead of a *B hand.*

See also HONOR and RESPECT for initialized signs formed in a similar manner.

GOD (B), LORD, HASHAYM (C), YAHWEH (Hebrew), YHWH (Hebrew)

The finger in this sign points up to God and then moves down in a movement similar to RESPECT.

Formation: Beginning with the right extended index finger, palm facing left, pointing up near the right side of the head, bring the hand downward in an arc toward the forehead and down in front of the face while changing into a *B hand*.

See also HONOR and RESPECT for initialized signs formed in a similar manner.

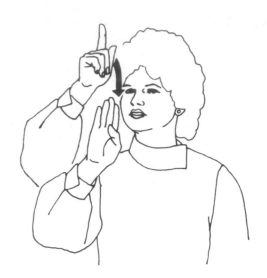

GOD (C) See ALLAH

GODLINESS

This sign is a combination of GOD and SAME, indicating an attitude and a style of life that seeks to live according to God's will.

Formation: Move the right *open hand,* palm facing left, from above the front of the head downward in an arc toward the forehead and down in front of the face. Then move the right *Y hand,* palm facing down, back and forth with a repeated movement.

See also CHRISTLIKE and LIKENESS for signs with similar meanings.

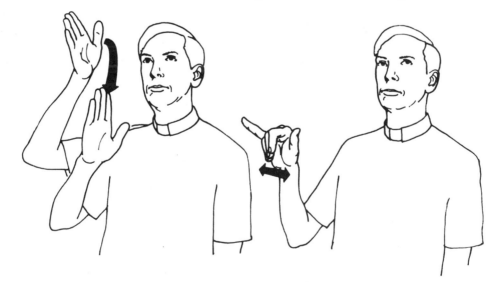

GOD'S IMAGE See IDOL

GOD'S MERCY See MERCY (B)

GOD'S WILL See WILL (A)

GOOD, WELL

The hand in this sign seems to take something desirable from the mouth and bring it forward.

Formation: Beginning with the fingers of the right *open hand* touching the mouth, palm in and fingers pointing up, move the hand down, landing the back of the right hand in the palm of the left *open hand* held in front of the body.

GOOD WORKS

This sign is a combination of GOOD and WORK and refers to Christian behavior that is a response to the belief that Christ is the Savior from sin.

Formation: Beginning with the fingers of the right *open hand* touching the mouth, palm in and fingers pointing up, move the hand down, landing the back of the right hand in the palm of the left *open hand* held in front of the body. Then, with a double movement, tap the heel of the right S *hand* on the back of the left S *hand,* both palms facing down.

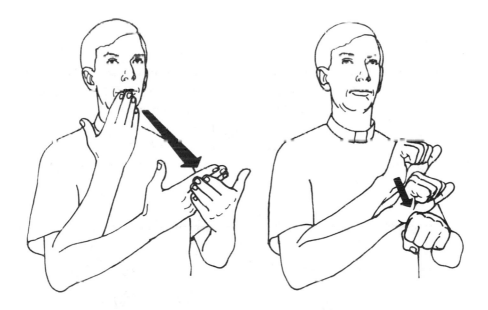

GOSPEL (A)

This sign is a combination of TELL and NEW and refers to the first four books of the New Testament, describing the life, death, and resurrection of Jesus Christ.

Formation: Beginning with the extended right index finger pointing to the mouth, palm facing in, bring the hand down in an arc while opening into an *open hand*, brushing the back of the right hand across the palm of the left *open hand*, held in front of the body, palm facing up.

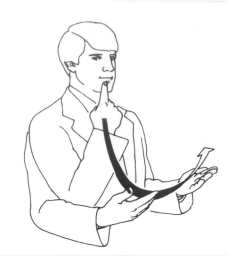

GOSPEL (B)

This sign is a combination of GOOD and NEW and refers to the translation of *Gospel* from the Latin word meaning "good news."

Formation: Beginning with the fingers of the right *open hand* pointing to the mouth, palm facing in, bring the hand down in an arc, brushing the back of the right hand across the palm of the left *open hand*, held in front of the body, palm facing up.

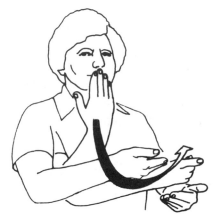

GOSPEL (C)

This sign is a combination of GOOD and INFORMATION and refers to the books of the New Testament that describe the message of Christianity and record Christ's life and teachings.

Formation: Beginning with the fingers of the right *open hand* touching the mouth, palm facing in and fingers pointing up, move the hand down, landing the back of the right hand in the palm of the left *open hand* held in front of the body. Then, beginning with the fingers of both *flattened O hands* near the forehead, palms facing in, move the hands forward while opening into 5 *hands*, palms facing up.

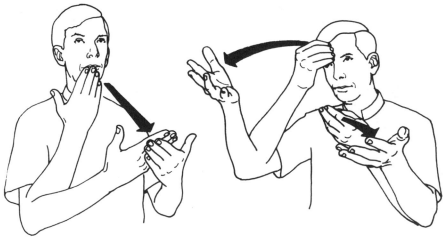

GRACE (A)

The hand seems to take something from God and shower it down, signifying God's divine love being bestowed freely upon mankind.

Formation: Beginning with the right *flattened O hand* above the right shoulder, palm facing forward, twist the wrist inward while spreading the fingers into a *5 hand* and moving down to the right side of the head.

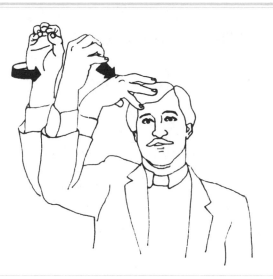

GRACE (B)

This is an initialized sign that indicates taking something from God and bringing it down to mankind.

Formation: Bring the right *G hand* from above the right shoulder, palm facing forward and fingers pointing up, downward, ending with the little-finger side of the right hand against the left side of the chest, palm facing up.

GRACIOUS, BENEVOLENT, MERCIFUL

This sign is a combination of GOOD and COMFORTABLE.

Formation: Move the right *open hand* from the lips, palm facing the body, down and forward over the left *open hand*, palm facing the chest and the fingers of both hands pointing toward each other in opposite directions. Then move the left hand up over the right hand exchanging places, keeping both hands close to the body.

GRATEFUL See THANKFUL

GRAVE See BURY

GREEDY, SELFISH

The hands seems to clutch at something, symbolizing an excessive desire to possess things.

Formation: With the *3 hands* apart in front of the waist, palms facing down, draw the hands toward the body while crooking the fingers and thumbs.

See also COVET (A) for a sign with a related meaning.

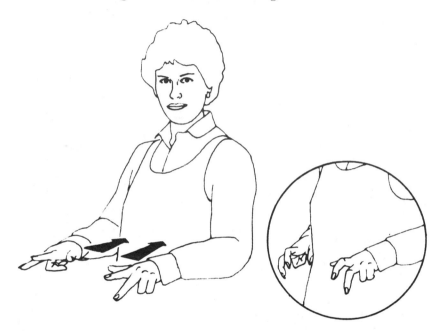

GRIEVE See MOURN

GUARD See PROTECT

GUIDE, LEAD

One hand pulls the other hand along such as when a person shows another the way by leading, directing, or advising the course to be pursued.

Formation: Grasp the fingertips of the left open hand, palm facing right, with the fingers of the right hand, palm toward the body. Let the right hand pull the left hand forward.

Note: This sign is sometimes formed with the right thumb and middle finger grasping the left hand instead of the entire right hand.

GUILT See CONSCIENCE (A)(B)

HADES See HELL (A)

HAGGADAH

This sign is a combination of PASSOVER and STORY and refers to the book containing the story of the Exodus read by Jewish people at the Passover Seder.

Formation: Knock the palm side of the right *A hand* near the elbow of the bent left arm held across the chest. Link the thumbs and index fingers of both *F hands* and pull them apart with a repeated movement.

Note: The illustration shows PASSOVER (A) for the first part of the sign, however PASSOVER (B) or (C) may be used, if preferred.

HAIL See HONOR

HAJJ *(Arabic),* PILGRIMAGE

This sign is used to refer to a Muslim's pilgrimage to Mecca in Saudi Arabia at least once in his or her lifetime, which is required as one of the Five Pillars of Islam. The hajj has ceremonies that symbolize the essence of the Islamic faith and commemorate the trials of the prophet Abraham and his family.

Formation: Beginning with the thumb and index finger of the right *A hand* pinched together in front of the right shoulder, palm facing forward, move the hand forward while opening into a *G hand*.

HALACHA (A) *(Hebrew)*

This sign is a combination of JEW and LAW and refers to the legal elements of Talmudic literature that assist in interpreting the Scriptures.

Formation: With the right *bent hand* near the chin, palm facing in and fingers pointing up, bring the fingertips downward from the chin with a double movement while closing the fingers to a *flattened O* hand each time. Then strike the palm side of the right *L hand* against the palm of the left *open hand*.

HALACHA (B) *(Hebrew)*

This initialized sign is formed like LAW and refers to decrees, ordinances, and customs that comprise Jewish tradition.

Formation: Move the thumb side of the right *H hand*, palm facing down, down the palm of the left *open hand*, palm facing right and fingers pointing up, touching first on the fingers and then on the heel.

See also COMMANDMENTS, LAW (B), MOSES, and TESTAMENT for other initialized signs formed in a similar manner.

HALLELUJAH See ALLELUIA

HALLOWED See HOLY (A), HONOR

HANUKKAH *(Hebrew)* See CHANUKAH *(Hebrew)*

HARDNESS OF HEART

This sign is a combination of HARD and HEART and refers to a stubborn attitude that leads a person to reject God's will.

Formation: Hit the middle-finger side of the right *bent V hand* on the back of the left *S hand*. Then touch the bent middle finger of the right *5 hand* to the chest near the location of the heart.

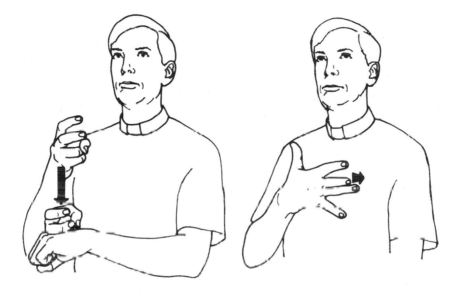

HASHAYM *(Hebrew)* See GOD (A)(B)

HASIDIC, CHASSIDIC

The fingers follow the shape of the long curls worn by certain observant Jewish sects.

Formation: Bring both extended index fingers from pointing up to each ear, palms facing back, downward in a circling movement, ending near each side of the chest.

Related forms: HASIDIM, CHASSIDIM

HATE See DESPISE

HEALING See MIGHTY (A)

HEART (A)

The fingers outline the traditional shape of the heart near its physical location.

Formation: Use the extended index fingers of both hands, palms facing in, to trace the outline of a heart on the left side of the chest.

HEART (B)

The middle fingers, considered the feeling fingers in American Sign Language, are used to form a heart shape. This sign is used for the emotional feeling of the heart, not for the physical organ.

Formation: Use the bent middle fingers of both 5 *hands,* palms facing in, to trace the outline of a heart on the left side of the chest.

HEAVEN (A), CELESTIAL, FIRMAMENT, PARADISE

The hands show a global movement above the head, signifying the firmament or traditional abode of God, the angels, and the souls of those already granted salvation.

Formation: Beginning with both *open hands* near each side of the head, palms facing each other and fingers pointing up, move the hands upward and toward each other. As the hands meet at the top of the head, pass the right hand under the left hand while turning both palms forward.

HEAVEN (B), CELESTIAL, FIRMAMENT, PARADISE

The hands seem to shield the body from the glory of God in heaven.

Formation: Starting with both *open hands* near each side of the head, palms facing each other and fingers pointing up, move the hands toward each other, crossing the right hand in front of the left in front of the forehead, ending with the palms facing forward.

Same sign for SKY, SPACE

HEAVENLY FATHER See FATHER (A)(B)

HEBREW (A)

This sign is a combination of JEW and LANGUAGE and refers to the Semitic language of Israel.

Formation: With the right *bent hand* near the chin, palm facing in and fingers pointing up, bring the fingertips downward from the chin with a double movement while closing the fingers to a *flattened O hand* each time. Then, beginning with the thumbs of both *L hands* near each other in front of the body, palms facing down, bring the hands apart while twisting the wrists with a double movement.

HEBREWS See ISRAELITES

HELL (A), HADES, SCHEOL *(Hebrew)*

This sign is a combination of DOWN and FIRE signifying the traditional location of hell and the place or state of torture and punishment of the wicked after death presided over by Satan.

Formation: Point the extended right index finger downward in front of the body. Then, while wiggling the fingers of both *5 hands,* palms facing in and fingers pointing up, move the hands in upward alternating circles.

HELL (B)

This is an initialized sign directed toward the traditional location of hell and signifies the abode of condemned souls and devils.

Formation: Thrust the right *H hand,* palm facing left and fingers pointing forward, from the center of the chest downward and outward to the right with a deliberate movement.

See also DAMN for an initialized sign formed in a similar manner.

HELL (C)

This sign is a combination of AREA and DEATH, signifying the place where people who experience true death—that is, a separation from God—go for eternity.

Formation: Move the right *open hand* in a large arc over the back of the left *open hand,* both palms facing down. Then, beginning with both *open hands* in front of the body, right palm facing down and left palm facing up and fingers pointing forward, flip the hands to the right so that the right palm faces up and the left palm faces down.

HELP

The right hand assists the left hand, symbolic of one who requires support during difficulty or distress.

Formation: With the little-finger side of the right *A hand,* palm facing left, in the palm of the left *open hand,* palm facing up, move both hands upward a short distance.

Same sign for AID, ASSIST

See also ADVOCATE and VICAR for signs formed in a similar manner.

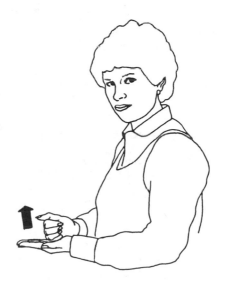

HENOTHEISM See POLYTHEISM

HERESY

This sign is a combination of **FALSE** and **TEACH** and refers to a doctrine or group considered contrary to correct doctrine from the Jewish or Christian perspective.

    Formation: Move the extended right index finger, palm facing left, from right to left across the nose, striking the nose as it passes. Then, with both *flattened O hands* in front of the head, palms down, move the hands forward with a short double movement.

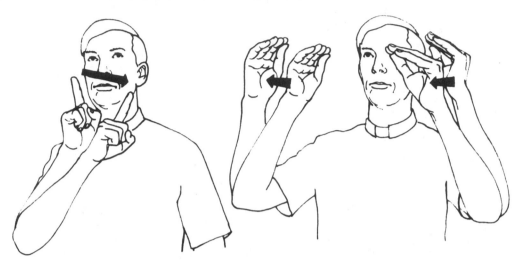

HIDDEN See MYSTERY

HIGH HOLY DAYS

This sign is a combination of **EXALT**, **HOLY**, and **DAY** and refers to Rosh Hashanah and Yom Kippur, the days designated for religious observance for Jews.

    Formation: Beginning with both *bent hands*, palms facing each other in front of each shoulder, move the hands upward simultaneously, stopping abruptly at about eye level. Then move the right *H hand* in a small circle in front of the chest and then across the palm of the left *open hand* from its base to the fingertips and outward. Then, beginning with the elbow of the bent right arm, right index finger pointing up, on the back of the left *open hand* held across the body, palm facing down, move the right index finger downward toward the left elbow.

HIGHER See EXALT (B)

HINDUISM, HINDU

This sign is a combination of INDIA and RELIGION and refers to the common religion of India, based on the religion of the original Aryan settlers.

Formation: Twist the thumb of the right *A hand* in the middle of the forehead. Then bring the fingertips of the right *R hand* from the left side of the chest downward and forward, ending with the palm facing down and the fingers pointing forward.

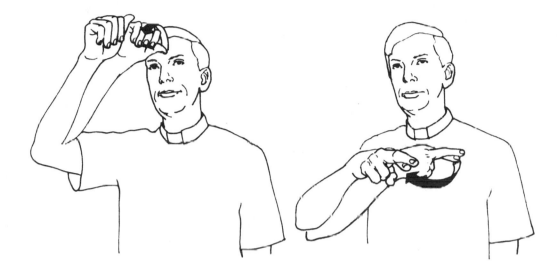

HOLY (A), DIVINE, HALLOWED, SACRED

This is an initialized sign formed similar to the sign for CLEAN and designates anything worthy of worship or high esteem.

Formation: Slide the little-finger side of the right *H hand* across the palm of the left *open hand* from its base to the fingertips and outward.

HOLY (B)

This is an initialized sign formed similar to the sign for CLEAN and refers to something set apart for a religious purpose.

Formation: Move the right *H hand* in a small circle in front of the chest and then across the palm of the left *open hand* from its base to the fingertips and outward.

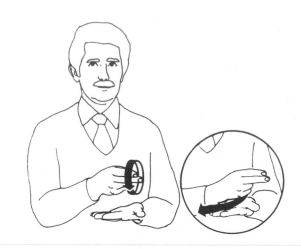

HOLY (C)

This is an initialized sign formed similar to the sign for CLEAN and refers to something set apart as sacred.

Formation: Move the right *H hand* in a small circle in front of the chest and then slide the palm of the right *open hand* across the palm of the left *open hand* from its base to the fingertips and outward.

HOLY COMMUNION See COMMUNION (A)(B)

HOLY DAY OF OBLIGATION

This sign is a combination of DAY and REQUIRE and refers to those days that, according to the Roman Catholic Church, should be observed by penitence and participation in a Mass.

Formation: Beginning with the elbow of the bent right arm, right index finger pointing up, on the back of the left hand held across the body, palm facing down, move the right index finger downward toward the left elbow. Then, with the index finger of the right *X hand* touching the palm of the left *open hand,* palm facing right, bring both hands toward the chest.

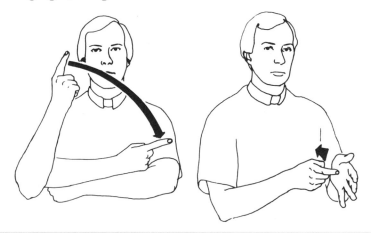

HOLY GHOST, HOLY SPIRIT

This sign is a combination of HOLY and SPIRIT and refers to the third person of the Trinity.

Formation: Move the right *H hand* in a small circle in front of the chest and then slide the palm of the right *open hand* across the palm of the left *open hand* from its base to the fingertips and outward. Then, with the fingertips of both *F hands* touching in front of the body, right hand above the left hand, pull the hands apart.

HOLY LAND

This sign is a combination of HOLY and LAND and refers to modern-day Israel and the historical locations where Christ lived and performed His ministry.

Formation: Move the right *H hand* across the palm of the left *open hand* from its base to the fingertips and outward. Then rub the thumb of both *curved hands* on each index finger with a repeated movement followed by moving the right *open hand* in a large arc over the back of the left *open hand*, both palms facing down.

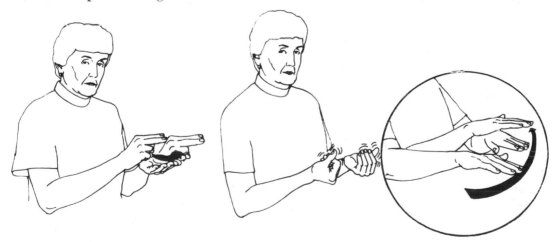

HOLY MATRIMONY See MARRIAGE

HOLY OF HOLIES

This sign is a combination of MOST, HOLY, and PLACE and refers to the innermost sanctuary of the Temple containing the Ark of the Covenant.

Formation: Move the knuckles of the right *A hand* upward on the knuckles of the left *A hand*, both palms facing in. Then move the right *H hand* across the palm of the left *open hand* from its base to the fingertips and outward. Then, with both *P hands* near each other in front of the chest, palms facing down, bring the hands outward in a circle, ending near each other close to the chest.

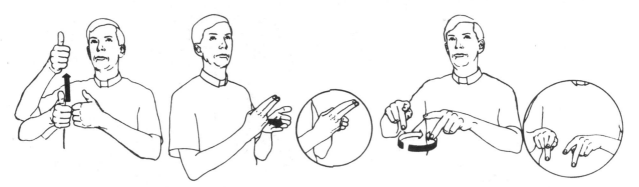

HOLY ORDERS See ORDAIN

HOLY QUR'AN *(Arabic)* See QUR'AN *(Arabic)*

HOLY SCRIPTURE See BIBLE (C)(D)

HOLY SPIRIT See HOLY GHOST

HOLY WEEK

This sign is a combination of HOLY and WEEK and refers to the week climaxing in Easter Sunday on which day the Christian church remembers the death and resurrection of Christ.

Formation: Move the right *H hand* across the palm of the left *open hand* from its base to the fingertips and outward. Then move the extended right index finger, palm facing down, across the left *open hand* from the heel to the fingertips.

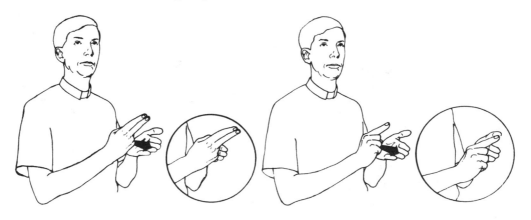

HOMILETICS See PREACH

HOMILY See PREACH

HONEST See TRUTH (A)

HONOR, HAIL, HALLOWED

This is an initialized sign formed similar to the sign for GOD and indicates the highest esteem, as for God.

Formation: Beginning with both *H hands* in front of the head, right hand higher than the left hand, palms facing each other and fingers pointing up, move the hands downward and in toward the chest.

Note: The head usually bows as the hands come down. This sign may be formed with only one hand.

See also GOD (A)(B) and RESPECT for signs with related meanings formed in a similar manner.

HOPE (A)

The hand seems to take a thought from the head and look at it in the future, as in anticipation of the Messiah's coming or the Last Judgment.

Formation: Beginning with the right *open hand* near the right side of the forehead and the left *open hand* forward of the left shoulder, palms facing each other, bend the fingers of both hands down with a double movement.

HOPE (B), EXPECT

The hand seems to be looking in anticipation to something in the future, such as the coming of the Messiah or the Last Judgment.

Formation: Beginning with the right extended index finger near the right side of the forehead and the left extended index finger forward of the left shoulder, palms facing each other, bring the right hand down to near the left hand while changing to *bent hands,* fingers pointing toward each other.

Related form: EXPECTATION
Same sign for ANTICIPATE, ANTICIPATION

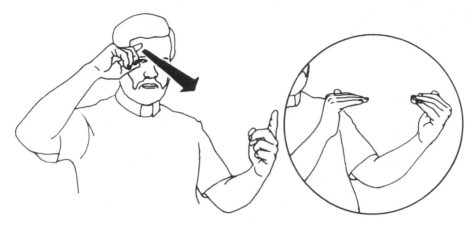

HOSANNA See PRAISE (A)(B)

HOST (A)

This is the sign for GROUP formed in two locations above the head and refers to large groups of angels in heaven.

Formation: Beginning with both *C hands* above the left side of the head, palms facing each other, twist the wrists in a circular movement to turn the palms in. Repeat above the right side of the head.

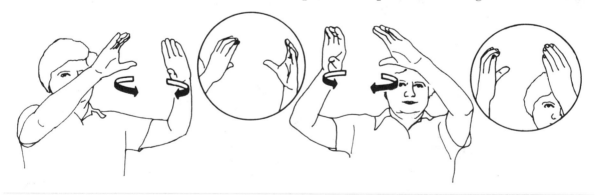

HOST (B) See BREAD, COMMUNION (B), MASS

HOUSE See TABERNACLE

HUMANITY See LAYPERSON

HUMBLE, LOWLY, MEEK

One hand moves to a position beneath the other and indicates deferential respect and an awareness of one's shortcomings.

Formation: Bring the right *B hand,* palm facing left and fingers pointing up, forward in an arc from the chin under the palm of the left *open hand* held in front of the face, palm facing down.

Related form: HUMILITY

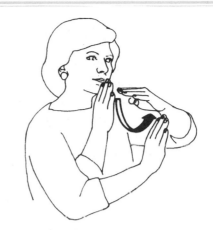

HYMN, ANTHEM, SONG

The hand follows a rhythmic movement indicating a song, as one intended for praise and worship of God.

Formation: Swing the right *open hand* back and forth in a large arc over the extended left forearm.

Same sign for MUSIC, MELODY

See also CANTOR, CHOIR (A), and PSALM for initialized signs formed in a similar manner.

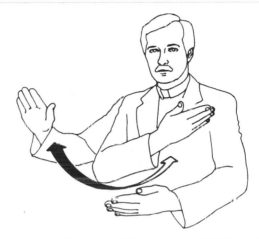

HYMNAL, HYMNBOOK

This sign is a combination of **HYMN** and **BOOK** and refers to a bound collection of church hymns.

Formation: Swing the right *open hand* back and forth in a large arc over the extended left forearm. Then, starting the palms of both *open hands* together in front of the chest, move the hands apart at the top, keeping the little fingers together.

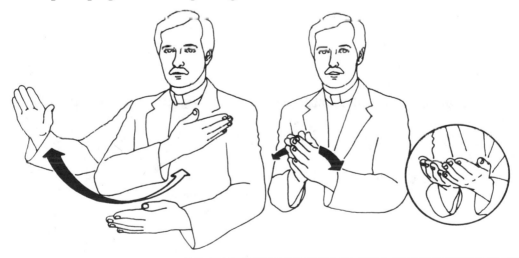

HYMNBOOK See HYMNAL

HYPOCRITE

The hands seem to cover up something not meant to be exposed and refers to a person who espouses beliefs that are not sincerely held.

Formation: With the right *open hand* on the back of the left *open hand*, both palms facing down, bend the right fingers down, pushing on the left fingers causing them to bend down.

Related form: HYPOCRISY

Same sign for IMPOSTER, FAKE

See also FALSE for a sign with a similar meaning.

HYSSOP, ASPERGILLUM

The hands mime holding an aspergillum, which is used for sprinkling in certain Hebraic and Catholic purification rights.

Formation: With the thumb and index finger of the right hand pinched together, palm facing left, move the hand downward and forward by bending the wrist first in front of the right side of the body and then in front of the body.

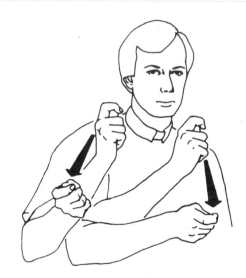

IBLIS *(Arabic)* See SATAN (A)

IBRAHIM See ABRAHAM

IDOL, GOD'S IMAGE

This initialized sign follows the shape of a graven image used for worship.

Formation: Beginning with both *I hands* near each side of the head, palms facing each other, bring the hands downward in a wavy movement to in front of the body.

See also STATUE for a sign with a related meaning formed in a similar manner.

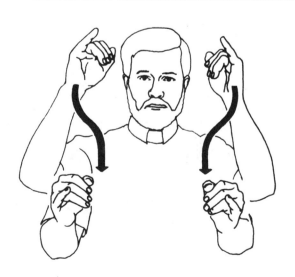

IDOLATRY

This sign is a combination of IDOL and WORSHIP and refers to the worship of graven or cast images used to represent a deity other than the one true God.

Formation: Beginning with both *I hands* near each side of the head, palms facing each other, bring the hands downward in a wavy movement to in front of the body. Then, beginning with the fingers of the right hand over the left *A hand,* both palms facing down, move the hands forward in an arc.

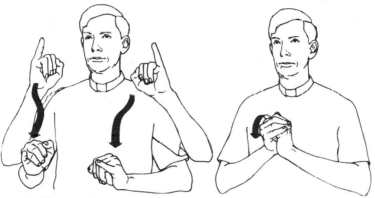

IMAGE See STATUE

IMAGE OF GOD See LIKENESS (A)

IMMACULATE CONCEPTION (A)

This sign is a combination of an initialized sign formed like CLEAN and BIRTH and signifies the Roman Catholic doctrine that Jesus was conceived in His mother's womb free from sin.

Formation: Form an *I* with the right hand above the left *open hand*, palm facing up. Then move the right *open hand* across the left palm from its base to off the fingertips. Then bring the palm of the right *open hand* from the stomach forward, landing the back of the right hand on the palm of the left *open hand*, palm facing up.

IMMACULATE CONCEPTION (B)

This sign is a combination of INNOCENT and BIRTH.

Formation: Move the fingers of both *H hands,* palms facing in and fingers pointing toward each other, outward across the lips, ending forward of each shoulder, palms facing each other and fingers pointing forward. Then bring the palm of the right *open hand* from the stomach forward, landing the back of the right hand on the palm of the left *open hand,* palm facing up.

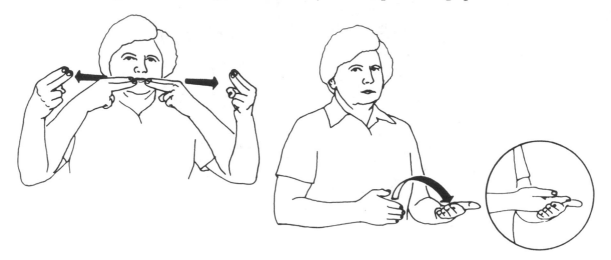

IMMANUEL See EMMANUEL

IMMERSION See BAPTIZE (A)

IMMORTAL See ETERNAL, ETERNAL LIFE

IMPURE, DEFILED, DIRTY, FILTHY, SOILED, STAINED

This sign is formed similar to the sign for PIG and is used to specify something that is in a state of immorality and sin.

Formation: With the back of the right *S hand,* palm facing down, under the chin, open the fingers deliberately into a *5 hand.*

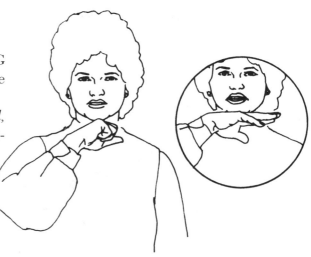

INCARNATE

This sign is a combination of BECOME and BODY and refers to Jesus Christ's assuming a human body.

Formation: With the palm of the right *open hand* on the palm of left *open hand*, twist the wrists to put the hands in reverse positions. Then touch the upper chest and then the lower chest with the palms of both *open hands*.

Related form: INCARNATION

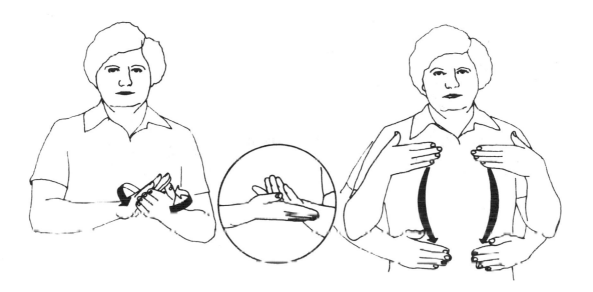

INCENSE, CENSER

The hands mime holding a censer, the vessel containing incense, a fragrant substance that is burned in religious worship.

Formation: Beginning with the left *S hand* held in front of the chest, palm facing down, swing the right *S hand* forward and back with a repeated movement while twisting the wrist under the left hand.

INDEED See VERILY

INDULGENCE See PURGATORY

INERRANT

This sign is a combination of WRONG and NONE, signifying that since the Scripture is inspired, it is fully trustworthy, complete, and does not wander from the truth.

Formation: Tap the chin with the middle fingers of the right Y *hand*. Then, beginning with both *O hands* side by side in front of the body, palms facing down, move the hands forward with a deliberate movement.

Related form: INERRANCY

See also INFALLIBLE for a similar sign with a stronger, but similar, meaning.

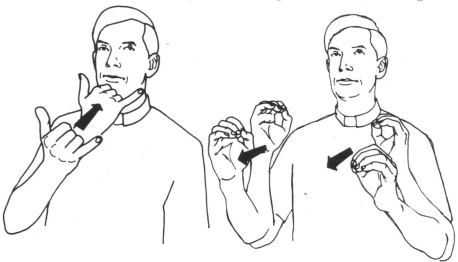

INFALLIBLE

This sign is a combination of NEVER and WRONG, signifying the absolute divine authority of the Scripture.

Formation: Move the right *open hand,* palm facing forward, from in front of the head downward in a large Z to in front of the waist. Then tap the chin with the middle fingers of the right Y *hand.*

Related form: INFALLIBILITY

See also INERRANT for a sign with a similar meaning.

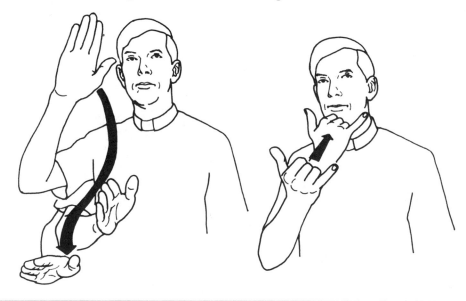

INFINITE (A)

This sign is a combination of WITHOUT and STOP and refers to God's attribute of existing without beginning or end.

Formation: Beginning with the palm sides of both *S hands* together in front of the body, pull the hands apart abruptly while opening to *5 hands*. Then bring the little-finger side of the right *open hand*, palm facing left, down sharply on the palm of the left *open hand*.

INFINITE (B) See ETERNAL

INIQUITY See SIN (A)(B)(C)(D)(E)

INNOCENT, BLAMELESS, SINLESS

This sign is used to refer to someone who is uncorrupted by wrongdoings.

Formation: Move the fingers of both *H hands*, palms facing in and fingers pointing toward each other, outward across the lips, ending forward of each shoulder, palms facing up and fingers pointing forward.

IN SHA ALLAH *(Arabic)*

This is a common Islamic expression meaning "God is willing" and indicating the absolute will and power of God over creation.

Formation: Beginning with the middle finger and thumb of the right *8 hand* together in front of the right shoulder, palm facing forward, flick the fingers open, forming an *open hand*.

INSPIRE, FILLED WITH

This sign shows some internal force seeming to rise in the body, as when a person becomes able to communicate because of divine influence.

Formation: Beginning with both *flattened O hands* in front of the body, palms facing up, bring the hands up in front of the chest while opening into *5 hands*.

Related form: INSPIRATION

INSTALL, CONFIRM

The hands mime the laying on of hands to bless the head of the person assuming a religious office.

Formation: Place the palms of both *open hands* on top of each side of the head.

Related forms: INSTALLATION, CONFIRMATION

See also CONFIRMATION (A)(B) and ORDAIN for signs with related meanings.

INSTITUTED See BEGINNING, FOUND

INSTRUCT See TEACH

INTERCEDE See BEG

INTERCESSION See PRAY

INTERCESSORY PRAYER

This sign is a combination of PRAY, FOR, and PEOPLE and refers to the act of intervening or pray-ing to God on behalf of another person.

Formation: With the palms of both *open hands* together, move the hands in toward the chest. Then move the right extended index finger from pointing to the forehead, palm facing in, forward by twisting the wrist, ending with the palm facing forward. Then make large alternating forward cir-cles with both *P hands*, palms facing each other, in front of each side of the body.

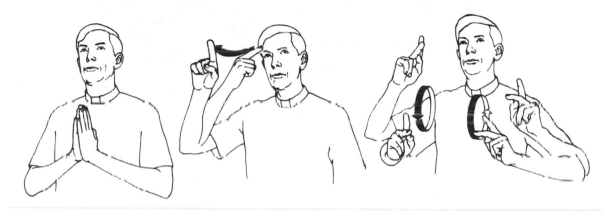

INTERPRET (A)

This sign is formed similar to the sign for CHANGE and indicates the process of explaining or sim-plifying the Bible so it is understandable to the layperson.

Formation: Beginning with the fingertips of both *F hands* touching in front of the body, twist the wrists in opposite directions with alternating movements toward and away from the body.

Related form: INTERPRETATION

See also CONVERT, REPENT, and TRANSLATE for signs formed in a similar manner.

INTERPRET (B), EXPLAIN

This sign is used for explaining a biblical reference for the purpose of clarifying it.

Formation: Move both *F hands,* palms facing each other, forward and back with an alternating movement in front of the body.

Related forms: EXPLANATION, INTERPRETATION

Same sign for DESCRIBE, DESCRIPTION

IN THE NAME OF GOD

This sign is a combination of TALK and ALLAH, referring to activities done by Muslims to follow divine orders.

Formation: Move the extended right index finger from the mouth, palm facing left and finger pointing up, forward and upward.

INVITE See CALL (B)

ISA *(Arabic)* See JESUS (B)

ISAIAH

This initialized sign is formed similar to the sign for PROPHET and the person marker and is used to refer to Isaiah, a Gideon prophet of the eighth century B.C.E. who foretold the Messiah's coming.

Formation: Move the right *I hand,* palm facing left, from near the chest forward in an arc under the palm of the left *open hand* held in front of the chest. Add the person marker.

See also PROPHET for a sign formed in a similar manner.

ISHA'A (Arabic)

This sign is a combination of FIVE and a gesture showing closing, or the end. The sign is used to refer to the fifth and last prayer of the required five daily prayers of salat. This prayer is recited before retiring for the night as Muslims take time to remember God's presence, guidance, mercy, and forgiveness.

Formation: Beginning with the right *5 hand* in front of the right shoulder, palm facing forward and fingers pointing up, move the hand downward while closing into an *S hand*.

ISLAM

This sign is used to refer to the monotheistic, Abrahamic religion that originated with the prophet Muhammad in the seventh century. The word *Islam* means "submission" in the Arabic language. A person who adheres to Islam is known as a Muslim.

Formation: Beginning with both *open hands* near each side of the face, palms facing each other and fingers pointing up, move the hands forward while changing to *10 hands*.

ISRAEL

This is an initialized sign that shows the location of a traditional Jewish beard and refers to the homeland of many Jewish people.

Formation: Bring the extended little finger of the right *I hand*, palm facing in, downward first on the left side of the chin and then the right side of the chin.

ISRAELITES, HEBREWS

This sign is a combination of JEW and PEOPLE.

Formation: With the right *bent hand* near the chin, palm facing in and fingers pointing up, bring the fingertips downward from the chin with a double movement while closing the fingers to a *flattened O hand* each time. Then make large forward circles with both *P hands*, palms facing each other, in front of each side of the body.

JEALOUS See COVET (A)

JEHOVAH'S WITNESS

This is an initialized sign that refers to the religious sect formed in the late nineteenth century characterized by active evangelism and belief in the imminent approach of the millennium.

Formation: Form a *J* with the right hand in front of the right shoulder, palm facing forward, and as the hand completes the *J* change to a *W hand*, palm facing back.

JERUSALEM (A)

This sign is a combination of *J* and the sign TOWN and is used to designate the town in ancient Israel whose temple was dedicated to the worship of God.

Formation: With the right hand, form a *J* near the right shoulder. Then, with palms facing each other and hands held at an angle, tap the fingertips of both *open hands* together, first in front of the left shoulder and then again in front of the right shoulder.

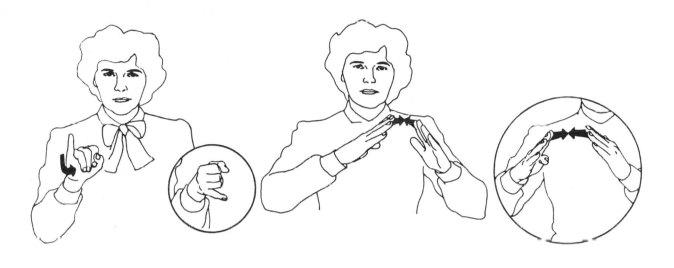

JERUSALEM (B)

The hand mimes kissing the ancient temple wall in Jerusalem.

Formation: Touch the fingertips of the right *open hand* first against the lips and then turn the palm and move the hand forward a short distance.

JESUS (A)

The fingers point to the nail prints in Jesus's hands. Jesus is regarded by Christians as the Messiah and the second member of the Trinity.

Formation: Touch the bent middle finger of the right *5 hand* to the center of the palm of the left *open hand.* Reverse the action by touching the bent middle finger of the left *5 hand* to the palm of the right *open hand.*

JESUS (B), ISA *(Arabic)*

This sign is used by Muslims to refer to Jesus, whom they believe has the true name of "Isa" according to the Qur'an. Muslims believe that Isa was a prophet and lawgiver and that the original disciples were Muslims.

Formation: Hold the right *H hand,* palm facing in and fingers pointing left, in front of the right side of the chest.

JEW (A), HEBREW

The hand follows the shape of a traditional Jewish beard.

Formation: With the right *bent hand* near the chin, palm facing in and fingers pointing up, bring the fingertips downward from the chin with a double movement while closing the fingers to a *flattened O hand* each time.

Related form: JEWISH

JEW (B)

This sign, used by Muslims, shows the placement of the knot of the head-worn part of the Jewish tefillin or phylacteries. The historical interaction of the Jews and Muslims is because they share a common origin in the Middle East through Abraham, with Muslims following the ancestry of Abraham's son by a maidservant, Ishmael; and Jews following Abraham's ancestry through his son Isaac.

Formation: Place the palm side of the right *G hand* on top of the head.

JOIN See UNITE

JOY See REJOICE (A)

JUDAISM (A)

This sign is a combination of JEW and RELIGION and designates the monotheistic religion of Jewish people, which traces its origins to Abraham.

Formation: With the right *5 hand* near the chin, palm facing in and fingers pointing up, bring the fingertips downward from the chin with a double movement while closing the fingers to a *flattened O hand* each time. Then bring the fingertips of the right *R hand* from the left side of the chest downward and forward, ending with the palm facing down and the fingers pointing forward.

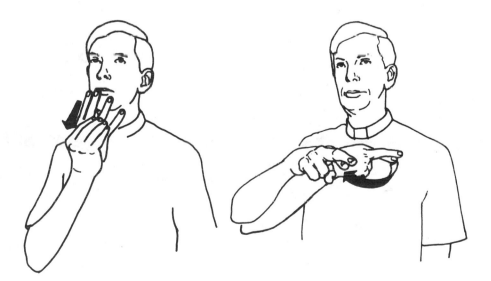

JUDAISM (B) See REFORM (B)

157

JUDGMENT (A), CONDEMN, TRIBUNAL

The hands seem to weigh a decision on the traditional balance of justice, as at God's final reck-
oning on Judgment Day.

Formation: Beginning with both *F hands* in
front of each side of the body, palms facing each
other and right hand higher than the left hand,
move the hands up and down in a repeated alternating movement.

Related form: JUDGE

See also CONDEMN for an alternate sign.

JUDGMENT (B) See CONDEMN (A)

JUDGMENT DAY, DAY OF JUDGMENT, LAST JUDGMENT

This sign is a combination of JUDGE and DAY and refers to the close of human history when Christ
will render verdicts on salvation or damnation on all human beings.

Formation: Beginning with both *F hands* in front of each side of the body, palms facing each
other and left hand higher than the right hand, move the hands up and down. Then, beginning with
the elbow of the bent right arm, right index finger pointing up, on the back of the left hand held
across the body, palm facing down, move the right index finger downward toward the left elbow.

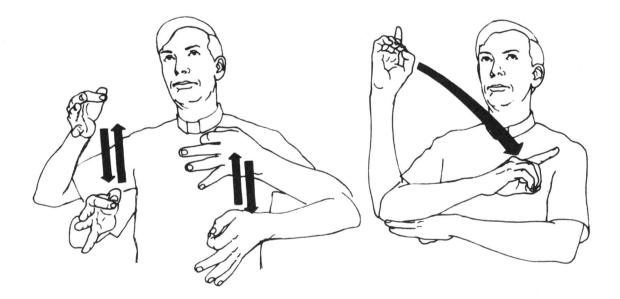

JUM'AH (Arabic), FRIDAY PRAYER, KHUBAH (Arabic)

This sign is used to refer to the required Islamic congregational prayer that is held at noon every Friday, in lieu of the dhuhr or zuhr prayer. The service begins with the *khubah,* or sermon, and concludes with two *rakas,* or units, of prayers.

Formation: Hold the thumb of the right *G hand,* palm facing left, against the chin.

JUSTIFICATION (A)

This sign is a combination of JUDGE and EQUAL and refers to the doctrine in which God judges believers as righteous despite sinful living.

Formation: Beginning with both *F hands* in front of each side of the body, palms facing each other and right hand higher than the left hand, move the hands up and down in a repeated alternating movement. Then tap the fingertips of both *bent hands* together in front of the chest, palms facing each other.

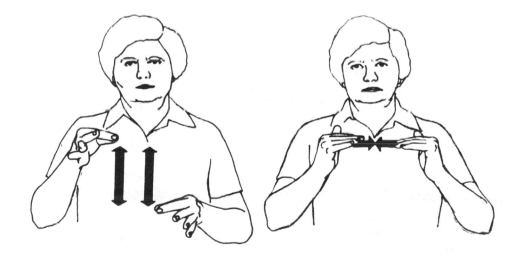

JUSTIFICATION (B)

This sign is a combination of ANNOUNCE and RIGHTEOUS and refers to the fundamental principle that salvation depends entirely on the grace of God rather than on human actions.

Formation: Start with both extended index fingers touching each side of the mouth, palms facing in. Twist the wrists to bring the fingers outward past the shoulders, palms facing forward and fingers pointing upward at an angle. Then slide the little-finger side of the right *open hand* across the palm of the left *open hand*.

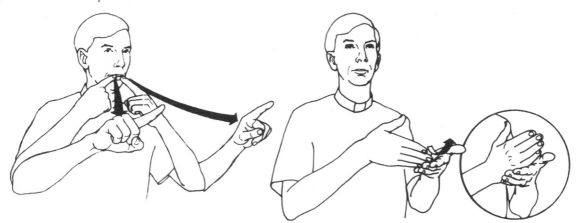

KHUBAH *(Arabic)* See JUM'AH *(Arabic)*

KIDDUSH *(Hebrew)*

The hand seems to hold an overflowing cup of wine over which the kiddush blessing is made for the Sabbath and festivals.

Formation: Bring the right *curved hand* straight upward in front of the right side of the body.

KILL, MURDER, SLAY

The finger makes a jabbing movement as if stabbing someone.

Formation: Push the index-finger side of the extended right index finger, palm facing down, downward across the palm of the left *open hand,* palm facing right.

KING

This initialized sign follows the shape of the sash worn by royalty and is used to refer both to the Old Testament monarchs and to Christ's designation as King of the Jews.

Formation: Touch the index-finger side of the right *K hand,* palm facing left, first to near the left shoulder and then to near the right hip.

See also CHRIST, DAVID, LORD (A), and MESSIAH for other initialized signs formed in a similar manner.

KING DAVID See DAVID

KING OF KINGS

This sign is a combination of KING, OVER, and KING and refers to the biblical teaching that Jesus fulfilled the Old Testament promises of a perfect king and reigns over His people and the universe. In the book of Revelation, Jesus is described as sitting on a throne and his name "King of Kings" is written on His thigh and vesture.

Formation: Touch the index-finger side of the right *K hand,* palm left, first to near the left shoulder and then to near the right hip. Then, starting with the palm of the right *open hand* lying on the back of the left *open hand,* elbows out and palms facing down, bring the right hand upward in a spiraling movement. Then touch the index-finger side of the right *K hand,* palm left, first to near the left shoulder and then to near the right hip.

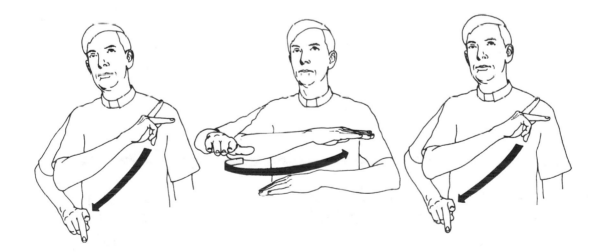

KINGDOM

This initialized sign is a combination of KING and a gesture showing an area of land and designates the realm of God's eternal spiritual sovereignty.

Formation: Touch the index-finger side of the right *K hand*, palm facing left, first to near the left shoulder and then to near the right hip. Then change the right hand to an *open hand* and move it upward in an arc to the left to circle over the left *open hand*, palm facing down.

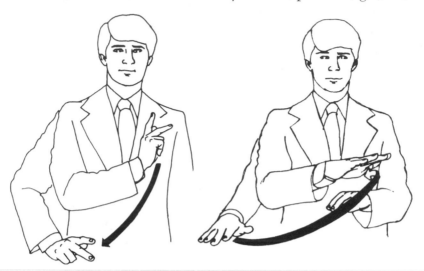

KIPPAH *(Hebrew)* See YARMULKE *(Hebrew)*

KNEEL

The fingers represent bended knees, a position of respect before God.

Formation: Place the knuckles of the bent right *V hand*, palm facing in, on the palm of the left *open hand*, palm facing up.

KORAN See QUR'AN *(Arabic)*

KOSHER

This is an initialized sign and indicates that something conforms to Jewish dietary laws and is properly prepared for eating.

Formation: Shake the right *K hand*, palm facing left, back and forth in front of the chest.

Note: Usually the mouthed word "kosher" accompanies the sign.

LAITY See LAYPERSON

LAMB See SHEEP

LAMB OF GOD

This sign is a combination of LAMB, a directional form of BELONG, and GOD and refers to John the Baptist identifying Jesus as "the Lamb of God" or "servant of God," fulfilling Isaiah's prophecy that described Jesus as one "brought as a lamb to the slaughter" as an offering for sin.

Formation: With the left arm extended, repeatedly sweep the back of the right *K hand,* palm facing up, up the inside of the left arm. Then, beginning with both *curved 5 hands* in front of the body, palms facing each other and right hand over the left, bring the hands together while touching the thumb and index fingertips of each hand and intersecting with each other. Then move the right *B hand,* palm left, from above the front of the head downward in an arc toward the forehead and down in front of the face.

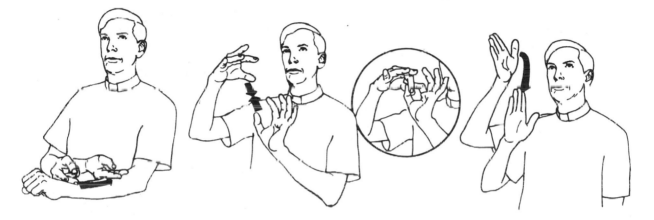

LAMENT See SUFFER (B)

LANGUAGE See TONGUE (A)

LAST JUDGMENT See JUDGMENT DAY

LASTING See ENDURE (B)

LATIN See ROMAN

LATTER-DAY SAINTS See MORMON (A)(B)

LAW (A)

This is an initialized sign showing something is forbidden.

Formation: Strike the palm side of the right *L hand* against the palm of the left *open hand*.

See also FORBID for a sign with a related meaning formed in a similar manner.

LAW (B)

This is an initialized sign and signifies the recording of laws on a tablet or book.

Formation: Move the right *L hand,* palm facing down, down the palm of the left *open hand,* palm facing right and fingers pointing up, touching first on the fingers and then on the heel.

See also COMMANDMENTS, HALACHA (A), MOSES, and TESTAMENT for other initialized signs formed in a similar manner.

LAYPERSON, HUMANITY, LAITY, MANKIND, PARISHIONER, PEOPLE

This is the sign for PEOPLE and is used to refer to members of a congregation as distinguished from the clergy.

Formation: Make large forward alternating circles with both *P hands,* palms facing each other, in front of each side of the body.

Note: The hands may circle inward instead of forward.

LEAD See GUIDE

LENT (A)

This is an initialized sign formed like FAST and indicates abstinence from a chosen substance during the Lenten season—the forty days before Easter—as a gesture of penitence.

Formation: Move the thumb tip of the right *L hand,* palm left, from left to right across the lips.

See also FAST for another initialized sign formed in a similar manner.

LENT (B) See ANOINT (A)

LEPROSY

This sign is a combination of SKIN and SICK to refer a skin disorder that leaves white patches on the skin, running sores, and sometimes the loss of digits on the hands and feet. Leprosy left its victims ceremonially unclean and therefore unfit to worship God, according to the Hebrews in biblical times.

Formation: Pinch and shake the loose skin on the back of the left *open hand,* with the bent thumb and index finger of the right 5 *hand,* both palms facing down. Then touch the bent middle finger of the right 5 *hand* to the forehead while touching the bent middle finger of the left 5 *hand* to the abdomen.

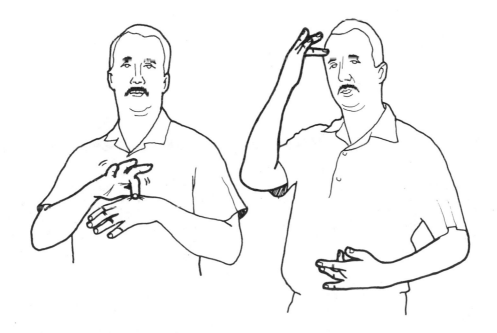

LESSON

The left hand represents a page and the right hand designates a portion of it.

Formation: Touch the little-finger edge of the right *bent hand*, palm facing in, first on the fingers and then on the heel of the left *open hand*, palm facing up.

LIE (A), FALSEHOOD, UNTRUTH

The finger's movement shows talking out of the side of the mouth.

Formation: Push the extended right index finger, palm facing down, across the chin from right to left.

See also FALSE for a sign with a related meaning.

LIE (B), FALSEHOOD, UNTRUTH

The hand shoves the truth to the side of the mouth and symbolizes any false information deliberately presented as being true.

Formation: Push the index-finger edge of the right *B hand*, palm facing down, across the chin from right to left.

See also FALSE for a sign with a related meaning.

LIFE, MORTAL

This sign symbolizes vitality surging through the body.

Formation: Bring both *L hands,* palms facing in and index fingers pointing toward each other, upward from the waist to the chest.

Related form: LIVING

See also LIVE for the verb form of this sign.

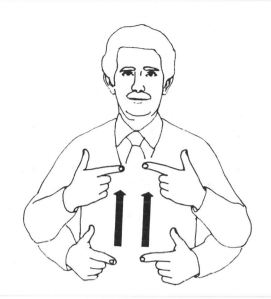

LIGHT (A), BRIGHT, LUMINOUS

The hands in this sign seem to clear away any haze in front of the eyes.

Formation: Beginning with the fingers of both *flattened O hands* touching in front of the chest, palms facing forward, move the hands upward and apart, opening into *5 hands* in front of each shoulder, palms facing forward and fingers pointing up.

Same sign for CLEAR, OBVIOUS

LIGHT (B) See EPIPHANY

LIKENESS (A), IMAGE OF GOD

This sign is a directional sign similar to SAME to indicate that although God cannot be properly compared to any likeness, humanity was created in the likeness of God in terms of the unique spiritual nature of man.

Formation: Move the right *Y hand,* palm facing forward, back and forth from the right side of the chest upward to the right.

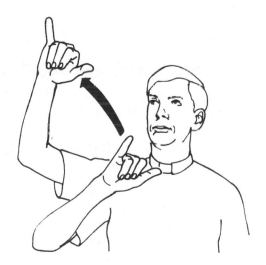

LIKENESS (B)

This sign is a directional sign similar to SAME, moving from God to the index finger, which represents man, to demonstrate that man shares a spiritual link to God.

Formation: Beginning with the left index finger pointing up in front of the chest, palm facing forward, move the right *Y hand*, palm facing forward, from near the right index finger upward to the right.

LITANY See PRAY

LITURGY

This is an initialized sign formed similar to MASS and refers to the rites of worship.

Formation: Beginning with the thumbs of both *L hands* touching in front of the body, palms facing forward and index fingers pointing up, move the hands upward in front of the face.

See also MASS for another sign formed in a similar manner.

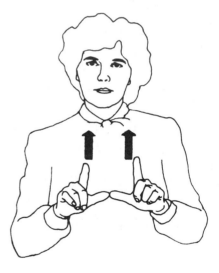

LIVE, ABIDE, ALIVE, DWELL, EXIST

This sign symbolizes vitality surging though the body.

Formation: Bring both *10 hands* with thumbs extended up, upward on each side of the body.

Same sign for ADDRESS, SURVIVE, RESIDE

See also LIFE for the noun form of this sign.

LOCUST

This sign is a combination of BUG and GRASSHOPPER to refer to an insect in the Middle East that periodically multiplies to astronomical numbers.

Formation: With the extended thumb of the right *3 hand* on the nose, palm facing left, bend the extended index and middle fingers with a repeated movement. Then, beginning with the fingertips of the right *bent V hand* near the wrist of the left bent arm held across the body, move the hand up while straightening the fingers and then down again near the left elbow while bending the fingers.

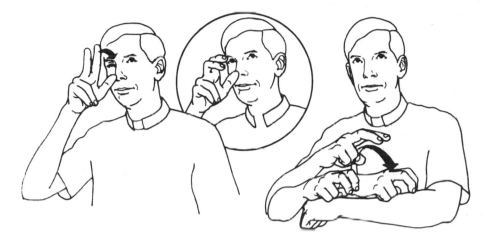

LOGOS See WORD

LONGING See DESIRE (A)(B)

LORD (A)

This is an initialized sign that follows the shape of the sash worn by royalty and refers to Christ's designation as the King of the Jews.

Formation: Touch the thumb of the right *L hand,* palm facing left, first to the left shoulder and then to the right hip.

See also CHRIST, DAVID, KING, and MESSIAH for other initialized signs formed in a similar manner.

LORD (B)

This is an initialized sign that gestures dramatically upward toward the traditional location of heaven. This sign is poetic and is often used in music.

Formation: Touch the thumb of the right *L hand*, palm facing left, to the left side of the chest. Then swing the hand upward and outward to the right in a large arc, ending near the right side of the head, palm facing forward.

LORD (C) See GOD (A)(B)

LORD'S SUPPER See COMMUNION (C)

LOVE (A), DEAR

This is a natural gesture for holding someone or something very dear near the heart.

Formation: Cross the arms of both *A hands* at the wrists across the chest, palms facing in.

Same sign for HUG

See also BELOVED for an alternate sign.

LOVE (B) See BELOVED

LOVING KINDNESS

This sign is a combination of LOVE and KIND referring to Christ's love and care of mankind.

Formation: Cross the arms of both *A hands* at the wrists across the chest, palms facing in. Then wipe the palm of the right *curved hand* down the fingers of the left *curved hand*, and then repeat with the palm of the left *curved hand* on the back of the right *curved hand*, both palms facing in.

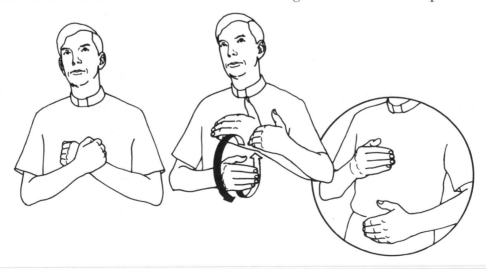

LOWLY See HUMBLE

LOYAL See FAITHFUL

LULAV *(Hebrew)*

The hands seem to hold the *etrog* (lemon) and the *lulav* (palm), symbolic of the festival of Sukkoth, which commemorates the temporary shelter of the Jews in the wilderness.

    Formation: With the right hand cupped tightly over the left *A hand,* shake both hands first on one side of the body, then the other side of the body, and then over the right shoulder.

LUMINOUS See LIGHT (A)(B)

LUTHER, MARTIN (A)

This is an initialized sign used to designate Martin Luther, a sixteenth-century German monk known as the founder of Protestantism.

    Formation: Tap the thumb of the right *L hand* to the center of the chest, palm facing left.

    See also LUTHERAN (A) for an alternate sign.

LUTHER, MARTIN (B)

This is an initialized sign for the name Martin
Luther, an Augustinian monk and Bible profes-
sor at Wittenburg University in Germany, who
was the pioneer of the Protestant Reformation.

Formation: With the right hand, form an *M*
and an *L* on the chest.

LUTHER, MARTIN (C) See LUTHERAN (A)

LUTHERAN (A), MARTIN LUTHER

This is an initialized sign and indicates Luther's
nailing of the Ninety-five Theses to the church
door at Worms, Germany, an act that led to a
separation from the Roman Catholic Church
and the establishment of the Lutheran Church.

Formation: Tap the thumb of the right *L*
hand, palm facing left, against the palm of the
left *open hand,* palm facing right.

LUTHERAN (B)

This is an initialized sign formed similar to the
sign for CHURCH.

Formation: Tap the heel of the right *L hand,*
palm facing forward, on the back of the left *S*
hand, palm facing down. Then tap the heel of
the right *S hand* on the back of the left *S hand,*
both palms facing down.

LUTHERAN (C)

This is an initialized sign formed similar to CHURCH and refers to those Christians who agree with Luther's teaching on justification by grace through faith alone.

Formation: Tap the thumb side of the right *L hand* on the back of the left *S hand,* palm facing down.

MAGHRIB *(Arabic)*

This sign shows the sun setting and refers to the fourth Islamic prayer of the day, recited at sunset. During Ramadan, the maghrib prayer signifies the end of fasting for the day.

Formation: Move the right *curved hand* in a wavy downward movement in front of the right shoulder.

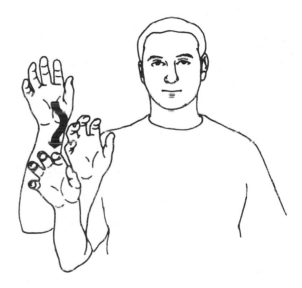

MAGNIFY See PRAISE (A)(B)

MAJESTY See GLORY, MESSIAH

MAKE See CREATE

MAKER See CREATOR

MANGER

The fingers form the shape of the traditional manger in which the baby Jesus was laid.

Formation: Thrust the middle finger of the right *V hand* between the index and middle fingers of the left *V hand,* palms facing each other.

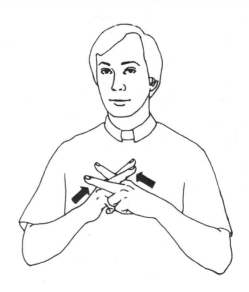

MANIFEST See REVEAL

MANKIND See LAYPERSON

MARRIAGE, HOLY MATRIMONY, NUPTIALS

This sign demonstrates the joining of hands, symbolic of the union of marriage.

Formation: Beginning with both *curved hands* a few inches apart in front of the chest, palms facing each other, bring the right hand down in a circular movement to clasp the left hand.

Related form: MARRY

See also WEDDING for the sign used to refer to the marriage ceremony.

MARTYR

The fingers seem to behead a person in this initialized sign, which is used to refer to anyone who endures extreme suffering, even death, because of religious beliefs.

Formation: Move the fingertips of the right *M hand,* palm facing down, across the neck from left to right.

MARVEL See MIRACLE, WONDER (A)

MARY (A), VIRGIN MARY

This is an initialized sign that follows the shape of the veil covering the head of Mary, the mother of Jesus.

Formation: Bring the right *M hand,* palm facing the head, from the top of the right side of the head down to the right shoulder.

Note: This sign may be formed with one *M hand* on each side of the head.

MARY (B), VIRGIN MARY

This is an initialized sign using the letters *V* and *M* to follow the shape of the veil covering the head of the Virgin Mary.

Formation: Bring the right *V hand*, palm facing right, from the left shoulder across the top of the head while changing to an *M hand*, ending on the right shoulder, palm facing down.

MASJID *(Arabic)* See MOSQUE

MASS, HOST

The fingers show the shape of the Host as the priest consecrates it during a Roman Catholic Mass.

Formation: With the thumb and index fingertips of both *F hands* touching in front of the chest, palms facing each other, lift both hands upward in front of the face.

See also LITURGY for an initialized sign formed in a similar manner.

MASTER

This is an initialized sign formed similar to the sign for OVER and indicates the Lord's authority over all things.

Formation: Move the right *M hand*, palm facing down, in a large circle over the left *open hand*, palm facing down.

See also DISTRICT (A)(B) and KINGDOM for signs formed in a similar manner.

MATZOH *(Hebrew)* See PASSOVER (A)

MEAT See FLESH (A)(B)

MEAT AND DAIRY, MILCHIG AND FLAYSHIG *(Hebrew)*

This sign is a combination of MEAT and MILK and signifies those foods that are forbidden by Jewish dietary laws to be eaten together.

Formation: Grasp the index-finger side of the left *open hand* with the bent thumb and index finger of the right *5 hand*. Then move both hands back and forth toward the chest with a repeated movement. Then, with the right *C hand* near the right shoulder, palm facing left, close the hand to form an *S hand* with a repeated movement.

MECCA

The hands in this sign show movement around a central point and refer to Mecca being the ritual center and origin point of Islam. Mecca is located in western Saudi Arabia. Muslims assert that Abraham resided in Mecca for a time. A required journey to Mecca at least once in a lifetime is one of the Five Pillars of Islam.

Formation: With the right *flattened O hand* above the left *flattened O hand*, palms facing each other, move the fingers around each other in opposite directions.

MEDITATE (A)

This initialized sign is formed similar to the sign for CONSIDER and represents the devotional exercise of contemplation.

Formation: Move the right *M hand*, palm facing toward the face, in a small circle near the right side of the forehead.

Related form: MEDITATION

See also PONDER for a sign with a similar meaning formed in a similar manner.

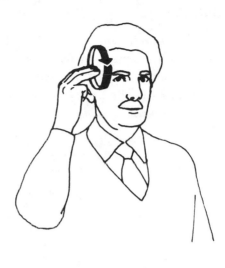

MEDITATE (B) See PONDER

MEEK See HUMBLE

MEETING, ASSEMBLY, CONFERENCE, CONVENTION, CONVOCATION, GATHERING

The fingers in this sign represent people coming together.

Formation: Beginning with the thumbs of both *5 hands* touching, palms facing each other, tap the other fingertips together with a repeated movement.

See also ASSEMBLE for the verb form of this sign.

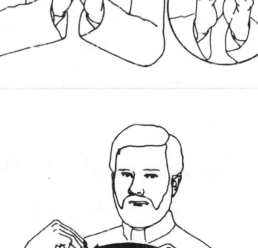

MEMBER (A)

This is an initialized sign used to refer to a person who belongs to an organization, such as a specific congregation.

Formation: Touch the fingertips of the right *M hand*, palm facing in, first near the left shoulder and then near the right shoulder.

Related form: MEMBERSHIP

See also BOARD, BOARD OF DEACONS, and DEACON (B) for other initialized signs formed in a similar manner.

MEMBER (B)

This sign is a combination of UNITE and the person marker and refers to a person who becomes affiliated with a particular congregation.

Formation: Beginning with a *5 hand* in front of each side of the chest, palms facing each other, bring the hands together, intersecting the closed index finger and thumb of each hand with the other. Add the person marker.

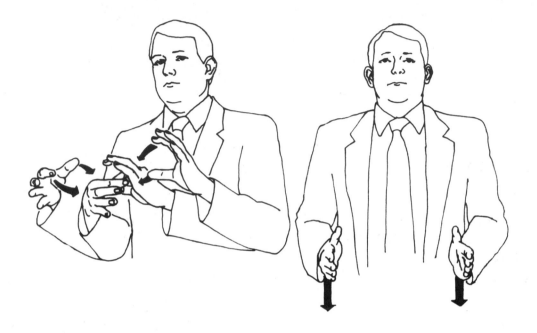

MEMORIAL, COMMEMORATE, REMEMBER

The hand in this sign seems to take a thought from the mind and place it in view for examination.

Formation: Bring the thumb of the right *10 hand* from the right side of the forehead down to touch the thumb of the left *10 hand* held in front of the chest, both palms facing down.

Related form: REMEMBRANCE

MENNONITE, AMISH

This sign mimes tying the bonnet traditionally worn by women who are Mennonites, a religious sect opposed to taking oaths, holding public office, or performing military service.

Formation: Bring a *modified X hand* from each side of the head down to meet under the chin, both palms facing down.

MENORAH See CHANUKAH

MERCIFUL See GRACIOUS

MERCY (A), COMPASSION, PITY, SYMPATHY

This sign uses the middle finger, which is used frequently in American Sign Language to denote feelings. The sign seems to take feeling from one's own heart and then caress the head of an unfortunate person. This is a directional sign made toward the person or thing being pitied.

Formation: Beginning with bent middle fingers of both *5 hands* pointing to the chest, stroke the right hand upward on the chest. Then turn the hands forward and stroke both hands downward with a double movement.

MERCY (B), GOD'S MERCY

This is a directional form of MERCY (A) and symbolizes God's mercy toward mankind.

Formation: With the bent middle fingers of both *5 hands* pointing down toward the chest, stroke the air toward the body with a repeated movement.

MERCY SEAT

This sign is a combination of MERCY and SIT. The term originally referred to the slab of pure gold that sat atop the Ark of the Covenant and symbolized the throne from which God ruled Israel. Now the term represents the place of God's presence and atonement.

Formation: Beginning with bent middle fingers of the right *5 hand* pointing to the chest, stroke the right hand downward on the chest. Then turn the hands forward and stroke both hands downward with a double movement. Then lay the bent fingers of the right *H hand* across the fingers of the left *H hand,* both palms facing down.

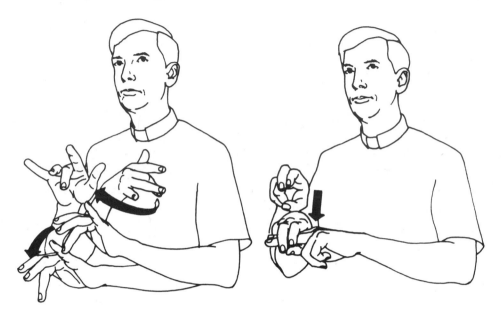

MERIT See DESERVE (A)

MESSAGE See PARABLE (A)

MESSENGER

The hand in this sign signifies a message from Allah to His people. Muslims believe that the difference between a messenger and a prophet is that a messenger has a direct revelation from God which he then reveals to the people, whereas a prophet follows what came before him without a direct revelation from God.

Formation: Bring the right *open hand,* palm facing left, from near the right side of the head downward in an arc to near the chest.

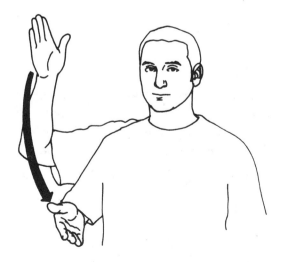

MESSIAH, MAJESTY

This is an initialized sign that follows the shape of the sash worn by royalty and refers to the Hebrew meaning of Messiah—"the anointed one."

Formation: Touch the index-finger side of the right *M hand,* palm facing down, first to the left shoulder and then to the right hip.

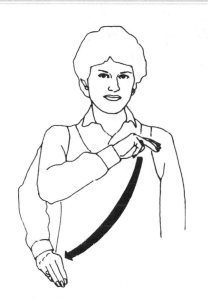

METASOMATOSIS See REINCARNATION

METHODIST, ZEAL

This sign is a natural gesture used by people who are enthusiastic or eager. It denotes the enthusiasm of the Methodist Revival Movement in the eighteenth century, which led to the establishment of the church based on the teachings of John and Charles Wesley.

Formation: Rub the palms of both *open hands* together with alternating back-and-forth movements.

Same sign for ENTHUSIASTIC, ANXIOUS, AMBITIOUS, EAGER

MEZUZAH (A) *(Hebrew)*

The fingers in this sign inscribe an imaginary mezuzah, the small container on the doorposts of Jewish homes that holds biblical passages written on parchment.

Formation: Move the fingertips of the right *G hand,* palm facing forward, downward a short distance in front of the head.

MEZUZAH (B) *(Hebrew)*

This sign refers to the custom of kissing the mezuzah on the doorpost of a home or other building before entering.

Formation: Pat the fingertips of the right *open hand* first against the lips and then forward against the palm of the left *open hand* held in front of the chest, palm facing in and fingers pointing up.

MIGHT See POWER (A)(B)

MIGHTY (A), COURAGE, HEALING, WHOLE

The hands in this sign seem to demonstrate health and strength.

Formation: Beginning with both *claw hands* on each side of the chest, bring the hands deliberately forward while changing into *S hands*.

Same sign for BRAVE, HEALTH, STRENGTH, STRONG, WELL

See also ALMIGHTY and POWER for related signs.

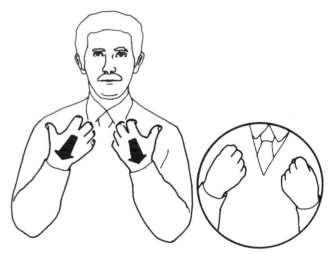

MIGHTY (B), AUTHORITY, POWERFUL

The hand in this initialized sign follows the shape of a flexed muscle as an indication of God's power to command and exact obedience from all things.

Formation: Move the right *curved hand* from near the left shoulder, palm facing down, in an arc to the crook of the left bent arm while turning the palm in.

Same sign for ENERGY, STRONG

See also ALMIGHTY and POWER for related signs.

MILLENNIUM

This sign is a combination of ONE, THOUSAND, and YEAR and signifies the belief regarding the thousand-year period of holiness during which Christ is to rule on earth.

Formation: Point the right extended index finger up, palm facing forward. Then tap the fingertips of the right *bent hand* in the palm of the left *open hand,* palms facing each other. Then, beginning with both *S hands* near each other in front of the body, palms facing each other, move the right hand forward in a circle around the left hand, ending with the little-finger side of the right hand on the index-finger side of the left hand.

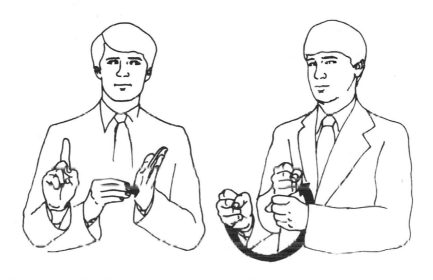

MINISTER (A)

This initialized sign is formed similar to the sign for SERVE and refers to duties and services performed by the clergy.

Formation: Move both *M hands,* palms facing up, forward and back with an alternating movement in front of the body.

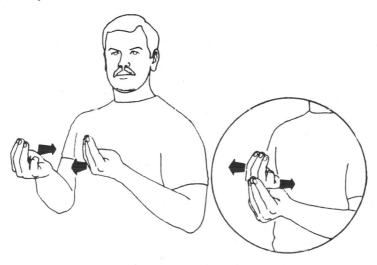

MINISTER (B) See PREACHER, SERVE

MINISTRY

This initialized sign has a movement similar to the sign for PREACH.

   Formation: With a repeated movement, tap the heel of the right *M hand*, palm facing forward, on the back of the left *S hand*, palm facing down.

MIRACLE, MARVEL

This is a combination of WONDERFUL and WORK and signifies an unexplainable event held to be an act of God or the supernatural.

   Formation: With a repeated movement, pat the air with a *5 hand* held in front of each shoulder, palms facing forward. Then, with a double movement, tap the heel of the right *S hand* on the back of the left *S hand*, both palms facing down.

   See also WONDER for an alternate sign.

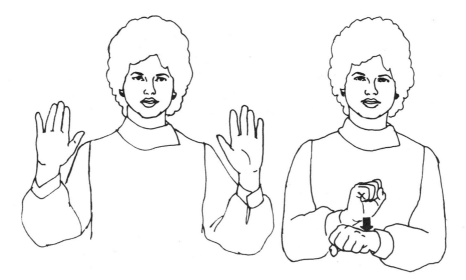

MISHKAN *(Hebrew)* See SYNAGOGUE, TABERNACLE

MISSAL

This sign is a combination of CATHOLIC and BOOK and refers to the book containing the prayers and responses necessary for celebrating the Roman Catholic Mass.

Formation: Bring the fingertips of the right *H hand* downward in front of the forehead, palm facing in and fingers pointing up, Then move the fingers from left to right in front of the forehead. Then, starting with the palms of both *open hands* together in front of the chest, move the hands apart at the top, keeping the little fingers together.

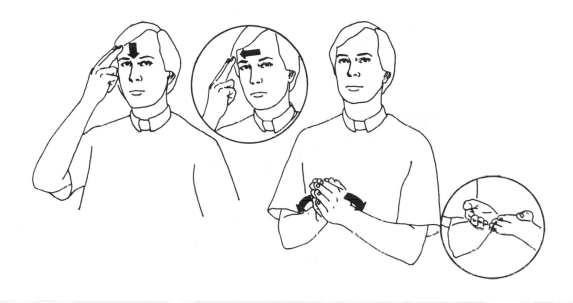

MISSION

This is an initialized sign formed near the heart to indicate that the heart motivates the religious or charitable work done either in foreign countries or in areas without assigned clergy.

Formation: Move the right *M hand*, palm facing left, in a small circle over the heart.

See also NATURE (B) for an initialized sign formed in a similar manner.

MISSIONARY

This initialized sign is a combination of MISSION and the person marker and refers to a person sent to do religious work in an unchurched area or foreign country.

Formation: Move the right *M hand*, palm facing left, in a small circle over the heart. Add the person marker.

MISTAKE See WRONG

MITER See BISHOP (B)

MITZVAH *(Hebrew)*

This initialized sign is formed similar to the sign for DO and refers to the 613 commandments in the Jewish faith which, according to tradition, Jews are obligated to observe.

Formation: Move both *M hands*, palms facing down, back and forth in front of the waist.

See also BAR MITZVAH, BAT MITZVAH, and WORKS for signs with related meanings.

MOCK, BETRAY, DECEIVE, REVILE, SCORN

The fingers in this sign seem to poke fun at someone.

Formation: With the index finger and little finger of each hand extended, place the right index finger on the side of the nose, palm facing left, and the left hand forward of the body, palm facing down. Move both hands forward with a short jabbing double movement.

MONK

The hands in this sign mime pulling up a hood, which is worn by members of a religious brotherhood devoted to the disciplines prescribed by their order.

Formation: Move both *modified A hands*, both palms facing in, from each side of the chin upward to each side of the forehead.

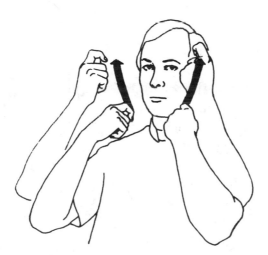

MONOTHEISM (A)

This sign is a combination of BELIEVE, ONE, and GOD, referring to the belief that there exists only one divine being or God.

Formation: Move the extended right index finger smoothly down from the right temple, palm facing in, to clasp the left hand held in front of the body, palms facing each other. Then hold up the extended right index finger in front of the chest, palm facing in. Then move the right *open hand,* palm facing left, from above the front of the head downward in an arc toward the forehead and down in front of the face.

See also POLYTHEISM for a sign with a contrasting meaning.

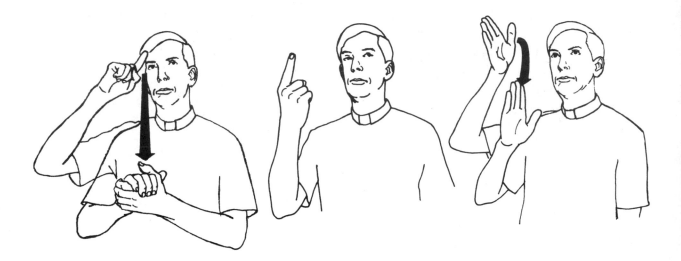

MONOTHEISM (B), TAWHID *(Arabic)*

This sign is a combination of gesture showing someone talking and ALLAH and refers to the doctrine of "Oneness of God" in Islam. The belief is that Allah is a unique, invisible being who is independent of the whole creation. This sign is not used by other monotheist religions that believe in the Trinity of God.

Formation: Beginning with the index finger and thumb of the right *A hand* together near the mouth, flick the index finger up. Then point the extended index finger up near the right side of the head, palm facing forward.

188

MONSIGNOR

The hand in this sign outlines the traditional red sash worn by monsignors in the Roman Catholic Church.

Formation: Bring the fingers of the right *C hand* around the waist from left to right.

MONSTRANCE

The hands hold an imaginary monstrance, the receptacle containing the Host in the Roman Catholic Church, and move it in the shape of a cross.

Formation: With the right *S hand* held on the top of the thumb side of the left *S hand*, palms facing each other, move both hands from in front of the face downward to in front of the chest. Then, keeping the hands in the same position, move them across in front of the face from left to right.

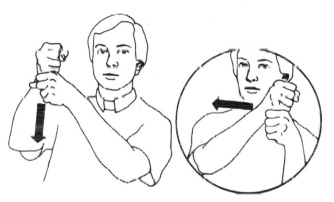

MORMON (A), LATTER-DAY SAINTS

This is an initialized sign used to refer to the church founded by Joseph Smith in 1830 in Fayette, New York.

Formation: Brush the fingertips of the right *M hand* downward and slightly outward with a repeated movement near the right side of the forehead.

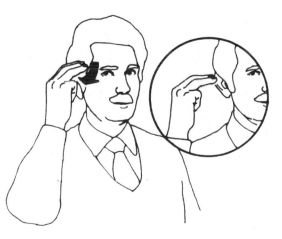

MORMON (B), LATTER-DAY SAINTS

This is an initialized sign referring to the Church of Jesus Christ of Latter-Day Saints, also known as the Mormon Church.

Formation: Form an *L, D,* and *S* with the right hand in front of the right shoulder, moving the hand slightly to the right for each letter.

MORTAL See LIFE

MOSES (A)

This is an initialized sign formed similar to the sign for LAW and refers to the lawgiver who led the Israelites out of Egypt.

Formation: Move the index-finger side of the right *M hand,* palm facing down, first against the fingers and then against the heel of the left *open hand,* palm facing right and fingers pointing up.

MOSES (B), MUSA *(Arabic)*

The movement in this sign shows Moses lowering his rod or walking stick to part the Red Sea so the Israelites could escape captivity by the Egyptians. This sign is used by Muslims who regard Moses as a prophet, with more references in the Qur'an than any other prophet.

Formation: Move the right *modified A hand* downward near the right side of the body, palm facing left.

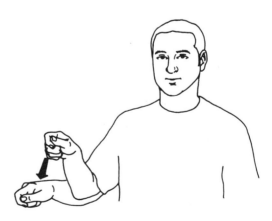

MOSES (C)

The hands in this sign show the tufts of Moses's hair as depicted in Michelangelo's sculpture of Moses located in a church in Rome. Jewish people find this sign offensive as it appears that the tufts of hair may be devil's horns.

Formation: Beginning with the fingertips of both *G hands* on each side of the head, pull the hands upward and outward a short distance, while pinching the fingers together.

MOSQUE, MASJID *(Arabic)*

This sign is used to refer to the site of assembly and worship for male Muslims. In the Arabic language *masjid* means a "place of ritual prostration."

Formation: Place the elbow of the bent right arm on the back of the left *open hand* held across the body, palm facing down, and form a *small C* with the right hand near the right side of the face.

MOURN, GRIEVE

This sign is a combination of the signs FEEL and AGONY, signifying the agony one feels when losing a loved one.

Formation: Touch the bent middle finger of the right *5 hand* to the center of the chest. Then, with the index-finger sides of both *S hands* together, right palm facing forward and left palm facing back, twist the hands, reversing the orientation of the palms.

Related form: GRIEF

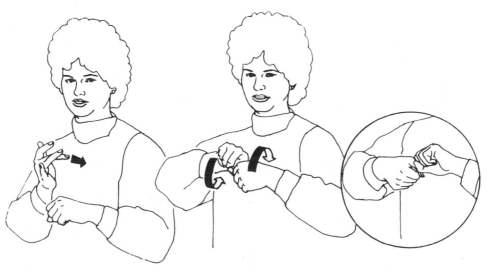

MUHAMMAD, THE PROPHET

This sign is a combination of a gesture showing Muhammad's beard and a movement that represents bringing Allah's revealed code of behavior down as law to Muslim people. In the Arabic language, *Muhammad* means "praised one."

  Formation: Bring the thumb of the right *5 hand,* palm facing in, down in front of the chest. Then, beginning with the right *open hand,* palm facing forward and fingers pointing up, near the right side of the face, bring the hand down while turning the fingers forward and palm facing left, and then closing into an *A hand* near the right side of the chest.

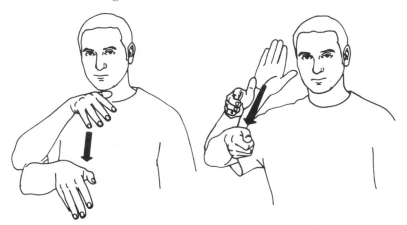

MULTITUDE, CROWD

This is the sign for HORDE, indicating rows of people. The sign is used to refer to the large number of people who showed up to hear Jesus wherever he was.

  Formation: Move both *curved 5 hands,* palms facing down, from in front of the sides of the chest forward with a simultaneous movement.

  Same sign for HORDE, MASS

MU'MIN *(Arabic)*

This sign is a combination of MUSLIM formed near the heart and STRONG, indicating a Muslim who holds the articles of Islamic faith in a higher degree than other Muslims. In the Arabic language, *mu'min* means "believer."

  Formation: Point the index finger of the right *G hand* to the heart and then pull the hand forward to the right while closing into an *S hand.*

MURDER See KILL

MUSA *(Arabic)* See MOSES (B)

MUSLIM

This sign refers to a person who submits to the will of Allah and practices Islam in daily life. In the Arabic language, *Muslim* means "one who submits."

Formation: Hold the right *G hand*, palm facing left, near the right shoulder.

MYSTERY, HIDDEN

This sign is similar to the sign for HIDE and denotes the hidden truths revealed through Christ to the elect. This sign is also used to signify any of the fifteen incidents in Christ's life regarded by the Roman Catholic Church as having mystical significance.

Formation: Beginning with the thumb of the right *A hand*, palm facing left, touching the lips, move the hand forward in an arc under the left *bent hand* held in front of the chest, palm facing down.

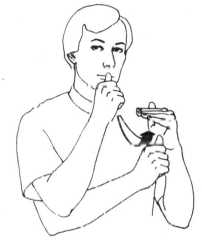

NATIVITY See BIRTH

NATURE (A)

This is an initialized sign used to indicate man's natural state, as opposed to a state of grace.

Formation: Move the fingertips of the right *N hand*, palm facing down, in a circle over and down on the back of the left *open hand*, palm facing down.

Note: The left hand may be an *S hand*.

Same sign for NATURALLY, NATION, NATIONAL, OF COURSE

NATURE (B)

This is an initialized sign formed near the heart and refers to the intrinsic characteristics and qualities of a person.

Formation: Move the right *N hand*, palm facing left, in a small circle over the heart.

See also MISSION for an initialized sign formed in a similar manner.

NAZARETH

This sign is a combination of an initialized sign and TOWN and is used to designate the town where Jesus spent his childhood.

Formation: Twist the right *N hand*, palm facing down, slightly outward near the right shoulder. Then with the palms of both *open hands* facing each other, tap the fingertips together first in front of the left side of the chest and then in front of the right side of the chest.

See also BETHLEHEM and JERUSALEM (A) for other initialized signs formed in a similar manner.

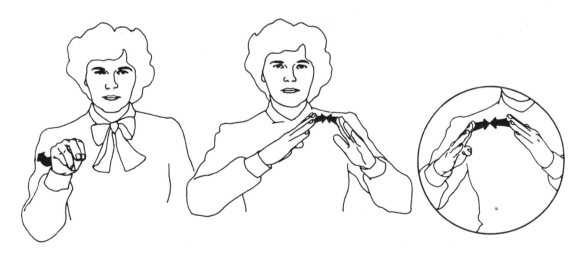

NEW COVENANT

This sign is a combination of NEW and PROMISE and refers to the covenant made in the New Testament whereby God redeems His people through Christ's resurrection and makes a new covenant with them that supersedes the covenant from the Old Testament.

Formation: Sweep the back of the right *open hand*, palm facing up, across the palm of the left *open hand*, held in front of the body, palm facing up. Then, beginning with the right extended index finger touching the mouth, palm facing left and finger pointing up, move the right hand down while changing to an *open hand*, ending with the palm of the right hand on the index-finger side of the left *S hand*, palm facing in.

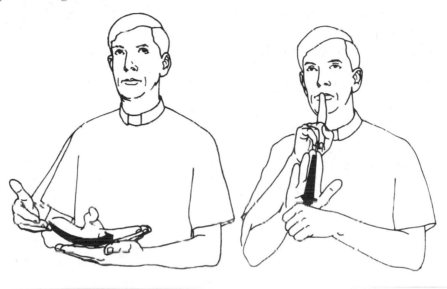

NEW TESTAMENT

This sign is a combination of NEW and TESTAMENT and is used to designate the Gospels, Acts of the Apostles, the Epistles, and the Book of Revelation, which together are considered by Christians as forming the record of the new dispensation of the church.

Formation: Sweep the back of the right *curved hand*, palm facing up, across the palm of the left *open hand*, held in front of the body, palm facing up. Then move the index-finger side of the right *T hand*, palm facing left, first against the fingers and then against the heel of the left *open hand*, palm facing right and fingers pointing up.

NEW YEAR See ROSH HASHANAH

NIQUAB *(Arabic)* See BURQA

NOEL See ANNOUNCE

NUN (A), SISTER

This is an initialized sign that follows the outline of the traditional headdress worn by nuns, women belonging to a religious order who have vowed a life of religious service in the Roman Catholic, Orthodox, or Anglican churches.

Formation: Move both *N hands,* palms facing each other, from touching each side of the forehead down to touching each shoulder.

NUN (B), SISTER

The hands of this sign follow the shape of the traditional headdress worn by nuns.

Formation: Move both *open hands,* palms facing the head, from on top of each side of the head down to touching each shoulder.

See also VEIL for an initialized sign formed in a similar manner.

NUPTIALS See MARRIAGE

OBEY

The hands in this sign represent putting one's own ideas in obeisance to another's.

Formation: Beginning with the right *flattened O hand* touching the forehead and the left *flattened O hand* somewhat forward of the head, both palms facing in, bring both hands forward and downward simultaneously while opening into *open hands,* palms facing up.

Related form: OBEDIENCE

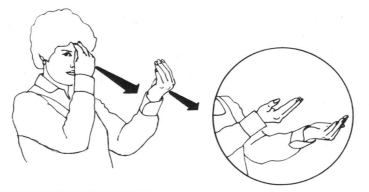

OBLATION See OFFERING

OBLIGATION, BEAR, BURDEN, FAULT, RESPONSIBILITY

The hands in this sign seem to place a heavy burden on the shoulder.

Formation: With the fingertips of both *bent hands* touching the chest near the left shoulder, drop the shoulder and left side of the body downward a short distance.

See also ACCUSE for a sign with a related meaning.

OBSERVANT See FRUM *(Hebrew)*

OBTAIN, ACQUIRE, GET, RECEIVE

The hands in this sign take something and bring it to oneself.

Formation: Beginning with both 5 *hands* in front of the body, right little finger across the left index finger, palms facing in opposite directions, bring both hands in to the body while changing to *S hands.*

See also CONCEIVE for a directional form of this sign.

OFFENSE See SIN (A)(B)(C)(D)(E)

OFFERING (A), OBLATION, PRESENT

The hands in this sign seem to lay something before another, as in an act of worship or thanksgiving to God.

Formation: Bring both *open hands,* palms facing up and one hand somewhat forward of the other hand, upward in a deliberate movement.

Related form: OFFER

Same sign for SUGGEST, PROPOSE

OFFERING (B) See COLLECTION, ZAKAT *(Arabic)*

OIL See ANOINT (B)

OINTMENT

The right hand in this sign seems to smooth an ointment on the other hand. Ointments in the Bible include salves used in cosmetics, medicine, and in religious ceremonies.

Formation: With the bent middle finger of the right *5 hand* in the palm of the left *open hand,* palms facing each other, rock the right hand from side to side with a double movement while keeping the middle finger in place. Move the fingers of the right *open hand* back and forth on the back of the left *open hand,* both palms facing down.

Same sign for SALVE

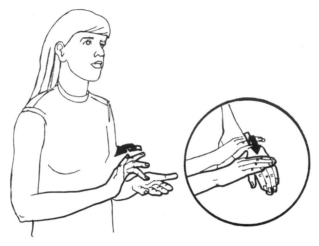

OLD TESTAMENT

This sign is a combination of OLD and TESTAMENT and is used to designate the Pentateuch, the Prophets, and the Hagiographa, which are shared with Christians as the first of two main parts of the Bible.

Formation: Beginning with the right *C hand,* palm facing left, near the chin, bring the hand downward while closing into an *S hand.* Then move the index-finger side of the right *T hand,* palm facing left, first against the fingers and then against the heel of the left *open hand,* palm facing right and fingers pointing up.

See also NEW TESTAMENT for a sign with a related meaning.

OMNIPOTENT See ALMIGHTY

OMNIPRESENT

This sign is a combination of ALL and HERE and signifies God's attribute of being present every-where.

    Formation: With the right *open hand,* palm facing forward, near the left shoulder, make a large loop to the right ending in the upturned palm of the left *open hand.* Then move both *open hands,* palms facing up, from side to side with repeated movements in front of each side of the waist.

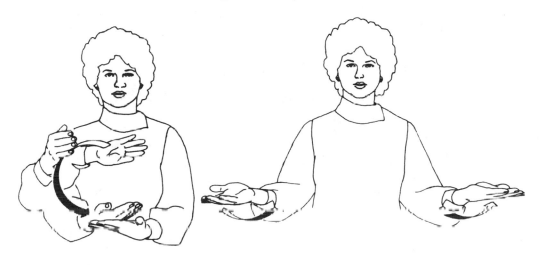

OMNISCIENT

This sign is a combination of KNOW, ALL, and THINGS, and refers to the attribute of total knowl-edge ascribed to God.

    Formation: Tap the fingertips of the right *bent hand* to the right side of the forehead. Then with the right *open hand,* palm facing forward, near the left shoulder, make a large loop to the right end-ing in the upturned palm of the left *open hand.* Then move both *open hands* from side to side with repeated movements, palms facing up, in front of each side of the body.

ONLY, SOLE

Shows being the only one of a kind, such as God's characteristics that set him apart from others.

Formation: Beginning with the right *1 hand* in front of the right shoulder, palm facing forward, twist the wrist to turn the palm in toward the body.

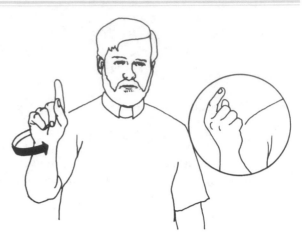

ORACLE See PROPHET (A)

ORDAIN, HOLY ORDERS

The hands symbolize the act of ordination, which invests a person with priestly or ministerial authority.

Formation: Move the right *open hand,* palm facing down, from the right side of the forehead down to on top of the left *open hand* held in front of the body, palm facing down.

Related form: ORDINATION

See also CONFIRMATION (A)(B) and IN-STALL for signs with related meanings.

ORDER (A)

This sign is a combination of RELIGION and ORGANIZATION and refers to certain monastic institutions.

Formation: Bring the fingertips of the right *R hand* from the left side of the chest downward and forward, ending with the palm facing down and the fingers pointing forward. Then move both *O hands,* palms facing each other in front of the chest, in an outward circular movement, ending with the little fingers together.

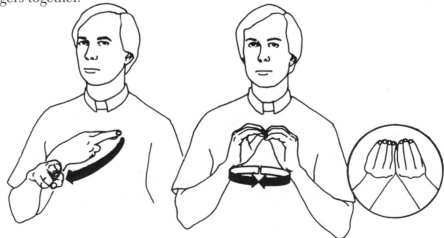

ORDER (B) See COMMAND (A)

ORGANIZATION See CONGREGATION

ORIGINAL SIN

This sign is a combination of BIRTH, HAVE, and SIN referring to the fact that sin is inherent to human nature and is present at birth as a result of the actions of Adam and Eve.

Formation: Bring the palm of the right *open hand* from the stomach forward, landing the back of the right hand on the palm of the left *open hand,* palm up. Then move the fingertips of both *bent hands* against the chest. Then, beginning with an *X hand* in front of each side of the body, both palms facing up, move the hands in repeated upward circular movements.

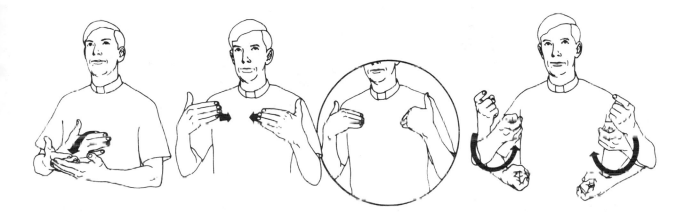

ORTHODOX

This is an initialized sign formed similar to the sign CLEAN and designates those Jews who adhere to strict traditional practices and beliefs.

Formation: Move the little-finger side of the right *O hand,* palm facing left, across the palm of the left *open hand,* palm facing up, from its base to off the fingertips.

See also CONSERVATIVE, DIVINE, HOLY (B), RIGHTEOUS, and SAINT (A) for initialized signs formed in a similar manner.

OVER See ABOVE

OVERCOME See CONQUER

PARABLE (A), MESSAGE, STORY

This sign is used to refer to the stories told by Jesus that illustrated moral or religious issues.

   Formation: Beginning with the index fingers and thumbs of both *8 hands* intersecting with each other, pull the hands apart to in front of each side of the chest. Repeat several times.

   Same sign for SENTENCE, TALE

PARABLE (B)

This sign is a combination of COMPARE and STORY and refers to stories told by Jesus to provide comparisons or disclosures.

   Formation: Beginning with both *curved hands* held several inches apart in front of the chest, right hand closer to the chest than the left hand and palms facing each other, twist the hands in opposite directions while keeping the palms facing each other. Then, beginning with the fingers of both *5 hands* near each other, pull the hands apart to in front of each side of the chest while closing into *flattened O hands*.

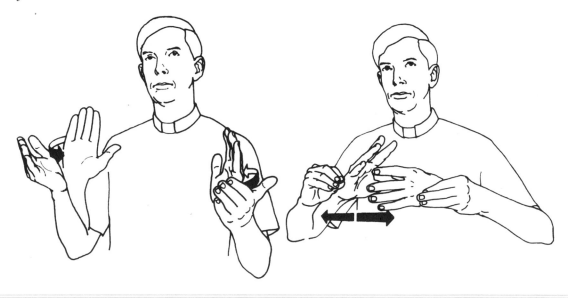

PARADISE See HEAVEN (A)(B)

PARDON See FORGIVE

PARISH

This is an initialized sign formed similar to the
sign for CHURCH and designates the area and
people in a diocese served by a Roman Catholic
Church.

Formation: Tap the heel of the right *P hand*
on the back of the left *S hand,* both palms facing
down.

See also CHURCH, LUTHERAN (B),
PETER, SYNAGOGUE, and TEMPLE for
other initialized signs formed in a similar manner.

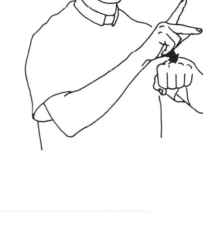

PARISHIONER See LAYPERSON

PASCHAL See EASTER

PASCHAL LAMB

This sign is a combination of PASSOVER and SHEEP and refers to the image of Christ's death
serving as the sacrifice to atone for the sins of the world similar to the Old Testament sacrifice of a
lamb in preparation for Passover.

Formation: Tap the thumb side of the right *S hand,* palm facing down, on the elbow of the bent
left arm held across the chest. Then, with the left arm extended, repeatedly sweep the back of the
right *K hand,* palm facing up, up the inside of the left arm.

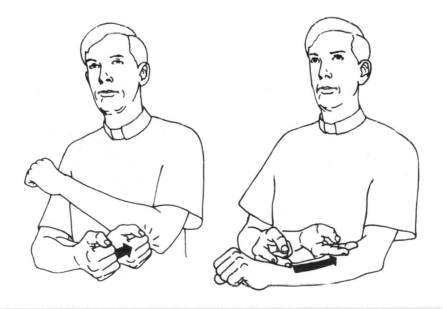

PASSION See SUFFER (B)

PASSOVER (A), MATZOH *(Hebrew)*,
PESACH *(Hebrew)*

This is the sign for CRACKER and refers to
matzoh, the unleavened bread eaten by Jewish
people during Passover.

    Formation: Knock the palm side of the right
A hand near the elbow of the bent left arm held
across the chest.

    Same sign for CRACKER

PASSOVER (B), PESACH *(Hebrew)*

This is an initialized sign showing one hand
passing over the other and representing the
angel of the Lord passing over the homes of
those with lamb's blood on the doorposts, thus
saving the life of the firstborn Jewish boy within.

    Formation: Move the right *P hand* forward
over the back of the left *S hand* held in front of
the body, both palms facing down.

PASSOVER (C), PESACH *(Hebrew)*

This is an initialized sign formed similar to the
sign for CRACKER and refers to matzoh, the
unleavened bread eaten at Passover.

    Formation: Tap the thumb side of the right
P hand, palm facing down, on the elbow of the
bent left arm held across the chest.

PASTOR See PREACHER

PATEN

The fingers in this sign encircle the plate used to hold the Eucharistic bread for Mass.

Formation: Move both *L hands,* fingers slightly curved and palms facing each other, downward a short distance.

Same sign for PLATE

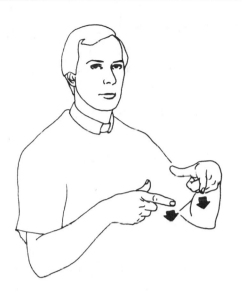

PATIENCE See ENDURE (A)

PATIENT See AFFLICTION

PAUL, SAINT PAUL

This is an initialized sign used to refer to Saul of Tarsus whose name was changed to Paul after his conversion and whose life and writing are recorded in the Acts of the Apostles and his epistles.

Formation: Tap the middle finger of the right *P hand* on the right side of the forehead with a repeated movement.

PEACE, SHALOM

This sign is a combination of BECOME and QUIET to indicate a calming serenity over everything.

Formation: Beginning with the palms of both *open hands* together in front of the chest, twist the hands in opposite directions while keeping the palms together. Then move the hands downward and apart from each other to each side of the body, both palms facing down.

PEACEFUL See SOLEMN

PENALTY See PUNISH

PENANCE See CONFESSION

PENITENT See ATONEMENT

PENTECOST (A), PONTIUS PILATE, WHITSUNDAY

This initialized sign refers to the descent of the Holy Spirit in tongues of fire on the head of the Apostles. It is used in Christian churches for the festival occurring on the seventh Sunday after Easter. It is also used to refer to Pontius Pilate, who was responsible for putting Jesus to death. The context will determine which meaning is intended.

Formation: Tap the middle finger of the right *P hand* down once in front of the body and again to the right.

See also CHARISMATIC (B) for a sign formed in a similar manner.

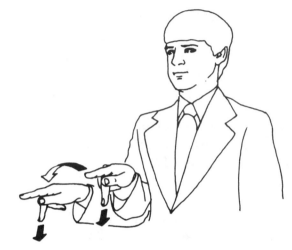

PENTECOST (B)

This sign shows the sign FIRE coming from the top of the head representing the Holy Spirit appearing as tongues of fire on the heads of early Christians on Pentecost.

Formation: With the thumb of the right 5 *hand* on the top of the head, palm facing forward and fingers pointing up, wiggle the fingers.

PEOPLE See LAYPERSON

PERIL See DANGER

PERISH See DEATH

PERPETUAL See ENDURE (B), ETERNAL

PERSECUTE

The hands in this sign seem to prod at a person in a repeated harassing manner.

Formation: Beginning with the right *X hand* held near the body and the left *X hand* somewhat forward, deliberately push the right little-finger side of the right hand across the thumb side of the left hand. Then reverse positions and repeat the action with the left hand.

Related form: PERSECUTION

Same sign for PROBATION, TORTURE

PERSONAL

This initialized sign follows the contour of the body.

Formation: Bring both *P hands*, palms facing each other, down along the body in a parallel movement.

Related form: PERSON

PESACH (*Hebrew*) See PASSOVER (A)(B)(C)

PETER, CEPHEUS, SAINT PETER, SIMON PETER

This is an initialized sign formed similar to the sign for ROCK and indicates the symbolic name conferred by Christ on Simon, which translated from the Aramaic and Greek means "rock."

Formation: Tap the middle finger of the right *P hand* on the back of the left *S hand*, both palms facing down.

See also CHURCH, LUTHERAN (B), PARISH, SYNAGOGUE, and TEMPLE for other initialized signs formed in a similar manner.

PHARAOH

This sign is a combination of the signs EGYPT and KING and refers to ancient kings of Egypt from 1500 B.C. until Persian domination about 500 B.C.

Formation: Bring the back of the right *X hand*, palm facing forward, against the center of the forehead. Then touch the index-finger side of the right *K hand*, palm facing left, first to near the left shoulder and then to near the right hip.

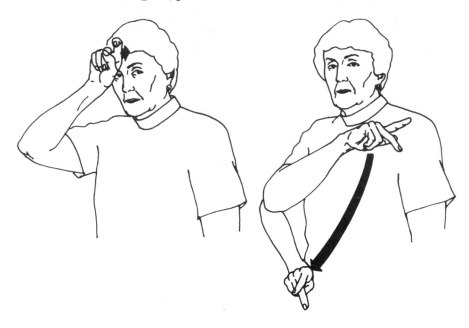

PHARISEE

This is an initialized sign in which the hands follow the form of the breastplate worn by members of the ancient Jewish sect that emphasized strict interpretation of Mosaic law.

Formation: Beginning with the middle fingers of both *P hands* touching the center of the chest, bring the hands straight outward, away from each other to the sides of the chest and then straight down to each side of the waist, ending with the palms facing up.

See also PRIEST and SADDUCEE for signs formed in a similar manner.

PHYLACTERIES See BAR MITZVAH

PILGRIMAGE See HAJJ *(Arabic)*

PILLAR, COLUMN

The hand in this sign shows the shape of a pillar or column. This sign can be used to refer either to structural supports, such as in the temple, or to stones set up as shrines or memorials.

Formation: Move the right *C hand* from in front of the right shoulder, palm facing left, downward a short distance.

PILLARS OF ISLAM, FIVE PILLARS

This sign is a combination of showing five fingers and MUSLIM and refers to the devotional acts required of all Muslims, which include the following: 1) shahada (witnessing); 2) salat (prayer service); 3) sawn (fasting); 4) zakat (almsgiving); and 5) hajj (pilgrimage to Mecca).

Formation: Touch the extended right index finger sequentially to the thumb and each finger of the left *5 hand* held in front of the chest, palm facing in and fingers pointing right. Then hold the right *G hand,* palm facing left, near the right shoulder.

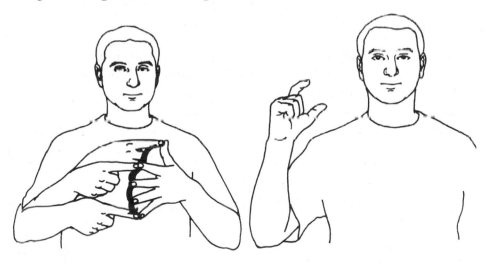

PIOUS See WORSHIP

PITY See MERCY (A)

PLAGUE

This sign is a combination of SICK and SPREAD and refers to mighty works of God that demonstrate God's sovereignty.

Formation: Touch the bent middle finger of the right *5 hand* to the forehead while touching the bent middle finger of the left *5 hand* to the stomach, both palms facing in. Then, beginning with the fingers of both *flattened O hands* together in front of the chest, both palms facing down, bring the hands forward and apart while opening into *5 hands*.

Same sign for EPIDEMIC

PLEAD See BEG

POLYTHEISM, HENOTHEISM

This sign is a combination of BELIEVE, MANY, and GOD, referring to the belief in a plurality of gods, whether coequal or existing under more superior divinities with authority over them.

Formation: Move the extended right index finger smoothly down from the right temple, palm facing in, to clasp the left hand held in front of the body, palms facing each other. Then, beginning with both *5 hands,* palms facing in, near each other in front of the chest, flick the fingers open to *5 hands* with a repeated movement. Then move the right *B hand,* palm facing left, from above the front of the head downward in an arc toward the forehead and down in front of the face.

See also MONOTHEISM for a sign with a contrasting meaning.

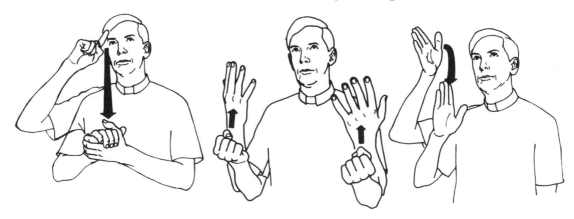

PONDER, MEDITATE, WONDER

The action of the hands in this sign show deep, thoughtful consideration of a matter.

Formation: Move the extended index fingers of both hands in small circles pointing at each side of the forehead.

Note: The sign may be made with one hand.

Same sign for CONTEMPLATE, CONSIDER

See also MEDITATE for an initialized alternate sign.

PONTIFF See POPE

PONTIUS PILATE (A)

This sign is a combination of ROME, RULE, and the person marker and refers to the Roman governor of Judea remembered as the magistrate under whom Jesus Christ suffered.

Formation: Move the right *II hand* from touching the center of the forehead down to touch the nose. Then move both *X hands,* palms facing each other several inches apart in front of the waist, in a double alternating movement forward and back. Add the person marker.

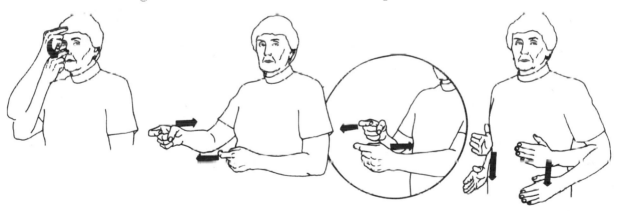

PONTIUS PILATE (B) See PENTECOST (A)

POOR, POVERTY

The hand in this sign shows the worn-out elbows on the clothes of poor people.

Formation: Beginning with the fingertips of the right *curved 5 hand* on the bent left elbow, bring the right hand down with a repeated movement closing into a *flattened O hand* each time.

POPE, PAPAL, PONTIFF

The hands follow the shape of the two-tiered miter traditionally worn by the Pope, the head of the Roman Catholic Church who acts as the vicar of Christ on earth.

Formation: With the palm of an *open hand* held near each side of the head, move the hands upward in and out in a double arc until the fingers touch above the head.

See also BISHOP for a sign formed in a similar manner.

POVERTY See POOR

POWER (A), ALMIGHTY, MIGHT, STRONG

This sign is a natural gesture of tightening the biceps by clenching the fists to show strength.

Formation: Move both *S hands,* palms facing in, from near the sides of the chest forward with a deliberate movement, ending abruptly.

Related forms: POWERFUL, MIGHTY, STRENGTH

See also ALMIGHTY and MIGHTY for alternate signs.

POWER (B), ALMIGHTY, MIGHT, STRONG

The hand in this sign outlines a large flexed biceps, symbolizing physical strength.

Formation: Move the right *A hand* from near the left shoulder, palm facing down, in an arc to the crook of the left bent arm while turning the palm in.

Note: The right extended index finger may be used instead of the *A hand.*

Related forms: POWERFUL, MIGHTY, STRENGTH

See also ALMIGHTY and MIGHTY for related signs.

POWERFUL See MIGHTY (B)

PRACTICE See DISCIPLINE (A)

PRAISE (A), HOSANNA, MAGNIFY

The hands in this sign mime applauding to extol or exalt God.

Formation: Beginning with the extended right index finger at the mouth, palm facing left, move the hand down while changing to an *open hand,* palm facing down, landing on the palm of the left *open hand,* palm facing up.

Same sign for ACCLAIM, APPLAUD, CLAP, COMMEND, OVATION

PRAISE (B), HOSANNA, MAGNIFY

This sign is a combination of hands miming applause and OFFER.

Formation: Beginning with right extended index finger at the mouth, palm facing left, bring the right hand forward while opening to an *open hand* to land on the palm of the left *open hand.* Then move both *open hands* apart and upward, palms facing up.

Same sign for ACCLAIM, APPLAUD

PRAISE TO ALLAH

This sign is a combination of kissing one's hand in devotion and ALLAH and is used in a multitude of circumstances by Muslims. The sign is used in greeting other Muslims, in responding about one's health, and in all prayers.

Formation: Touch the palm of the right *open hand* to the mouth and then quickly flip the hand over and touch the back of the hand to the mouth, ending with the palm facing forward and fingers pointing left. Then move the right extended index finger from in front of the right shoulder upward near the right side of the head, palm facing forward and finger pointing up.

PRAY, AMEN, COLLECT *(noun)*, INTERCESSION, LITANY, PETITION, SUPPLICATION

The hands of this sign mime a natural pleading movement to indicate any communion with God, such as confession, petition, or praise.

Formation: With the palms of both *open hands* together, move the hands in toward the chest and downward a short distance with a double movement.

Related form: PRAYER
See also WORSHIP for an alternate sign.

PREACH, ENLIGHTEN, HOMILETICS, HOMILY, SERMON

This sign is formed similar to the sign for LEC-TURE and refers to a speech that gives religious or moral instruction.

Formation: Beginning with a right *F hand*, palm facing forward, in front of the right shoulder, move the hand forward a short distance with several small, jerky movements.

See also EVANGELISM for another sign formed in a similar manner.

PREACHER, MINISTER, PASTOR

This sign is a combination of PREACH and the person marker and designates Protestant clergy.

Formation: Beginning with a right *F hand*, palm facing forward, in front of the right shoulder, move the hand forward a short distance with several small, jerky movements. Add the person marker.

PREDESTINATION, ELECTION

This sign is a combination of BEFORE and DECIDE and refers to the belief of some Christian sects that God has chosen in advance those who will be saved.

Formation: Beginning with the back of the right *open hand,* palm facing in and fingers pointing left, across the back of the fingers of the left *B hand,* palm facing forward and fingers pointing up, bring the right hand back toward the chest. Then move both *F hands,* palms facing each other and fingers pointing forward, downward in front of the chest.

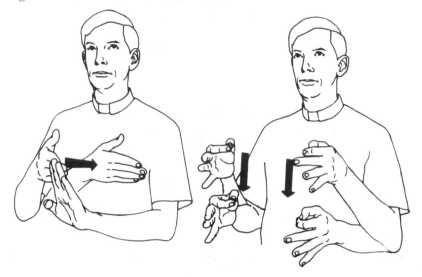

PREDICT See PROPHECY

PREPARE

The hands in this sign seem to be clearing different paths and symbolize mankind's preparation for eternal life.

Formation: Move both *open hands,* palms facing each other several inches apart with fingers pointing forward, from left to right in front of the body in several arcs.

Related form: PREPARATION

PRESBYTERIAN

This is an initialized sign used to designate various Protestant churches, which are traditionally Calvinist in doctrine and governed by presbyters and elders.

Formation: Tap the middle finger of the right *P hand,* palm facing left, on the palm of the left *open hand,* palm facing right and fingers pointing forward.

PRESENCE, APPEARANCE, BEFORE, COME BEFORE

The hands in this sign represent a person coming before another person. If referring to the presence of God, the left hand is held somewhat higher than the right to indicate God's elevated position. This is a directional sign.

Formation: Beginning with an *open hand* in front of each side of the body, left palm facing down and right palm facing up, simultaneously bring the hands upward in an arc, ending with the palms facing each other in front of the chest.

Related form: APPEAR

PRESENT See GIFT, GIVE, OFFERING (A)

PRESERVE (A)

This is an initialized sign in which the hands symbolize eyes watching in all directions to keep something safe.

Formation: Tap the little-finger side of the right *K hand* on the index-finger side of the left *K hand,* palms facing in opposite directions and move the hands downward in front of the chest.

Same sign for KEEP

PRESERVE (B)

This sign is used to refer to long-term care for something and refers to God's care over his children.

Formation: With the fingers of the right *V hand* on the back of the left *S hand*, both palms facing in, move both hands toward the chest.

Same sign for STORE, KEEP, SAVE

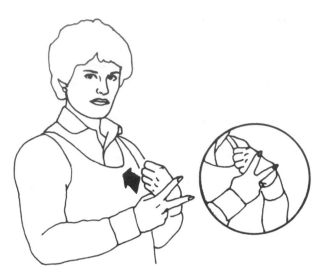

PRESERVE (C) See ENDURE (B)

PRIEST (A)

This sign is formed similar to the sign for pharisee and designates the ancient priests of the Scriptures.

Formation: Beginning with the extended index fingers of both hands touching the center of the chest, bring the hands straight outward away from each other to the sides of the chest and then straight down to each side of the waist, ending with the palms facing up.

See also PHARISEE for a sign formed in a similar manner.

PRIEST (B), FATHER

The fingers follow the shape of the clerical collar worn by those members of the clergy in the Roman Catholic, Episcopal, and some other churches who have authority to pronounce absolution and administer the Sacraments.

Formation: Move the fingertips of the right *G hand* from the left side of the neck around the neck to the right.

Note: This sign may be formed with both hands beginning in the middle of the neck, moving apart from each other around the neck.

PROCESSION

The hands in this sign represent the feet of people marching and moving forward in an orderly and formal manner.

Formation: Beginning with the fingers of both *4 hands* pointing down, palms facing in and right hand forward of the left hand, flip the fingers of both hands forward from the wrists with a double movement.

Same sign for PARADE, MARCH

PROCLAIM See ANNOUNCE

PROFANATION See SACRILEGE (A)(B)

PROMISE See VOW (A)(B)

PROMISED LAND

This sign is a combination of PROMISE and LAND and refers to the land of Canaan to which the Israelites returned following the Exodus. This term is often used today in referring to heaven.

Formation: Beginning with the right extended index finger touching the mouth, palm facing left and finger pointing up, move the right hand down while changing to an *open hand,* ending with the palm of the right hand on the index-finger sign of the left *S hand,* palm facing in. Then rub the thumb of both *curved hands* on each index finger with a repeated movement followed by moving the right *open hand* in a large arc over the back of the left *open hand,* both palms facing down.

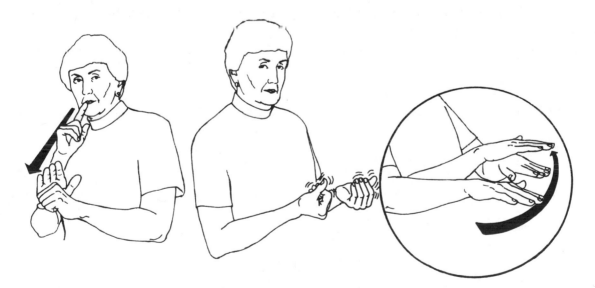

PROOF, EVIDENCE

The hand in this sign takes something that is known and lays it out for examination to verify its truth or existence.

Formation: Bring the extended right index finger from near the right eye downward while changing to an *open hand* and landing in the palm of the left *open hand,* both palms facing up.

Note: The right hand may begin as an *open hand,* palm facing in, on the right cheek.

See also WITNESS (A) for a sign with a related meaning formed in a similar manner.

PROPHECY, FORETELL, PREDICT

This sign is a combination of SEE and a movement toward the future and refers to the inspired revelations of the messianic prophets.

Formation: Beginning with the fingers of the right *V hand* pointing to the eyes, move the right hand forward and downward under the palm of the left *open hand* held in front of the chest, both palms facing down.

Related form: PREDICTION

See also VISION for a sign with a related meaning formed in a similar manner.

PROPHET (A), ORACLE

This sign is a combination of PROPHECY and the person marker and refers to those who, through divine inspiration, predict the future.

Formation: Beginning with the fingers of the right *V hand* pointing to the eyes, move the right hand forward and downward under the palm of the left *open hand* held in front of the chest, palm facing down. Add the person marker.

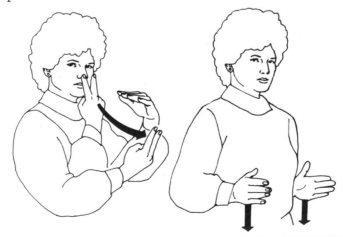

PROPHET (B)

This is the sign for RAISE and refers to a person who is a specialist in divine-human communication. In the Islamic religion this sign is used to refer to Moses, Jesus, and others who are considered prophets.

Formation: Move the right *open hand*, palm facing up, upward near the right side of the body.

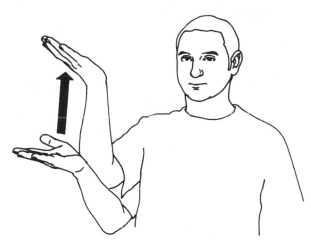

PROPHET, THE See MUHAMMAD

PROPITIATION, EXPIATION

This sign is a combination of CHRIST, SACRIFICE, and PAY to signify that Jesus's death canceled or paid for the sins of the world in God's eyes and averted God's wrath toward sin.

Formation: Touch the index-finger side of the right *C hand*, palm left, first to near the left shoulder and then to near the right hip. Then, beginning with both *S hands*, palms facing up, in front of each side of the waist, move the hands upward and forward while opening into *5 hands*, palms facing up. Then move the extended index finger of the right hand across the palm of the left *open hand* from the heel to the fingers and outward.

See also ATONEMENT for a sign with a similar meaning.

PROSELYTE

This sign is a combination of JOIN and CONVERT and refers to a person who accepts a religion and joins it.

Formation: Beginning with the fingers of the right *H hand*, palm facing left, in front of the chest, move the fingers downward to inside the thumb side of the left *C hand*. Then, with the thumb of the right *C hand* on the thumb of the left *C hand*, twist the hands in opposite directions, ending with the hands in reverse positions.

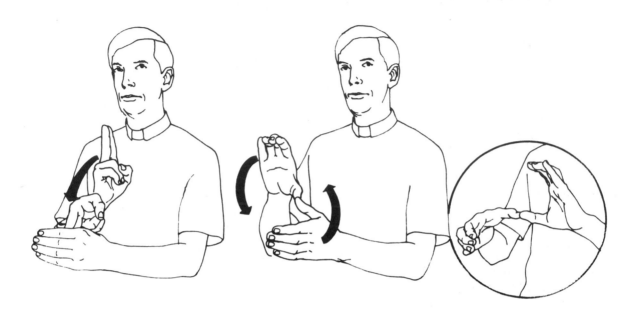

PROTECT, DEFEND, GUARD

The hands in this sign are held up as a shield to protect the body.

Formation: Beginning with the wrists of both *S hands* crossed in front of the chest, both palms facing down, move both hands forward with a short double movement.

PROTESTANT

The fingers in this sign represent bended knees. The sign is used to refer to Christians belonging to any sect descending from those that seceded from the Roman Catholic Church at the time of the Reformation.

Formation: Tap the knuckles of the bent right *V hand,* palm facing in, on the palm of the left *open hand,* palm facing up, with a double movement.

See also GENUFLECT and KNEEL for signs with related meanings formed in a similar manner.

PROTESTANT EPISCOPAL
See EPISCOPAL

PROVERB

This sign is a combination of WISE and STORY, referring to stories and poems that can be used to compare abstract principles with concrete facts. Proverbs, though similar to parables, are usually shorter.

Formation: Bring the bent index finger of the right *X hand* downward with a double movement in front of the forehead. Then, beginning with the fingers of both *5 hands* near each other, pull the hands apart in front of each side of the chest while closing into *flattened O hands.*

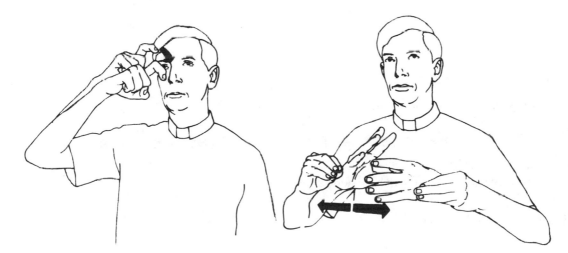

PROVIDENCE, DIVINE PROVIDENCE

This is the sign for TAKE CARE OF and refers to God's faithful and effective care and guidance of everything that He has made toward the end that He has chosen.

Formation: With the little-finger side of the right *K hand* across the index-finger side of the left *K hand,* palms facing in opposite directions, move the hands in a repeated flat circle in front of the body.

Same sign for CARE, MONITOR, PATROL, SUPERVISE, TAKE CARE OF

PSALM

This is an initialized sign formed like SONG and indicates any of the hymns collected in the Old Testament book of Psalms.

Formation: Swing the right *P hand* back and forth in a large arc over the extended left forearm.

Same sign for POEM, POETRY

See also CANTOR, CHOIR, and HYMN for initialized signs formed in a similar manner.

PUNISH, DISCIPLINE, PENALTY

The hand in this sign mimes a punishing movement.

Formation: Strike the extended right index finger downward with a deliberate movement on the elbow of the bent left arm held across the chest.

Related form: PUNISHMENT

PURE (A)

This is an initialized sign formed similar to the sign for CLEAN and refers to the state of being sinless and perfect in God's eyes.

Formation: Slide the middle finger of the right *P hand* across the palm of the left *open hand* from its base to the fingertips and outward.

  Related form: PURITY

  Same sign for CHASTITY

  See also CONSERVATIVE, DIVINE, HOLY (B), ORTHODOX, RIGHTEOUS (A), and SAINT (A) for other initialized signs formed in a similar manner.

PURE (B)

This initialized sign is a combination of *P* and CLEAN and refers to something that is without defilement.

Formation: Beginning with the right *P hand* over the heel of the palm of the left *open hand*, change to a right *open hand* and bring the right palm across the palm of the left *open hand* from its base to the fingertips and outward.

  Related form: PURITY

  See also HOLY (A)(C) and SANCTIFY (A) for other initialized signs formed in a similar manner.

PURGATORY, INDULGENCE

This initialized sign is formed similar to the sign for COIN and refers to the former practice of selling indulgences in the sixteenth century to expiate the sins of souls in purgatory who died in grace.

Formation: Move the middle finger of the right *P hand* in a small circle in the palm of the left *open hand*, palms facing each other.

PURIM

The fingers in this sign form a mask that represents the Jewish holiday celebrating the deliverance of the Jews from massacre by Haman.

Formation: Beginning with the fingers of both *V hands* near the outside of each eye, palms facing back and fingers pointing toward each other, pull the hands outward away from the face with a short double movement.

QUAKERS (A), FRIENDS, SOCIETY OF FRIENDS

This sign is a combination of SOCIETY and FRIEND and signifies the preferred name of this religious sect founded by George Fox in 1650 in England which rejects ritual, formal sacraments, a formal creed, a priesthood, and violence. They distinguish themselves from other Christians through their doctrine of the "Inward" or "Inner Light," which is the manifestation of the divine within each individual.

Formation: Move both *S hands,* palms facing forward in front of the chest, in a outward circular movement, ending with the little fingers together. Then hook the bent index finger of the right *X hand,* palm facing down, down over the bent index finger of the left *X hand,* palm facing up. Turn the hands to repeat the action in reverse.

See also FRIEND for an alternate sign.

QUAKERS (B), FRIENDS, SOCIETY OF FRIENDS

The hands in this sign mime twiddling thumbs to indicate the reputed patience of members of the Quaker Church as they await the Holy Spirit. The name "Quaker" is not used by members of the church, founded by George Fox, who admonished the members "to tremble at the word of the Lord."

Formation: Beginning with the fingers of both hands intertwined with each other, revolve the thumbs around each other with a repeated movement.

QUAKERS (C) See FRIENDS (A)

QUR'AN *(Arabic)*, HOLY QUR'AN, KORAN

This sign is a combination of BOOK and ALLAH and refers to the Muslim record of God's revelation to Muhammad. In Arabic, the word *Qur'an* means "recitation" or "reading." Muslims view the Qur'an as God's full and final disclosure to the last of his prophets, Muhammad, and that the Qur'an records God's very words as revealed in the Arabic language.

Formation: Beginning with the palms of both *open hands* together in front of the chest, move the hands apart at the top, keeping the little fingers together. Then move the extended right index finger, palm facing left and finger pointing up, upward in front of the right shoulder.

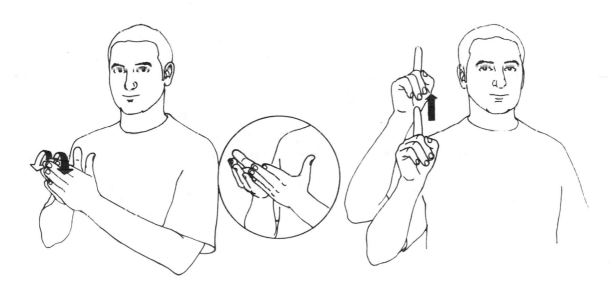

RABBI

The hands of this initialized sign indicate the location of the tallith, the pray shawl, worn by the ordained spiritual leader of a Jewish congregation.

Formation: Bring the fingertips of both *R hands* from near each shoulder straight down each side of the chest.

See also BROTHER and TALLITH for signs formed in a similar manner.

RAGE See ANGER

RAISE See EXALT (A)(B)

RAMADAN

This sign shows closing one's mouth to eating as is practiced by Muslims during daylight hours in the month of Ramadan. Ramadan is one of two canonical feasts observed in the ninth month of the Muslim year.

Formation: Beginning with the right *G hand* in front of the mouth, fingers pointing left, pinch the extended index finger and thumb together.

REAL PRESENCE

This sign is a combination of JESUS, TRUE, and THERE and refers to the belief of some Christian sects that Christ's body and blood are present in the bread and wine taken during the Eucharist.

Formation: Touch the bent middle finger of the right *5 hand* to the center of the palm of the left *open hand.* Reverse the action by touching the bent middle finger of the left *5 hand* to the palm of the right *open hand.* Then move the extended right index finger, palm facing left and finger pointing up, from the mouth forward, ending with the finger pointing forward. Then move the right *open hand,* palm facing up, forward a short distance in front of the body.

REBEL See DISOBEY (A)(B)

REBIRTH See REINCARNATION

RECEIVE See OBTAIN

RECONCILIATION (A), ATONEMENT, COVENANT

This is a directional sign made like the sign for UNITY and indicates Christ's role in uniting God with man.

Formation: With the thumb and index finger of each hand touching and intersecting with the other hand, palms facing each other, move the hands upward and back toward the chest with a double movement.

Related forms: RECONCILE, ATONE

See also COMMUNION OF SAINTS and UNITY for signs formed in a similar manner.

RECONCILIATION (B)

This sign is formed similar to the sign WELCOME, formed with both hands, and symbolizes bringing two things together such as God's relationship with man because of Christ's redemptive work.

Formation: Beginning with an *open hand* in front of each side of the body, palms facing up and fingers pointing toward the other hand, bring the hands together in front of the waist.

Related form: RECONCILE

Same sign for INTRODUCE, INTRODUCTION

RECONSTRUCTIONISM

This sign is a combination of fingerspelling R-E and BUILD and signifies a religious movement in the United States that developed out of the Conservative branch of Judaism.

Formation: Form *R* and *E* with the right hand near the right shoulder. Then, with the fingertips of both *bent hands* overlapping slightly, palms facing down, alternately move the right and left hands over each other several times, moving the hands upward each time.

RECTOR, CHIEF, SUPREME

This is the sign for CHIEF and indicates a Roman Catholic priest appointed the spiritual head of a parish or seminary.

Formation: Move the right *10 hand* upward from in front of the right side of the chest, palm facing in.

See also EXALT for a sign with a related meaning.

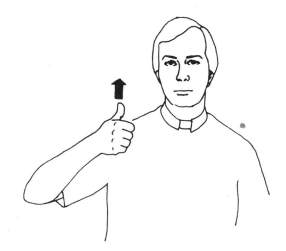

REDEEM

This initialized sign shows the hands breaking free from bondage and refers to the freedom from sin given though Christ's redemptive work.

Formation: Bring both *R hands,* wrists crossed in front of the chest and palms facing in, away from each other by twisting the wrists, ending with the palms facing forward in front of each side of the body.

Related form: REDEMPTION

See also DELIVER, REFORM (B), and SALVATION for initialized signs with related meanings formed in a similar manner.

REDEEMER

This sign is a combination of REDEEM and the person marker and refers to Christ's role in redeeming mankind from a state of sinfulness.

Formation: Bring both *R hands,* wrists crossed in front of the chest and palms facing in, away from each other by twisting the wrists, ending with the palms facing forward in front of each side of the body. Add the person marker.

See also SAVIOR for a sign formed in a similar manner

REFORM (A) See CONVERT

REFORM (B), JUDAISM

This initialized sign shows the hands breaking free from bondage and refers to the branch of Judaism introduced in the nineteenth century that does not require strict observance of traditional Jewish laws.

Formation: Bring both *R hands* from near each other in front of the chest, palms facing in, away from each other by twisting the wrists, ending with the palms facing forward in front of each side of the body.

See also DELIVER, REDEEM, and SALVATION for initialized signs formed in a similar manner.

REGENERATION See BORN AGAIN (A)(B)

REGRET See ATONEMENT

REIGN See RULE

REINCARNATION, METASOMATOSIS, REBIRTH

This sign is a combination of BIRTH and CYCLE and refers to the Hindu belief in the rebirth of the soul in successive life-forms.

Formation: Bring the palm of the right *open hand* from the stomach forward, landing the back of the right hand on the palm of the left *open hand,* palm up. Then move the right extended index finger in a repeated circular movement, around the extended left index finger.

See also BORN AGAIN (A) for a sign formed in a similar manner.

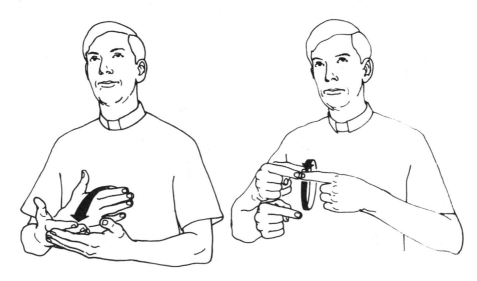

REJECT (A), EXCOMMUNICATION

The hand in this sign brushes away a rejected object and signifies dismissing someone from participation in the religious community.

Formation: Beginning with the little-finger side of the right *open hand,* palm facing left, on the palm of the left *open hand,* palm facing up, brush the right hand across and upward off the left palm while twisting the palm forward.

Related form: REJECTED

REJECT (B), EXCOMMUNICATION

The fingertips in this sign brush away an unwanted object or person and refer to cutting a person off from church rites as directed by ecclesiastical authority.

Formation: Brush the fingertips of the right *open hand* from the heel to off the fingertips of the palm of the left *open hand* with a flick of the wrist.

Related form: REJECTED

REJOICE (A), JOY

The hands in this sign have an upward movement that indicates bringing up happiness from within.

Formation: Bring the palms of both *open hands,* fingers pointing toward each other, upward and forward from the chest with circular alternating movements.

Note: This sign may be formed with only one hand.

Same sign for DELIGHT, GLAD, HAPPY, HAPPINESS, MERRY

See also REVIVAL for an initialized sign with a related meaning and formed in a similar manner.

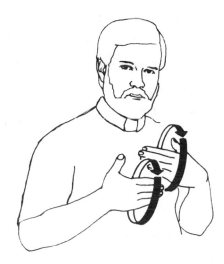

REJOICE (B) See CELEBRATE

RELATIVISM

This sign is a combination of TEACH, VAGUE, and SO-SO and refers to the view that knowledge and morals are relative to historical epoch, to societal or scientific worldview, or to personal conviction.

Formation: With both *flattened O hands* in front of the head, palms facing down, move the hands forward with a short double movement. Then rub the palm of the right 5 *hand* on the palm of the left 5 *hand* with a circular movement. Then move the right 5 *hand* in a repeated up-and-down movement by twisting the wrist in front of the right shoulder, palm facing down.

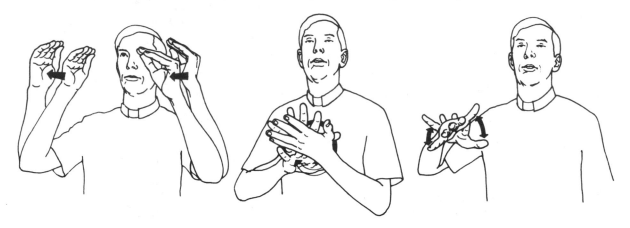

RELIGION

This is an initialized sign that indicates an inward faith from the heart as well as outward sincere observance of rituals.

Formation: Bring the fingertips of the right *R hand* from the left side of the chest downward and forward, ending with the palm facing down and the fingers pointing forward.

Note: The *R hand* may begin on the right side of the chest instead of the left.

Related form: RELIGIOUS

See also DENOMINATION, THEOLOGY (A)(B) for signs formed in a similar manner.

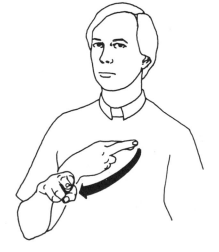

RELIGIOUS See FRUM *(Hebrew)*

REMEMBER See MEMORIAL

REMOVE See TAKE AWAY

RENOUNCE, SUBMIT, SURRENDER

The hands in this sign demonstrate a natural gesture of surrender and symbolize a pledge to turn away from sin and the devil's power.

Formation: Beginning with both *S hands* near each side of the body, palms facing down, bring the hands up abruptly while changing into *5 hands,* ending near each side of the head, palms facing forward and fingers pointing up.

Related form: SUBMISSION
Same sign for GIVE UP, RELINQUISH

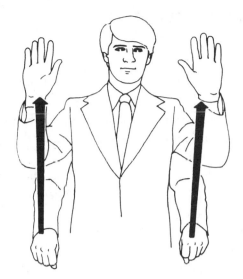

REPENT (A)

This initialized sign is formed similar to the sign CHANGE and indicates a repentant person's regret for past behavior and intent to abjure future sins.

Formation: Beginning with the palms of both *R hands* touching in front of the body, twist the wrists in opposite directions, ending with the hands in reverse positions.

Related form: REPENTANCE

See also CONVERT, INTERPRET, and TRANSLATE for signs formed in a similar manner.

REPENT (B) See ATONEMENT

REPLY See ANSWER

REQUEST See ASK

REQUIRE See COMMAND (B)

RESPECT, REVERE

This initialized sign is formed similar to the sign HONOR and signifies a deep respect for God.

Formation: Beginning with both *R hands* in front of the head, right hand higher than the left hand, palms facing each other, and fingers pointing up, move the hands downward and in toward the chest.

Note: The head usually bows as the hands come down. This sign may be formed with only the right hand.

Related form: REVERENT

See also HONOR for a sign with a related meaning and formed in a similar manner.

RESPOND See ANSWER

RESPONSIBILITY See OBLIGATION

RESURRECTION, ARISE

The fingers in this sign demonstrate getting on one's feet and refers to the rising of Christ after the Crucifixion and of the dead at the Last Judgment.

Formation: Beginning with the right V *hand* near the left *open hand,* both palms facing up, bring the right hand up in an arc, ending with the fingertips of the right hand on the left palm.

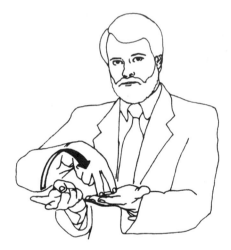

RETREAT

This initialized sign signifies a period of seclusion used for discussing religious practices or issue.

Formation: Move the right *R hand,* palm facing in and fingers pointing up, from touching the forehead down to touch the chin.

Note: As a variation of this sign, the hand may change to a *T hand* at the chin.

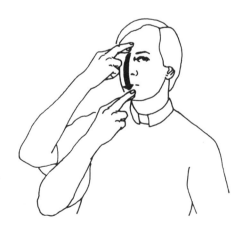

REVEAL, EXAMPLE, MANIFEST

The hand in this sign seems to bring out something into view for examination. This is a directional sign.

Formation: With the extended right index finger touching the palm of the left *open hand*, palms facing each other, move both hands forward a short distance.

Note: The left palm may face forward with the fingers pointing either up or down as a variation of this sign.

Related forms: MANIFESTATION, REVELATION

Same sign for DEMONSTRATE, EXPRESS, SHOW, REPRESENT

See also SYMBOL and WITNESS (B) for initialized signs formed in a similar manner.

REVERE See BELOVED, RESPECT

REVILE See MOCK

REVIVAL

This is an initialized sign formed similar to the sign REJOICE and signifies the reawakening of faith that frequently occurs at religious revivals.

Formation: Bring the palms of both *R hands*, fingers pointing up, upward and forward from the chest with circular alternating movements.

See also REJOICE for an initialized sign with a related meaning and formed in a similar manner.

RIGHTEOUS (A)

This initialized sign is formed similar to the sign CLEAN and refers to the righteous being cleansed through Christ's redemptive power.

Formation: Slide the middle finger of the right *R hand* across the palm of the left *open hand* from its base to the fingertips and outward.

Related form: RIGHTEOUSNESS

See also CONSERVATIVE, DIVINE, HOLY (B), ORTHODOX, PURE (A), and SAINT (A) for other initialized signs formed in a similar manner.

RIGHTEOUS (B)

This sign is formed like the sign for ALL RIGHT and refers to those people who have been declared right with God.

Formation: Slide the little-finger side of the right *open hand,* palm facing left, across the palm of the left *open hand,* palm facing up, from its base to the fingertips and outward.

Related form: RIGHTEOUSNESS

ROBE

The hands in this sign show the flow of garments worn by church officials.

Formation: Beginning with the fingers of a *flattened O hand* touching near each shoulder, bring the hands down to near each other at the waist, ending with the palms facing up.

See also VESTMENTS for a related sign.

ROMAN, LATIN, ROME

This initialized sign follows the shape of a traditional Roman nose and refers to the location of the headquarters of the Roman Catholic Church in Italy.

Formation: Move the right *R hand* from touching the center of the forehead down to touch the nose.

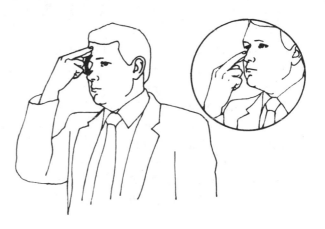

ROMAN CATHOLIC See CATHOLIC

ROME See ROMAN

ROSARY

The fingers of this initialized sign follow the shape of the beads on which prayers of devotion are counted while praying to the Virgin Mary.

Formation: Beginning with the fingers of both *R hands* touching in front of the chest, palms facing forward and fingers pointing up, bring the hands apart and down in arcs, ending with the fingers touching in front of the waist, palms facing down.

ROSH HASHANAH *(Hebrew)*, NEW YEAR

This sign is a combination of HAPPY, NEW, and YEAR and refers to the Jewish New Year, a solemn occasion celebrated in late September or early October.

Formation: Bring the palm of the right *open hand*, fingers pointing left, upward and forward from the chest with a double circular movement. Then sweep the back of the right *curved hand*, palm facing up, across the palm of the left *open hand*, held in front of the body, palm facing up. Then, beginning with both *S hands* near each other in front of the body, palms facing in, move the right hand forward in a circle around the left hand, ending with the little-finger side of the right hand on the index-finger side of the left hand.

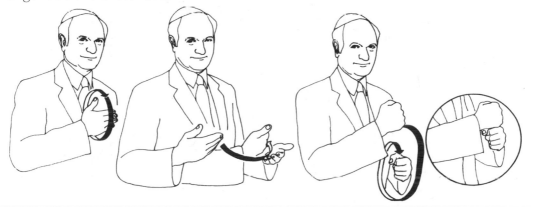

RULE, DIRECT, REIGN

The fingers in this sign seem to hold the reins of a horse to control it. The sign refers to God's control over the lives of mankind.

Formation: Move both *X hands,* palms facing each other several inches apart in front of the waist, in a double alternating movement forward and back.

Same sign for CONDUCT, CONTROL, GOVERN, MANAGE, OPERATE

SABBATH (A)

This sign is a combination of REST and DAY and refers to the last day of the week, observed by Jews and some Christian sects as a day of rest and worship.

Formation: Lay the palms of both *open hands* on the chest near the opposite shoulder, crossing the arms at the wrists. Then, beginning with the elbow of the bent right arm, right index finger pointing up, on the back of the left hand held across the body, palm facing down, move the right index finger downward toward the left elbow.

SABBATH (B), SHABBAT *(Hebrew)*

This is the sign for SATURDAY, the seventh day of the week, designated by some religions as a day of rest and worship.

Formation: Move the right *S hand*, palm facing in, in a small circle in front of the right side of the chest.

Same sign for SATURDAY

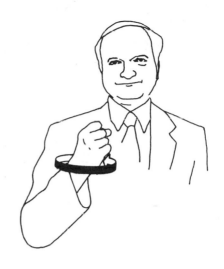

SABBATH (C), SHABBAT *(Hebrew)*

The hand represents the sun going down behind the horizon and signifies the beginning of the Jewish Sabbath on Friday at sundown.

Formation: Bring the right *F hand*, palm facing left, down in front of the chest behind the left *open hand* held in front of the chest, palm facing down.

SABBATH (D), SUNDAY

This sign is formed similar to the sign WONDERFUL and is used to designate the first day of the week, observed by most Christian churches as a day of rest.

Formation: Move both *open hands*, palm facing forward in front of each shoulder, in circular movements upward and outward away from each other.

SACRAMENT

This initialized sign is made in the form of a cross and designates those rites mediating grace that are considered to have been instituted by Christ.

Formation: Move the right *S hand,* palm facing forward, from above the right shoulder downward. Then move the right *S hand* from in front of the right shoulder outward to the right.

SACRED See HOLY (A)

SACRIFICE

This sign is formed similar to the sign for OFFER and indicates that a sacrifice is the offering of something of value to God. This is a directional sign toward God.

Formation: Beginning with an *S hand,* palm facing up, in front of each side of the waist, move the hands upward and forward while opening into *5 hands,* palms facing up.

SACRILEGE (A), PROFANATION

This sign is a combination of the sign MOCK and GOD and refers to the act of desecrating objects or space set apart as sacred.

Formation: With the index finger and little finger of each hand extended, place the right index finger near the side of the nose, palm facing left, and the left hand forward of the body, palm facing down. Move both hands forward with a short jabbing double movement. Then move the right *open hand,* palm facing left, from above the front of the head downward in an arc toward the forehead and down in front of the face.

Related form: SACRILEGIOUS

SACRILEGE (B), PROFANATION

This is a directional sign toward God formed similar to the sign DON'T CARE and indicates an irreverence toward anything sacred.

   Formation: Move the extended index fingers from the nose upward in an arc, ending with the finger pointing up and the palm facing forward above the right side of the head.

   Related form: SACRILEGIOUS

SACRISTY See SANCTUARY

SAD See SORROWFUL

SADDUCEE

This initialized sign is formed similar to PRIEST, designating a Jewish group of aristocrats that was in charge of the Temple and its services during the period 200 B.C.E. to 70 A.D., when the Temple was destroyed.

   Formation: Beginning with both *S hands*, each near the center of the chest, palms facing each other, bring the hands straight outward away from each other to the sides of the chest and then straight down to each side of the waist, ending with the palms facing down.

   See also PHARISEE and PRIEST for signs formed in a similar manner.

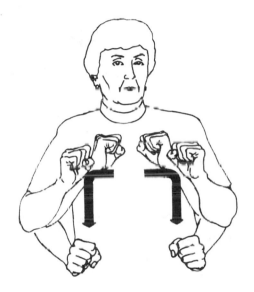

SAINT (A)

This is an initialized sign formed like HOLY and indicates a baptized believer in Christ or, in the Catholic Church, a person who has been canonized and is therefore entitled to public veneration.

   Formation: Slide the palm side of the right *S hand* across the palm of the left *open hand* from its base to the fingertips and outward.

SAINT (B)

This sign is a combination of HOLY and PEOPLE and signifies all believers on earth and those who have died and gone to heaven.

Formation: Move the right *H hand* in a small circle in front of the chest and then slide the little-finger side across the palm of the left *open hand* from its base to the fingertips and outward. Then make large alternating forward circles with both *P hands,* palms facing each other, in front of each side of the body.

SAINT PAUL See PAUL

SAINT PETER See PETER

SALAT *(Arabic)*

Salat means "prayer" in Arabic and refers to the five prayers a day required of practicing Muslims. The prayer is a short, highly formalized worship service performed in total prostration with the forehead touching the floor.

Formation: Beginning with both *curved 5 hands,* palms facing each other, near each side of the head, move the hands forward and downward with a double movement.

244

SALAT-UL-ASR *(Arabic)* See ASR *(Arabic)*

SALUTATION See CALL (B)

SALVATION, DELIVER, SAVE

The hands of this initialized sign seem to break free of bondage and symbolize the deliverance of man's soul through Christ's redemption from the penalty of sin.

Formation: Bring both *S hands*, wrists crossed in front of the chest and palms facing in, away from each other by twisting the wrists, ending with the palms facing forward in front of each side of the body.

See also DELIVER, REDEEM, and RE-FORM for initialized signs with related meanings formed in a similar manner.

SANCTIFY (A)

This is an initialized sign formed similar to the sign CLEAN and signifies the act of making something clean or holy.

Formation: Beginning with the right *S hand* over the heel of the palm of the left *open hand*, change to a right *open hand* and wipe the right palm across the palm of the left *open hand* from its base to the fingertips and outward.

Related form: SANCTIFICATION

See also HOLY (A) and PURE (B) for other initialized signs formed in a similar manner.

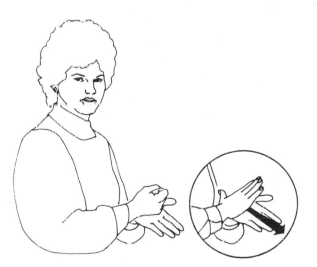

SANCTIFY (B), CONSECRATE

This sign is a combination of MAKE and HOLY and signifies the practice of setting something aside as holy.

Formation: With the little-finger side of the right *S hand* on the index-finger side of the left *S hand*, palms facing in opposite directions, twist the wrists in opposite directions several times, touching the hands together after each twist. Then form an *H* with the right hand above the left *open hand*, palm up. Then move the right *open hand* across the left palm from its base to off the fingertips.

Related forms: SANCTIFICATION, CONSECRATION

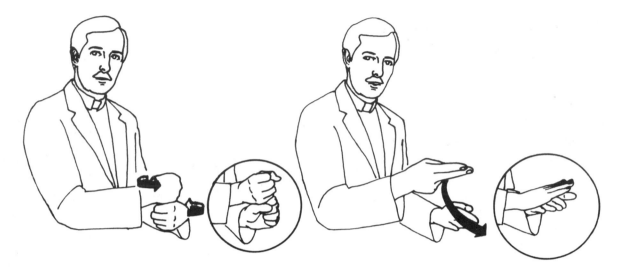

SANCTUARY, SACRISTY, SHRINE, VESTRY

This sign is a combination of HOLY and PLACE and refers to a sacred place, such as a church, temple, or mosque, or a most holy place within that place.

Formation: Make a circle with the right *H* above the left *open hand,* palm up. Then move the right *open hand* across the left palm from its base to off the fingertips. Then with the middle fingers of both *P hands* touching, palms facing each other, bring the hands outward in a circle, ending by touching the fingers again near the body.

See also SHRINE (A) for a sign with a similar meaning.

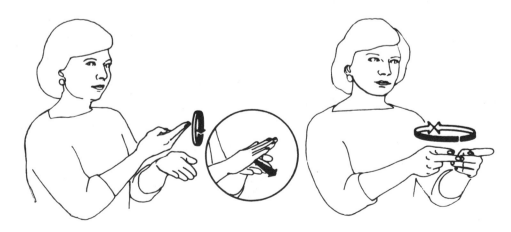

SATAN (A), DEVIL, IBLIS *(Arabic)*

This sign showing the horns of an evil being in Islam refers to Iblis, the chief of the legions of devils, who are trying to lead humans astray and will serve as tormentors in the fires of hell.

Formation: With the index finger and little finger of the right hand extended, touch the index finger on the side of the nose and then move the hand to the top of the right side of the head.

SATAN (B) See DEVIL (A)

SATISFACTION

The hands demonstrate controlling inner feelings and refer to reparation in the form of penance for sin.

Formation: Bring the thumb side of both *open hands,* palms facing down and right hand above the left hand, back against the chest.

Related form: SATISFY

SAVE See SALVATION

SAVIOR

This sign is a combination of SALVATION and the person marker and designates Christ's role in rescuing mankind from its sins.

Formation: Bring both *S hands,* wrists crossed in front of the chest and palms facing in, away from each other by twisting the wrists, ending with the palms facing forward in front of each side of the body. Add the person marker.

Related form: SAVIOUR

See also REDEEMER for an initialized sign with a related meaning formed in a similar manner.

SAWN (*Arabic*) See FAST (B)

SCHEOL (*Hebrew*) See HELL (A)

SCORN See MOCK

SCRIBE

The right hand seems to write something on the other hand, plus the person marker. This sign refers to persons trained in writing skills who recorded events of the time.

Formation: Slide the palm of the right *modified A hand*, across the palm of the left *open hand* with a double movement. Add the person marker.

Same sign for JOURNALIST, PLAYWRIGHT, RECORDER, REPORTER, WRITER

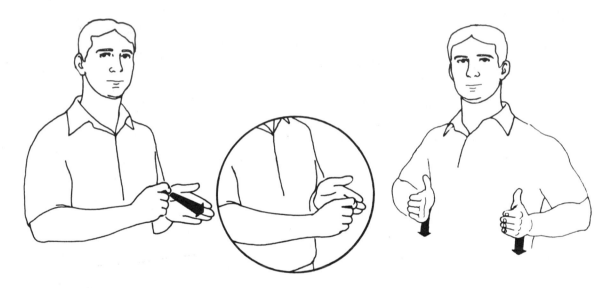

SCRIPTURE, WRITE

The hand in this sign mimes writing and signifies the sacred writings contained in the Holy Scriptures.

Formation: With the right index finger and thumb pinched together, move the fingertips across the palm of the left *open hand*, from the heel to off the fingers.

Related form: WRITINGS

SCROLL See TORAH (A)

SECT

The hands in this sign encompass an identifiable group. The sign is used to refer to a group having established its own identity and teachings separate from the larger group to which it belongs, such as the different sects making up Judaism in the New Testament.

Formation: Beginning with the thumbs of both *C hands* near each other in front of the chest, palms facing each other, bring the hands away from each other in outward arcs while turning the palms in, ending with the little fingers near each other.

Same sign for CATEGORY, CLASS, GROUP

SEDER

This sign is a combination of PASSOVER and FEAST and represents the feast celebrated on the first two days of Passover, which commemorate the exodus of the Israelites from Egypt.

Formation. Tap the thumb side of the right *P hand*, palm facing down, on the elbow of the bent left arm held across the chest. Then, with alternating circular movements, bring the fingertips of each *flattened O hand* to the mouth.

Note: You may use either PASSOVER (A) or (B) for the first position of this sign.

SELECT See APPOINT (A)(B)

SELF-DENIAL See DENY (C)

SELFISH See GREEDY

SEMINARY

This is an initialized sign formed similar to the sign COLLEGE and indicates a theological school of higher education for the training of priests, ministers, or rabbis.

Formation: Beginning with the palm side of the right *S hand* on the palm of the left *open hand,* bring the right hand upward in a circular movement in front of the chest.

See also YESHIVA (A) for another initialized sign formed in a similar manner.

SERAPH See ANGEL

SERAPHIM See ARCHANGEL

SERMON See PREACH, TESTIMONY (A)

SERVANT

This is a combination of SERVE and the person marker and designates someone who expresses submission to God.

Formation: Move both *open hands,* palms facing up, forward and back with an alternating movement in front of the body. Add the person marker.

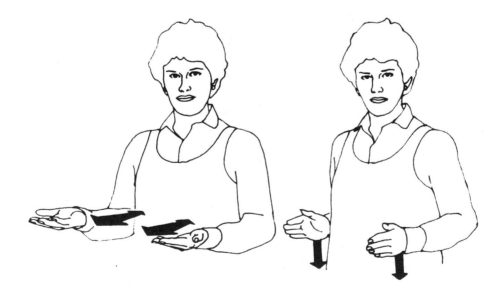

SERVE, MINISTER (*verb*)

The hands in this sign seem to carry a tray while serving, representing performing acts of benefit to others as evidence of love of God.

Formation: Move both *open hands,* palms facing up, forward and back with an alternating movement in front of the body.

Related form: SERVICE

See also MINISTER for an initialized sign with a related meaning formed in a similar manner.

SEVENTH-DAY ADVENTIST (A)

This initialized sign refers to the Adventist Church, which believes that Christ's second coming and the end of the world are near and that the Sabbath should be observed on Saturday.

Formation: Form the fingerspelled letters *S, D,* and *A* with the right hand in front of the right shoulder, palm facing forward and moving slightly to the right with each letter.

SEVENTH-DAY ADVENTIST (B)

This sign is a combination of SEVENTH, DAY, and CHURCH and refers to the members of the Adventist sect that observes its Sabbath on Saturday.

Formation: Form a right *7 hand* in front of the right shoulder, palm facing forward, and then twist the palm sharply to the left so the palm faces the head. Then, beginning with the elbow of the bent right arm, right index finger pointing up, on the back of the left hand held across the body, palm facing down, move the right index finger downward toward the left elbow. Then tap the thumb side of the right *C hand* on the back of the left *S hand,* palm facing down.

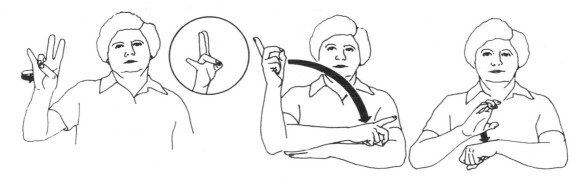

SHABBAT *(Hebrew)* See SABBATH (B)(C)

SHAHADAH *(Arabic)*

This sign is a combination of a sign showing a person witnessing to his faith and the sign ALLAH. This sign is used to refer to the sincere utterance of the first pillar of faith in Islam by declaring, "There is no god but Allah, and Muhammad is His messenger." The ultimate gesture of bearing witness to the faith is to perish as a martyr.

   Formation: Beginning with both extended index fingers pointing toward the face, bring the hands forward while bending the fingers into *X hands.* Then move the extended right index finger, palm facing left and finger pointing up, upward in front of the right shoulder.

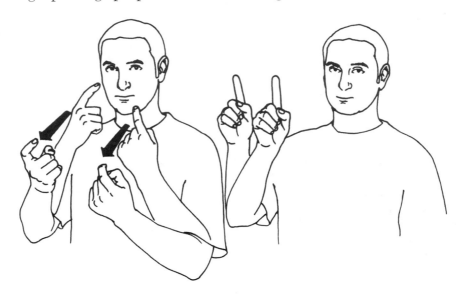

SHALOM *(Hebrew)* See PEACE

SHAVUOT *(Hebrew),* **FEAST OF WEEKS**

This sign is the same as SEVEN WEEKS and refers to the Jewish holiday that commemorates the revelation of the Law on Mount Sinai and the celebration of the wheat festival in ancient times.

   Formation: Move the palm side of the right *7 hand* across the palm of the left *open hand* from the heel to off the fingers.

SHED See BLEED

SHEEP, LAMB

The hands in this sign mime shearing wool from sheep.

Formation: With the left arm extended, repeatedly sweep the back of the right *K hand*, palm facing up, up the inside of the left arm.

Note: The sign SMALL may be added before the sign SHEEP to refer to a LAMB.

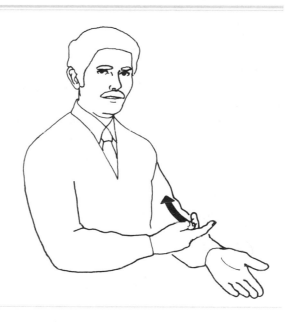

SHEPHERD

This sign is a combination of SHEEP, SUPERVISE, and the person marker and indicates a person who herds, guards, and cares for sheep.

Formation: With the left arm extended, repeatedly sweep the back of the right *K hand*, palm facing up, up the inside of the left arm. Then, with the little-finger side of the right *K hand* on the index-finger side of the left *K hand*, palms facing in opposite directions, move the hands in a outward circle in front of the body. Then add the person marker.

SHIA (*Arabic*) See SHIITE

SHIITE, SHIA *(Arabic)*

This sign refers to one of two major branches of Muslim doctrine that strictly adheres to the belief that Muhammad is the political and religious authority of the faith, which upon his death was passed on to Ali, as the senior male in Muhammad's family, who then served as *Imam,* a religiously inspired leader.

Formation: Place the thumb side of the right *G hand* against the forehead.

SHIVAH *(Hebrew)*, SITTING SHIVAH

This sign is a combination of SIT and MOURN and signifies the seven-day period of formal mourning observed after the death of a close Jewish relative.

Formation: Lay the fingers of the right *H hand* across the fingers of the left *H hand,* both palms facing down. Then, with the index-finger sides of both *S hands* near each other, right palm facing forward and left palm facing back, twist the hands, reversing the orientation of the palms.

SHOFAR

The hands in this sign follow the shape of the trumpet made of a ram's horn that is sounded in the synagogue at Rosh Hashanah and Yom Kippur.

Formation: Beginning with both *C hands* in front of the mouth, left hand closer to the mouth than the right hand and palms facing in opposite directions, move the right hand upward in an arc, ending with the palm facing forward.

SHRINE (A)

This sign is a combination of PLACE and WORSHIP and refers to a temple or any place of worship, including roadside memorial sites.

Formation: With *P hands* near each other in front of the chest, palms facing each other, bring the hands outward in a circle, ending near the body. Then, beginning with the fingers of the right hand over the left *A hand*, both palms facing down, move the hands forward in an arc back from the chest.

See also SANCTUARY for a sign with a similar meaning.

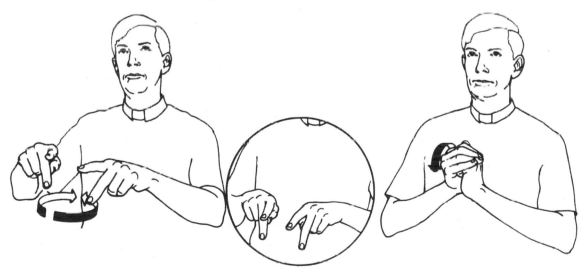

SHRINE (B) See SANCTUARY

SHUL *(Hebrew)* See SYNAGOGUE, TEMPLE

SIGN See SYMBOL

SIMON PETER See PETER

SIN (A), INIQUITY, OFFENSE, TRANSGRESSION, TRESPASS

This sign is a combination of TELL and HURT, symbolizing how the sin of lying hurts others.

Formation: Move both extended index fingers from pointing to each side of the mouth, palms facing in, down in an outward arc to jab at each other in front of the chest.

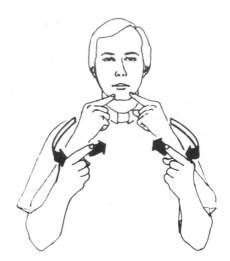

SIN (B), INIQUITY, OFFENSE, TRANSGRESSION, TRESPASS

The fingers in this sign move in opposition to each other, signifying the way that sin violates religious or moral laws.

Formation: Beginning with both extended index fingers pointing toward each other in front of the body, both palms facing in, move the fingers in repeated circular movements toward and away from each other.

SIN (C), INIQUITY, OFFENSE, TRANSGRESSION, TRESPASS

The hands in this sign seem to churn up an inner turmoil caused by a deliberate violation of God's laws.

Formation: Beginning with an *X hand* in front of each side of the body, both palms facing up, move the hands in repeated upward circular movements.

SIN (D), INIQUITY, OFFENSE, TRANSRESSION, TRESPASS

This sign is a combination of WRONG and DO, indicating that sin is doing something that violates moral or religious laws.

Formation: Tap the chin with the middle fingers of the right *Y hand*. Then move both *C hands*, palms facing down, back and forth in front of the waist.

SIN (E), INIQUITY, OFFENSE, TRANSGRESSION, TRESPASS

This sign is a combination of BREAK and LAW and refers to an offense against the laws of God.

Formation: Beginning with the index-finger side of both *S hands* together in front of the chest, both palms facing down, bring the hands apart by twisting the wrists to each side, ending with the palms facing each other. Then hit the right *L hand*, palm facing left, on the palm of the left *open hand*, palm facing right and fingers pointing up.

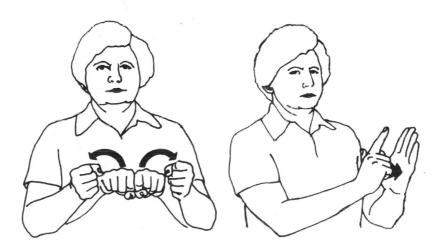

SINLESS (A)

This sign is a combination of SIN and NONE, referring to Jesus, who was without sin even in his human nature.

Formation: Beginning with an *X hand* in front of each side of the body, both palms facing up, move the hands in repeated upward circular movements. Then, beginning with an *O hand* in front of each side of the chest, palms facing down, move the hands forward.

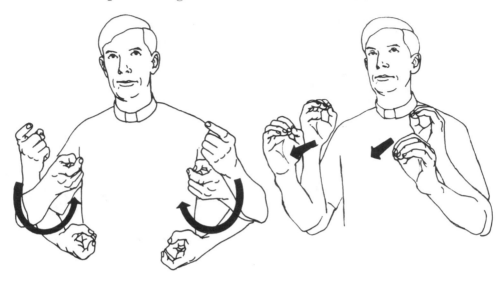

SINLESS (B) See INNOCENT

SINNER (A)

This sign is a combination of SIN (C) and the person marker.

Formation: Beginning with an *X hand* in front of each side of the body, both palms facing up, move the hands in repeated upward circular movements. Add the person marker.

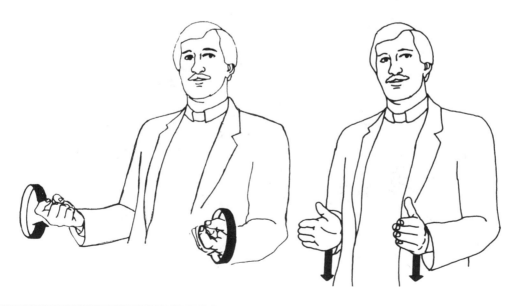

SINNER (B)

This sign is a combination of SIN (B) and the person marker.

   Formation: Beginning with both extended index fingers pointing toward each other in front of the body, both palms facing in, move the fingers in repeated circular movements toward and away from each other. Add the person marker.

SISTER See NUN (A)(B)

SITTING SHIVAH See SHIVAH *(Hebrew)*

SKULLCAP See YARMULKE *(Hebrew)*

SLAVERY, BONDAGE, CAPTIVITY

The wrists in this sign seem to be bound together, signifying the years of captivity of the Jews by the Egyptians.

   Formation: With the heel of the right *S hand* on the back of the left *S hand*, both palms facing down, move the hands in a repeated flat circle in front of the body.

SLAY See KILL

SOCIETY (A)

This is an initialized sign formed similar to CLASS and indicates a group of people sharing a similar culture.

Formation: Beginning with both *S hands* near each other in front of the chest, palms facing each other, move the hands in a circle outward and then together until the little fingers meet, ending with the palms facing in.

SOCIETY (B) See CONGREGATION

SOCIETY OF FRIENDS See QUAKERS (A)(B)

SOILED See IMPURE

SOLE See ONLY

SOLEMN, PEACEFUL, SILENCE

The hands move down in a natural gesture of quieting a group, as during a religious ceremony.

Formation: Beginning with both *B hands* crossed in front of the mouth, bring the hands smoothly apart and down to each side of the body, ending with both palms facing down.

SON

This sign is a combination of BOY and a modification of the sign BABY and is used to refer to Jesus as the Son of God and the second person of the Trinity.

Formation: Bring the right *B hand* down from the right side of the forehead to rest in the crook of the left bent arm held across the body.

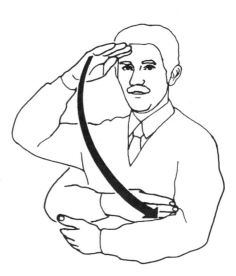

SONG See HYMN

SOOTHE See COMFORT

SORROWFUL, DEJECTED, SAD

The hands and posture in this sign demonstrate a dejected and downcast posture.

Formation: Bring both 5 *hands* from in front of the forehead down in front of the face, both palms facing in and fingers pointing up.

Note: The head and shoulders should be slightly bowed.

Same sign for FORLORN, DOWNCAST, DESPONDENT

See also SORROW for the noun form of this sign.

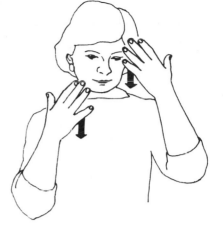

SORRY See ATONEMENT

SOUL (A), SPIRIT

The fingers reach deep inside, the traditional location of the immortal spiritual nature of man.

Formation: Beginning with the fingers of the right *F hand* in the hole formed by the left *O hand*, bring the right hand straight up in front of the chest.

Related form: SPIRITUAL

See also SPIRIT for an alternate sign.

SOUL (B)

The hand brings GOD into the body.

Formation: Bring the right *bent hand* from the front of the right shoulder, palm facing forward, and flip the hand in toward the chest, ending with fingers pointing in.

SOUL (C)

This is a Muslim sign.

Formation: Beginning with the right *curved 5 hand* near the right cheek, move the hand upward to the right while closing into an *S hand* above the right side of the head.

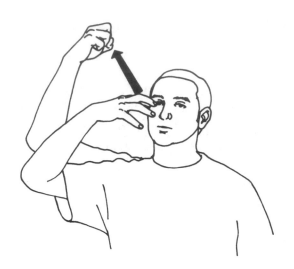

SOUL (D) See SPIRIT

SPEAKING IN TONGUES See TONGUE (B)

SPIRIT (A), SOUL

The fingers of this sign seem to hold something thin and filmy, symbolic of a supernatural being such as the Holy Spirit.

Formation: Beginning with the fingertips of both *F hands* touching in front of the body, right hand above the left hand, pull the hands apart.

    Related form: SPIRITUAL

    Same sign for GHOST

    See also HOLY GHOST for a sign with a related meaning.

SPIRIT (B) See SOUL

SPIRITUAL LIFE

This sign is a combination of SPIRIT and LIFE and pertains to living a life of a moral and religious nature.

Formation: Beginning with the fingertips of both *F hands* touching in front of the body, right hand above the left hand, pull the hands apart. Then bring both *L hands*, palms facing in and index fingers pointing toward each other, upward from the waist to the chest.

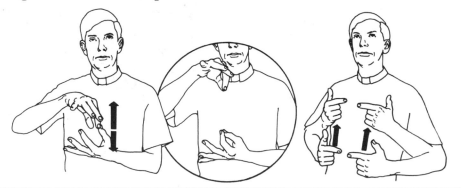

STAINED See IMPURE

STAR

The fingers in this sign mime the twinkling rays from stars, such the rays that led the Wise Men to Christ's birthplace in Bethlehem.

Formation: Brush the sides of both extended index fingers, palms facing forward, up and down with a double alternating movement.

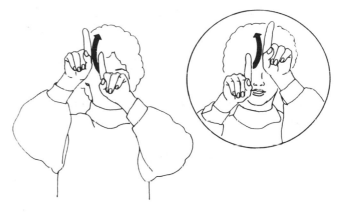

STATIONS OF THE CROSS

This sign is a combination of FOURTEEN and several crosses. The sign refers to meditating before fourteen crosses set up to commemorate the fourteen events in the Passion of Jesus.

Formation: Wiggle the fingers of the right *B hand,* palm facing in and fingers pointing up. Then, with the right extended index finger pointing up, palm facing left, hold the left extended index finger across it, palm facing down and index finger pointing right. Repeat to the right.

See also WAY OF THE CROSS for a sign with a related meaning.

STATUE, IMAGE

The hands in this sign follow the form of an imaginary statue, such as those that represent religious figures.

Formation: Beginning with an *A hand* in front of each side of the head, palms facing forward, bring the hands downward in a wavy movement to in front of the body, ending with the palms facing down.

Same sign for FIGURE, SCULPTURE

See also IDOL for a sign with a related meaning formed in a similar manner.

STEAL

Formation: Beginning with the index-finger side of the right *V hand,* palm facing down, on the elbow of the bent left arm, held at an upward angle across the chest, pull the right hand toward the left wrist with a double movement while bending the fingers in tightly each time.

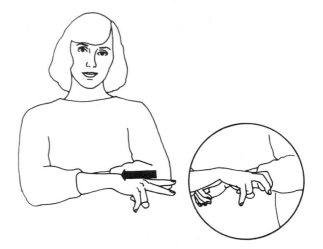

STEEPLE

This sign shows the shape of a church's steeple pointing to the heavens.

Formation: Beginning with both *open hands* near each other in front of the chest, palms facing each other and fingers pointing up, move the hands upward at an angle until the fingers meet above the head.

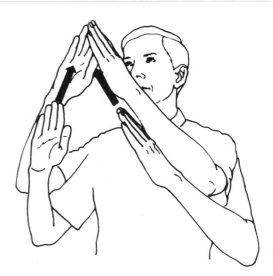

STEWARD

This sign is a combination of KEEP and the person marker and refers to a person who manages God's gifts and uses them for God's glory.

Formation: With a repeated movement tap the little-finger side of the right *K hand* on the index-finger side of the left *K hand*, palms facing in opposite directions. Add the person marker.

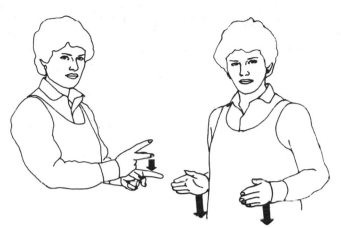

STORY See PARABLE (A)

STRAY (A), APOSTASY

The hands in this sign mime being diverted from the "straight and narrow" as occurs when one abandons one's religious faith

Formation: Beginning with both extended index fingers side by side in front of the body, palms facing down and fingers pointing forward, move the right finger forward and off to the right at an angle.

See also BACKSLIDE for an alternate sign.

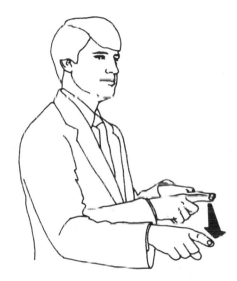

STRAY (B) See BACKSLIDE

STRONG See POWER (A)(B)

SUBDUE See CONQUER

SUBMIT See RENOUNCE

SUFFER (A), BEAR, ENDURE

This sign is formed similar to ENDURE but with a twist of the hand indicating sustained toleration of emotional or physical pain.

Formation: Twist the thumbnail of the right *A hand,* palm left, on the lips, ending with the palm facing back.

Related form: SUFFERING
Same sign for TOLERATE
See also MOURN and ATONEMENT for signs with related meanings.

SUFFER (B), AGONY, LAMENT, PASSION

The hands in this sign mime deep inner turmoil, as in the Passion of Christ prior to His Crucifixion.

Formation: Bring the right *A hand,* palm facing left, from in front of the mouth down in an arc in front of and in a complete circle around the left *A hand* held in front of the body, palm facing right.

Note: Keep the hands close to the body. The first position at the mouth may be omitted.

Related form: SUFFERING

SUFFER (C) See AFFLICTION

SUKKOTH *(Hebrew),* FEAST OF TABERNACLES

The hands of this initialized sign follow the shape of a hut and symbolize the eight-day festival commemorating the dwelling in huts by the Jews during the exodus through the desert.

Formation: Beginning with the thumb sides of both *S hands* together in front of the forehead, palms facing forward, bring the hands straight outward to each side and then straight downward to each side of the body.

See also CHUPPAH for another sign formed in a similar manner.

SUNDAY See SABBATH (D)

SUNDAY SCHOOL (A)

This is an initialized sign that refers to religious instruction for children on Sunday.

Formation: Form the fingerspelled letters *S* and *S* with the right hand in front of the right shoulder, palm facing forward and moving slightly to the right with each letter.

SUNDAY SCHOOL (B)

This sign is a combination of SUNDAY and SCHOOL.

Formation: Move both *open hands,* palms facing forward and fingers pointing up in front of each shoulder, upward and outward in small arcs toward each other. Then, with a double movement, clap the right *open hand,* palm facing down and fingers angled left, on the palm of the left *open hand,* palm facing up and fingers angled right.

SUNNI

This sign refers to the majority branch of the Muslim faith that believe that Muhammad died without designating his successor. Thus, historically, elders of the faith elect a caliph as the political leader of the community, who serves to protect and defend Islam as guided by Allah's law.

Formation: Hold both *open hands,* palms facing each other and fingers pointing forward, apart in front of the body, left hand forward of the right hand.

SUPERIOR See EXALT (B)

SUPPLICATION See BEG, PRAY

SUPPORT See ADVOCATE

SUPREME See EXALT (B), RECTOR

SURRENDER See RENOUNCE

SWEAR See BLASPHEMY (A)(B)

SYMBOL, SIGN

This initialized sign is formed similar to SHOW and directs attention to something in the hand.

Formation: With the thumb side of the right *S hand,* palm facing down, against the palm of the left *open hand,* palm facing right and fingers pointing up, move both hands forward a short distance.

See also REVEAL and WITNESS (B) for signs formed in a similar manner.

SYMPATHY See MERCY (A)

SYNAGOGUE, MISHKAN *(Hebrew),* SHUL *(Hebrew)*

This is an initialized sign formed similar to CATHEDRAL used to designate a place for Jewish worship and religious instruction.

Formation: Beginning with the heel of the right *S hand* on the back of the left *S hand,* both palms facing down, move the right hand upward in a small arc.

See also CATHEDRAL, CHURCH, LUTHERAN (B), PARISH, PETER, and TEMPLE for other initialized signs formed in a similar manner.

SYNOD See CONGREGATION

TABERNACLE, DWELLING, HOUSE, MISHKAN *(Hebrew)*

This is the sign for HOUSE and is used to specify both a Jewish temple and the portable shrine that the Hebrews carried with them during the Exodus.

Formation: Beginning with the fingertips of both *B hands* touching at an angle in front of the chest, palms angled toward each other, bring the hands apart from each other at an angle and then straight down in front of each side of the body.

TAKE AWAY, REMOVE

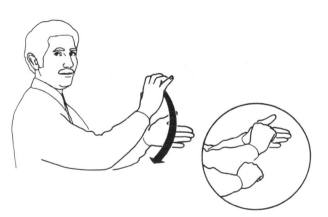

The hands in this sign seem to sweep something away from the other hand and symbolize Christ's redemption which removed mankind's sins.

Formation: Sweep the right *curved hand* down across the palm of the left *open hand,* while changing to an *S hand* as it passes the left palm.

Same sign for SUBTRACT

TAKE AWAY SIN

This sign is a combination of REMOVE and SIN and refers to Jesus's act of atonement in dying on the cross to remove mankind's sins from God's perspective.

Formation: Beginning with the palm side of the right *A hand* on the palm of the left *open hand,* move the right hand deliberately to the right while opening to a *5 hand,* palm facing down and fingers pointing forward. Then, beginning with an *X hand* in front of each side of the body, both palms facing up, move the hands in repeated upward circular movements.

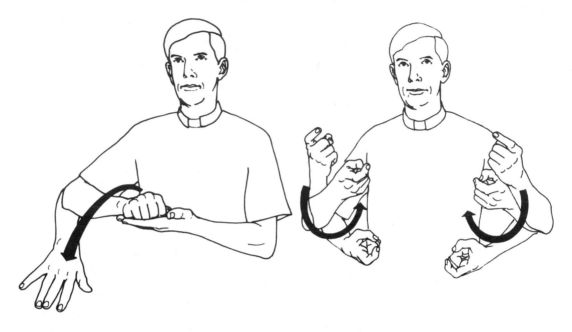

TALLITH *(Hebrew)*

The hands in this sign follow the shape of the fringed prayer shawl that has bands of blue or black and that is worn by Jewish men at prayer.

Formation: Beginning with the thumb and index fingers of a *modified C hand* touching each side of the chest, move the hands downward on the body simultaneously.

Related form: TALLIS

See also BROTHER and RABBI for signs formed in a similar manner.

TANACH *(Hebrew)* See BIBLE (C)(D)

TAWHID *(Arabic)* See MONOTHEISM (B)

TEACH, EDIFY, INSTRUCT

The hands in this sign seem to direct information to another person.

Formation: Move both *flattened O hands*, palms facing forward in front of the sides of the chest, forward with a short double movement.

Related forms: TEACHINGS, EDIFICATION, INSTRUCTION

Note: INSTRUCT may be initialized.

TEFILLIN See MITZVAH

TEMPLE, SHUL *(Hebrew)*

This is an initialized sign formed similar to CHURCH and signifies both ancient and modern buildings set apart for the presence of a deity and for ritual activities.

Formation: Tap the heel of the right *T hand* on the back of the left *S hand*, both palms facing down.

See also CATHEDRAL, CHURCH, LUTHERAN (B), PARISH, PETER, and SYNAGOGUE for other initialized signs formed in a similar manner.

TEMPT

The finger in this sign taps on the elbow of a person in order to divert attention, as when a person is enticed to do an immoral act, often with the promise of earthly rewards.

Formation: With a double movement, tap the elbow of the bent left arm with the index finger of the right *X hand*.

Related form: TEMPTATION

TEN COMMANDMENTS See DECALOGUE

TENEBRAE

This sign is a combination of DARK and WORSHIP and refers to any of various worship services during Holy Week, in which all candles are gradually extinguished, to commemorate the darkness at the Crucifixion.

Formation: Beginning with an *open hand* in front of each side of the head, palms facing back and fingers pointing up, move the hands toward the opposite shoulder in front of the face, ending with the wrists crossed. Then, beginning with the fingers of the right hand over the left *A hand,* both palms facing down, move the hands forward in an arc away from the chest.

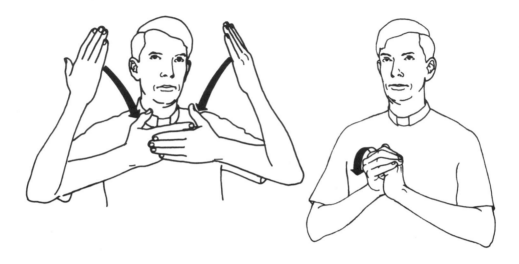

TERRESTRIAL See EARTH

TESTAMENT

This initialized sign is formed similar to LAW and is used to denote the two main divisions of the Bible. Translated from the Greek, *testament* means "a binding covenant between God and man."

Formation: Move the index-finger side of the right *T hand* down the palm of the left *open hand,* touching first the fingertips and the heel of the left hand.

See also COMMANDMENTS, HALACHA (B), LAW (B), and MOSES (A) for other initialized signs formed in a similar manner.

TESTIMONY (A), SERMON, WITNESS

The hand in this sign follows the gesture often used when speaking from a lectern, as when giving a public affirmation of one's faith.

Formation: Shake the right *open hand,* palm facing left and fingers pointing up, forward and back with a repeated short movement.

Related form: TESTIFY

Same sign for LECTURE, PRESENT

See also BEHOLD for the verb forms of WITNESS and PREACH and for an alternate sign for SERMON.

TESTIMONY (B)

This is an initialized sign and refers to a declaration regarding a religious experience.

Formation: Shake the right *T hand,* palm facing left and fingers pointing up, forward and back with a repeated short movement.

Related form: TESTIFY

See also PREACH for a sign formed in a similar manner.

THANKFUL, GRATEFUL

The hands in this sign bring words of gratitude from the mouth upward toward God.

Formation: Beginning with the right *open hand* near the mouth and the left *open hand* slightly forward, both palms facing in, move the hands forward and upward a short distance.

Related forms: THANKS, GRATITUDE

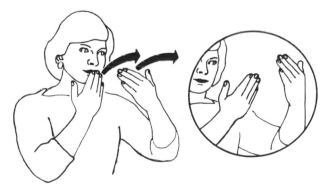

THANKSGIVING

This sign is a combination of THANKFUL and
GIVE and refers to an expression of gratitude to
God and to the national holiday celebrated in
some countries.

Formation: Beginning with the left *open hand*
near the mouth and the right *open hand* slightly
forward, both palms facing in, move the hands
forward and upward a short distance. Then, beginning with both *flattened O hands*, palms facing up, in front of the body, move the hands
forward in an arc while opening into 5 *hands*.

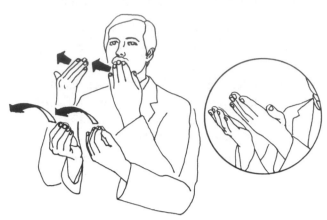

THEE

This directional sign is a natural gesture for the
second-personal pronoun when it is used to
refer to God.

Formation: Move the right *open hand* from
above the right shoulder a short distance upward, palm angled left and fingers pointing up.

Related form: THOU

See also THINE for the possessive pronoun
referring to God.

THEOLOGY (A)

This initialized sign is formed similar to RELI-
GION and refers to the study of God, His
attributes, and opinions concerning man's relationship with God.

Formation: Touch the palm side of the right *T
hand* to the left side of the chest. Then move the
right hand smoothly forward while twisting the
wrist, ending with the palm facing forward.

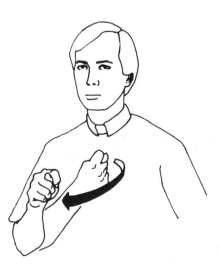

THEOLOGY (B)

This initialized sign is formed similar to RELIGION and refers to the study of the nature of God and religious truth.

Formation: Touch the palm side of the right *L hand* to the left side of the chest. Then move the right hand smoothly forward while changing into a *T hand*, palm facing down.

See also RELIGION for another initialized sign with a related meaning formed in a similar manner.

THINE

This is a directional sign with the open palm moving toward God, which is the sign formation used for possessive pronouns in American Sign Language.

Formation: Move the right *open hand* upward a short distance from near the right shoulder.

Related form: THY

See also THEE for the second-person pronoun referring to God.

TITHE

This sign is a combination of ONE and TEN formed as a fraction and refers to the payment of one-tenth of one's income to God for the support of a church.

Formation: Beginning with the right extended index finger pointing up in front of the chest, palm facing forward, move the hand downward a short distance while changing to a *10 hand*, palm facing left and thumb extended up.

TOMB

This sign is a combination of BURY and a gesture that appears to be a rolling stone door and refers to the garden tomb of Joseph of Arimathea where Jesus's body was laid to rest.

Formation: Insert the extended fingers of the right *H hand,* palms facing up and fingers pointing left, into the palm side of the left *C hand,* palm facing right. Then move the fingers of the right *H hand,* palm facing up, into the palm-side opening of the left *C hand,* palm facing right. Then move the palm of the right *open hand* against the index-finger side of the left *C hand,* palm facing right.

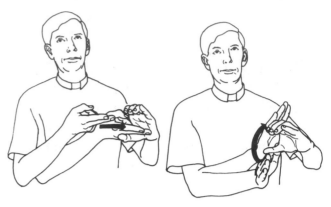

TONGUE (A), LANGUAGE

This is an initialized sign for TONGUE formed similar to SENTENCE and refers to a medium for the transmission of communication.

Formation: Beginning with the thumbs of both *L hands* touching in front of the waist, palms facing down, bring the hands apart in an arc to each side.

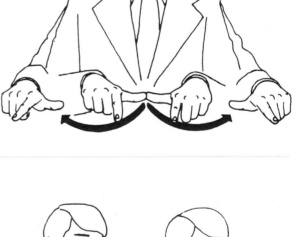

TONGUE (B), SPEAKING IN TONGUES

This sign is a combination of TELL and SPEAK and refers to the gift of the Holy Spirit to declare the Gospel to all people.

Formation: Touch the extended right index finger to the lips, palm facing in. Then beginning with both *4 hands* in front of the mouth, right hand closer to the mouth than the left and palms facing each other, move both hands forward repeatedly with short movements while wiggling the fingers.

See also CHARISMATIC (A)(B) and PENTECOST for signs with related meanings.

TORAH (A), SCROLL

The hands unroll an imaginary scroll referring to the parchment scroll on which the Pentateuch is written and used during services in a synagogue.

Formation: Move both *S hands* from near each other in front of the waist, palms facing each other, away from each other by twisting the wrists up and down.

TORAH (B)

The hands in this initialized sign seem to unroll a scroll.

Formation: Move both *T hands* from near each other in front of the body, palms facing down, away from each other by twisting the wrists up and down.

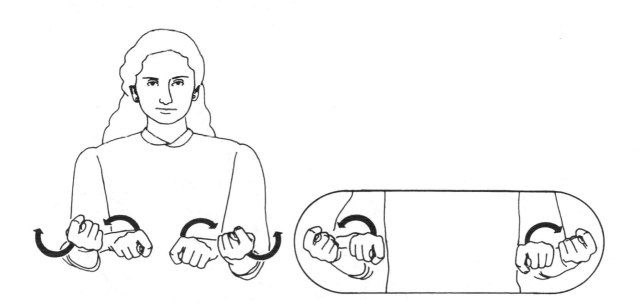

TRADITION

This initialized sign is formed similar to AN-CESTOR with the hands moving from a location used to show time in the past in American Sign Language to the present, symbolizing the handing down of unwritten religious precepts from generation to generation.

Formation: Move the right and left *T hands* over each other from in front of the right shoulder downward to in front of the waist, palms facing the body.

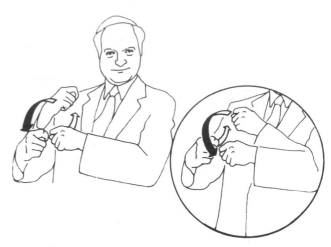

TRAINING See DISCIPLINE (A)

TRANSFIGURATION

This sign is a combination of BODY, CHANGE, and SHINE and refers to the event when Jesus was visibly glorified in the presence of three disciples.

Formation: Touch the upper chest and then the lower chest with the palms of both *open hands.* Then. with the palm side of the right *modified A hand* on top of the palm side of the left *modified A hand,* twist the hands in opposite directions, ending with the hands in reverse positions. Then, beginning with both *5 hands* touching each side of the chest, middle fingers bent down, move the hands upward in a wiggly movement.

TRANSGRESSION See SIN (A)(B)(C)(D)(E)

TRANSLATE

Formation: With the palms of both *T hands* together at angles in front of the chest, twist the wrists in opposite directions.

Related form: TRANSLATION

See also CONVERT, INTERPRET, and REPENT for other signs formed in a similar manner.

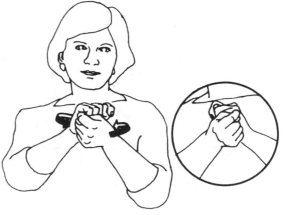

TRESPASS See SIN (A)(B)(C)(D)(E)

TRIBULATION

This is an initialized sign formed similar to
TROUBLE and refers to great distress or suffering.

Formation: With an alternating movement,
bring both *T hands,* palms facing each other,
from the forehead downward across the face
several times.

See also TROUBLE for a sign with a related
meaning formed in a similar manner.

TRIBUNAL See JUDGMENT (A)

TRINITY

This sign is a combination of THREE and ONE.
The movement shows the *three* being changed
or integrated into *one* and symbolizes the union
of three divine beings—Father, Son, and Holy
Spirit—in one godhead.

Formation: With the back of the right *3 hand*
resting in the palm of the left *open hand,* palms
facing toward the chest, pull the right hand
down behind the left hand while changing into a
1 hand, which then moves in a big arc in front of
the left hand, right index finger pointing up and
palm facing in

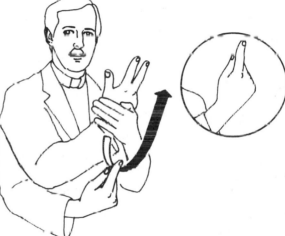

TRIUMPH (A), ATTAIN, FINALLY

This sign is a natural gesture for expressing
success.

Formation: Beginning with both index fingers
pointing toward each other near each side of the
head, both palms facing back, twist the wrists
forward, ending with the index fingers pointing
upward and palms facing forward.

Related form: TRIUMPHANT

Same sign for AT LAST, SUCCEED, SUC-
CESS, SUCCESSFUL

See also VICTORY and CELEBRATE for
signs with a related meaning.

TRIUMPH (B) See CELEBRATE

TROUBLE, CARE, WORRY

The hands in this sign represent things coming from all sides causing worry.

Formation: With an alternating movement bring both *B hands* down from in front of the forehead across the face several times, palms angled toward each other.

Same sign for CONCERN

See also TRIBULATION for an initialized sign with a related meaning formed in a similar manner.

TRULY See TRUTH (B), VERILY

TRUST (A), CONFIDENCE

The hands in this sign seem to grab hold of something and indicate confidence or reliance on something unseen.

Formation: Beginning with both *C hands* in front of the body, right hand a few inches above the left hand and palms facing each other, bring the hands together and toward the body while changing into *S hands* as they move.

See also FAITH (A) for an alternate sign.

TRUST (B) See FAITH (A)

TRUTH (A), HONEST

This is an initialized sign that indicates presenting something in a straightforward and honest way.

Formation: Move the fingertips of the right *H hand* across the palm of the left *open hand,* from the heel forward toward the fingertips.

Related form: HONESTY

TRUTH (B), TRULY

This sign is a combination of TRUE and HON-EST and indicates that something said is factual.

Formation: Move the right extended index finger forward from the mouth a short distance, palm facing left. Then move the fingertips of the right *H hand* across the palm of the left *open hand,* from the heel forward toward the fingertips.

See also VERILY for a sign with a similar meaning.

TZEDAKAH (*Hebrew*)

This sign is a combination of MONEY and a gesture that seems to put money into a container and refers to the traditional acts of charity performed by observant Jews.

Formation: Tap the back of the right *open hand* on the palm of the left *open hand,* both palms facing up. Then insert the thumb and index finger of the right *F hand* into the thumb-side opening of the left *O hand* with a repeated movement.

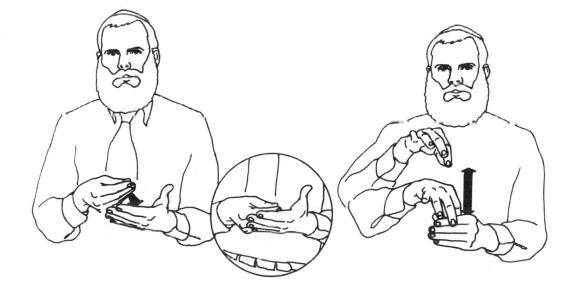

TZITZIT (*Hebrew*) See ZIZITH (*Hebrew*)

UNBELIEF, DISBELIEF, DOUBT

This sign is a combination of NOT and BELIEVE and refers the refusal to believe in God or a religious principle.

Formation: Bring the thumb of the right *10 hand* forward from under the chin. Then move the extended right index finger smoothly down from the right temple, palm facing in, to clasp the left hand held in front of the body, palms facing each other.

See also BELIEVE for a sign with an opposite meaning.

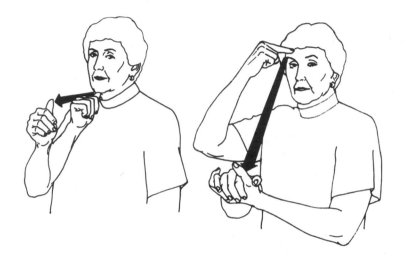

UNBELIEVER

This sign is a combination of NOT and BELIEVE and the person marker, referring to a person who does not believe in God or a religious principle.

Formation: Bring the thumb of the right *10 hand* forward from under the chin. Then move the extended right index finger smoothly down from the right temple, palm facing in, to clasp the left hand held in front of the body, palms facing each other. Add the person marker.

See also BELIEVER for a sign with an opposite meaning.

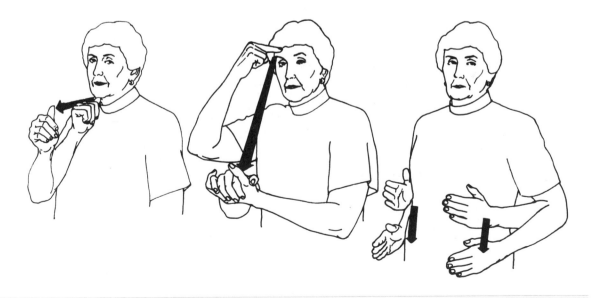

UNITE, AFFILIATE, BELONG, JOIN

The hands in this sign come together and intertwine as a symbol of coming together for a common purpose or interest.

Formation: Beginning with both *C hands*
apart in front of the chest, palms facing each
other, bring the hands together while changing
into *F hands* and intersecting the thumbs and
index fingers of both hands together.

UNITY, CATHOLIC, COMMUNION OF SAINTS, UNIVERSAL

This sign is a modification of UNITE and represents the common religious faith that unites
Christians.

Formation: With the thumbs and index fingers of each hand intersecting with each other,
move the hands in a flat circle in front of the
body.

See also COMMUNION OF SAINTS (A)
for an alternate sign.

UNIVERSAL See UNITY

UNIVERSE

This is an initialized sign formed similar to the
sign WORLD and signifies the sphere of all created things.

Formation: Bring the right *U hand* upward in
a circle over and around the left *U hand,* palms
facing each other.

Related form: UNIVERSAL

See also WORLD for another initialized sign
with a related meaning formed in a similar
manner.

UNLEAVENED BREAD

This sign is a combination of BREAD and FLAT.

Formation: Move the fingertips of the right *bent hand* down over the back of the left *bent hand* several times, both palms facing in. Then, beginning with the thumb of the right *bent hand* on the back of the fingers of the left *open hand,* both palms facing down, close the right fingers to the thumb, forming a *flattened O hand.*

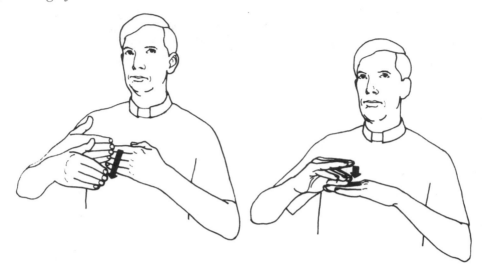

UNTRUTH See LIE (A)(B)

UPRIGHTNESS

This sign is a combination of GOOD and INSIDE and is used to describe a person who adheres to religious, honest, or just principles.

Formation: Beginning with the fingers of the right *open hand* touching the mouth, palm facing in and fingers pointing up, move the hand down, landing the back of the right hand in the palm of the left *open hand* held in front of the body. Then insert the fingertips of the right *flattened O hand* inside the opening of left *C hand* held in front of the chest, both palms facing in.

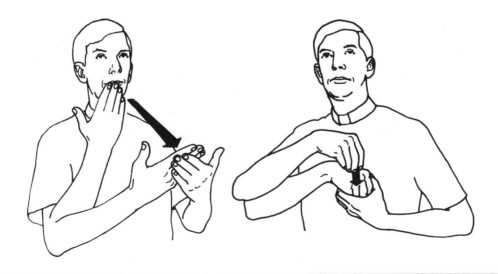

VEIL

This is an initialized sign formed similar to the sign NUN with the hands following the shape of a veil worn by women.

Formation: Move both *V hands*, palms facing back, from touching the top of each side of the head down to touch each shoulder.

See also NUN for another initialized sign formed in a similar manner.

VERILY, INDEED, TRULY

This sign indicates speaking straightforward with factual accuracy.

Formation: Move the side of the extended right index finger, palm facing left, from the lips straight forward.

Same sign for ACTUALLY, CERTAINLY, REALLY, SURELY

See also TRUTH for a sign with a related meaning.

VERSE

The fingers of this sign seem to measure out a short passage of text such as one of the numbered subdivisions of a chapter of the Bible.

Formation: Move the right *G hand*, palm facing down, across the palm of the left *open hand* from the base to the fingertips, palm facing up.

VESPERS, EVENING PRAYER

This sign is a combination of NIGHT and PRAY and refers to worship or prayers held in the late afternoon or evening.

Formation: Tap the wrist of the right *bent hand,* palm facing down, on top of the wrist of the left *open hand* held across the body. Then, with the palms of both *open hands* together, move the hands in toward the chest and downward a short distance.

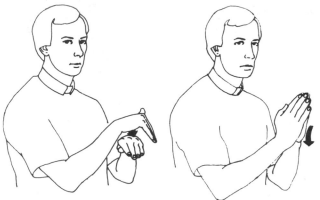

VESTMENTS

The hands of this sign indicate the location of the ritual robes worn by the clergy during church services.

Formation: Beginning with the thumbs of both *5 hands* at each side of the chest, fingers pointing toward each other, move the thumbs downward with a repeated sweeping movement.

See also ROBE for a sign with a related meaning.

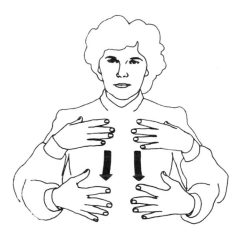

VESTRY See SANCTUARY

VICAR

This sign is formed similar to HELP and is used to refer to a seminarian in the Lutheran Church who is assigned to a parish prior to graduation.

Formation: Move the index-finger side of the right *V hand,* palm facing right, upward against the little-finger side of the left *S hand* with a double movement.

See also ADVOCATE and HELP for signs formed in a similar manner.

VICARIOUS See ATONE (A)(B)

VICTORY (A)

This initialized sign is a combination of PRAISE and CELEBRATE and symbolizes the final defeat of an enemy, such as Satan.

Formation: Pat the palms of both hands together, fingers pointing up. Then make small circles near each shoulder with a *V hand*, palms facing each other and fingers pointing up.

VICTORY (B) See CELEBRATE

VIRGIN MARY See MARY (A)(B)

VISION

This sign is a combination of a modification of FAITH and a gesture showing the expansion of something envisioned and indicates the appearance of a mental image of a supernatural being.

Formation: Move the extended right index finger from touching the right side of the forehead down smoothly while changing into an *S hand*, ending with the little-finger side of the right *S hand* on the thumb side of the left *S hand* held in front of the body, palms facing in opposite directions. Then move the hands apart to in front of each shoulder while opening into *curved hands*.

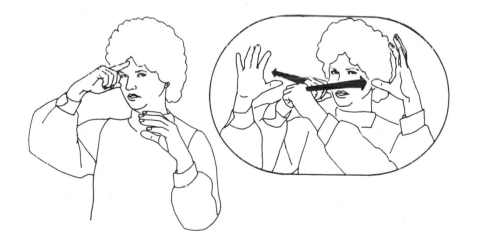

VOCATION (A)

This initialized sign is formed similar to WORK and refers to the urge or predisposition to work in a religious field.

Formation: Tap the base of the right *V hand,* palm facing forward, on the back of the left *S hand,* palm facing down, with a double movement.

See also CALL (A) for an alternate sign.

VOCATION (B), WORK

This is the sign for WORK and refers to a calling to undertake a religious career.

Formation: Tap the base of the right *S hand* on the back of the left *S hand,* both palms facing down, with a double movement.

Same sign for EMPLOYMENT

See also CALL (A) for an alternate sign.

VOCATION (C) See CALL (A)

VOW (A), PROMISE

This sign is a combination of TRUE and a natural gesture indicating a promise to tell the truth. This sign is used to refer to a solemn promise to live and act in accordance with the prescriptions of a religious body.

Formation: Bring the extended right index finger, palm facing left, forward from the lips, while changing to an *open hand,* palm facing forward, with the right bent elbow resting on the back of the left *open hand,* palm facing down.

Same sign for LOYAL, OATH, PLEDGE, SWEAR

VOW (B), PROMISE

This sign is an initialized form of VOW (A) and indicates a solemn promise.

Formation: Bring the extended right index finger, palm facing left, forward from the lips, while changing to a V *hand,* palm facing forward, ending with the base of the right V *hand* resting on the index finger side of the left *open hand,* palm facing down.

WANT See DESIRE (A)

WARN See ADMONISH

WASH See CLEANSE

WATCH See BEHOLD (A)

WAY See AISLE

WAY OF THE CROSS

This sign is a combination of WAY and CROSS and refers to the route Christ followed from his trial to his Crucifixion.

Formation: Move both *open hands,* palms facing each other and fingers pointing forward, forward in a parallel movement in front of the waist. Then move the right C *hand,* palm facing forward, first down from above the right side of the head and then from left to right in front of the right shoulder.

See STATIONS OF THE CROSS for a sign with a related meaning.

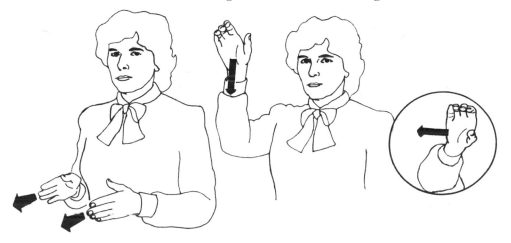

WEDDING

This sign shows bringing the hands together, symbolizing the union of two lives during a wedding ceremony.

Formation: With the *5 hands* hanging down from bent wrists, swing the hands toward each other and grasp the fingers of the left hand with the right fingers.

See also MARRIAGE for a sign with a related meaning.

WELL See GOOD

WHITSUNDAY See PENTECOST (A)

WHOLE See MIGHTY (A)

WICKED (A)

This is the sign for DEVIL repeated and refers to something very evil.

Formation: With the thumbs of both *3 hands* touching the temples, palms facing forward, crook the extended index and middle fingers with a repeated movement.

See also BAD and DEVIL for signs with related meanings.

WICKED (B) See BAD

WILDERNESS, DESERT

This sign is a combination of DRY and LAND and refers to the barren regions of the Holy Land.

Formation: Bring the index finger of the right *X hand,* palm facing down, across the chin from left to right. Then rub the thumbs of both *flattened O hands* across the fingertips, palms facing up. Then flip the *flattened O hands* over and open them into 5 *hands,* palms facing down and fingers pointing forward, while pushing them forward and outward.

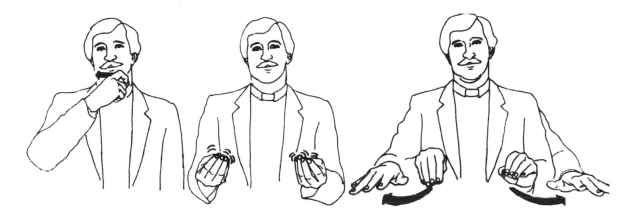

WILL (A), GOD'S WILL

This is an initialized sign formed like LAW and refers to God's commandments for mankind.

Formation: Hit the index-finger side of the right *W hand* against the palm of the left *open hand,* palms facing each other.

See also DESIRE (A) for an alternate sign.

WILL (B) See DESIRE (A)

WINE

This is an initialized sign.

Formation: Move the right *W hand* in small circles near the right cheek.

WISDOM, WISE

The movement of this sign shows deep thinking.

Formation: Move the index finger of the right *X hand* down with a repeated movement in front of the forehead.

WISE See WISDOM

WISH See DESIRE (B)

WITNESS (A)

This is an initialized sign that signifies seeing something and presenting it for view as evidence.

Formation: Bring the right *W hand* from touching near the right eye down to touch the palm of the left *open hand*, palm facing right.

See also PROOF for a sign with a related meaning formed in a similar manner.

WITNESS (B)

This is an initialized sign formed similar to SHOW and indicates the idea of presenting evidence.

Formation: With the index finger of the right *W hand* touching the palm of the left *open hand*, move both hands forward with a short repeated movement.

See also REVEAL and SYMBOL for signs formed in a similar manner.

WITNESS (C) See BEHOLD (A)(B), TESTI-MONY (A)

WONDER (A), MARVEL

This sign is a natural gesture for exclaiming delight.

Formation: Repeatedly push both *5 hands* forward with a short movement, palms facing forward and fingers pointing up in front of each shoulder.

Related form: WONDERFUL

Same sign for FANTASTIC, GRAND, GREAT, MARVELOUS, TERRIFIC

See also PONDER for the verb form of this sign and MIRACLE for an alternate sign for MARVEL.

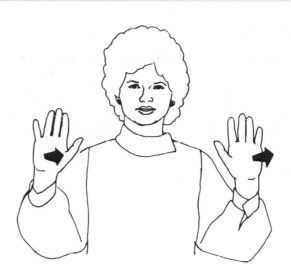

WONDER (B) See PONDER

WORD, LOGOS *(Greek)*

The fingers in this sign demonstrate a small portion of a sentence. This sign is used to refer to the Word of God as presented in the Scriptures.

Formation: Touch the fingertips of the right *G hand* to the extended left index finger pointing up in front of the chest, palms facing each other.

WORK See VOCATION (B)

WORKS, DEEDS, DO

This is the sign for DO and signifies moral or righteous actions.

Formation: Swing both *C hands*, palms facing down, back and forth in opposite directions to and from each other in front of the waist.

Same sign for ACT, ACTION

See also MITZVAH for an initialized sign formed in a similar manner.

WORLD

This is an initialized sign that traces the shape of the globe.

Formation: Beginning with the right *W hand* above the left *W hand,* bring the right hand in a complete circle around the left hand, ending with the little-finger side of the right hand on the thumb side of the left hand.

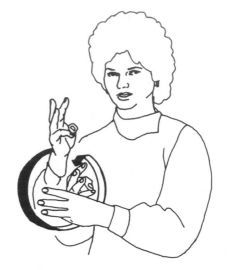

WORLDLY

This sign is a combination of WORLD and SIN and is used to describe a person who is connected to the sensual aspects of life as contrasted to heaven and a spiritual life.

Formation: Bring the right *W hand* in a circle over and around the left *W hand,* palms facing each other and fingers pointing in opposite directions. Then, beginning with an *X hand* in front of each side of the body, both palms facing up, move the hands in repeated upward circular movements.

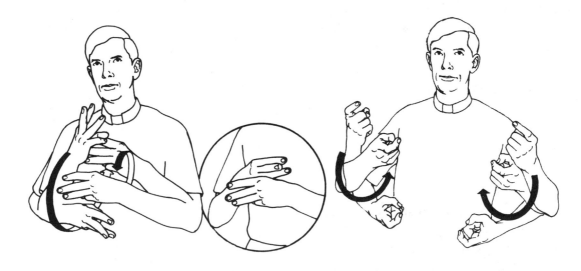

WORRY See TROUBLE

WORSHIP, ADORE, DEVOUT, PIOUS

The hands in this sign mime a worshipful pose and show reverence for a deity.

Formation: Beginning with the fingers of the right hand over the left *A hand,* both palms facing down, move the hands in an arc back toward the chest.

Related form: ADORATION

See also PRAY for an alternate sign.

WORTHY (A), DESERVE

The hands in this sign seem to bring something of value or worth to the top of the pile for examination or recognition.

Formation: Beginning with both *F hands* in front of the body, palms facing up, bring the hands upward in two large arcs upward and then together, ending with the thumbs touching and palms facing down.

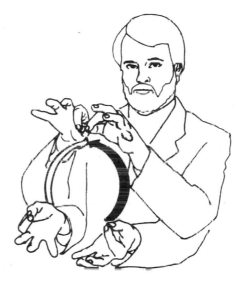

WORTHY (B) See DESERVE (A)

WRATH See ANGER

WRITE See SCRIPTURE

WRONG, ERROR, MISTAKE

Formation: Tap the chin with the middle fingers of the right *Y hand,* palm facing in.

YAHWEH *(Hebrew)* See GOD (B)

YARMULKE (Hebrew), KIPPAH (Hebrew), SKULLCAP

The hand in this sign demonstrates the shape of the traditional head covering worn by Jewish males.

Formation: Tap the fingertips of the right *C hand,* palm facing down, on top of the head with a double movement.

YESHIVA (A) (Hebrew)

This initialized sign is formed similar to COLLEGE and refers to an institute of Talmudic learning.

Formation: Beginning with the palm side of the right *Y hand* on the palm of the left *open hand,* palm facing up, bring the right hand upward in an arc.

See also SEMINARY for another sign formed in a similar manner.

YESHIVA (B) (Hebrew)

This is an initialized sign.

Formation: Move the right *Y hand,* palm facing forward, in a small circular movement near the right shoulder.

YHWH *(Hebrew)* See GOD (B)

YOM KIPPUR (A) (Hebrew), DAY OF ATONEMENT

This sign is a combination of DAY and SORROW.

Formation: Place the elbow of the bent right arm, index finger pointing up, on the back of the left *open hand.* Move the extended right finger down toward the elbow of the bent left arm held across the body. Then rub the palm side of the right *A hand* over the heart with a repeated movement.

YOM KIPPUR (B) (Hebrew), DAY OF ATONEMENT

The hand in the sign beats on the chest as a sign of sorrow and refers to the Jewish holiday on which fasting and prayer for the atonement of sins is prescribed.

Formation: Knock the palm side of the right *A hand* against the left side of the chest with a quick double movement.

See also FRUM for a sign formed in a similar manner but with a slower movement.

ZAKAT (Arabic), CHARITY, OFFERING

The hands in this sign seem to show putting money in a place of offering. Zakat, one of the five pillars of Islam, is the obligatory alms paid by self-sufficient Muslims to aid the Islamic community. Zakat also contributes to purify the giver of selfishness and greed.

Formation: Move the fingers of the right *flattened O hand,* palm facing left, to the left to touch the palm of the left *curved hand,* palm facing right.

ZEAL See METHODIST

ZIZITH (Hebrew), TZITZIT (Hebrew)

The fingers in this sign seem to pull on the tassels of thread located on the four corners of prayer aprons worn by Jewish males which serve as reminders of God's commandments.

Formation: With the fingertips of both *G hands* touching each hip, bring the hands down and out while pinching the thumb and index fingers together as the hands move.

ZUHR (Arabic), DHUHR (Arabic)

The second of the ritual prayers, offered in the middle of the morning by Muslim worshippers every day.

Formation: Move the right *X hand,* palm facing down, from left to right across the forehead.

PRAYERS AND BLESSINGS

THE LORD'S PRAYER

Our Father, who art in heaven, hallowed be Thy name. Thy kingdom come. Thy will be done on earth as it is in heaven. Give us this day our daily bread. And forgive us our trespasses, as we forgive those who trespass against us. And lead us not into temptation, but deliver us from evil. For thine is the kingdom, and the power, and the glory forever. Amen.

Matthew 6

Our

Father

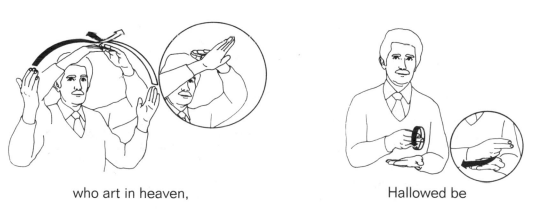

who art in heaven,

Hallowed be

Thy

name.

Thy

kingdom

come.

Thy

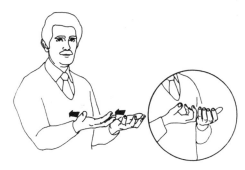

will

be done

on earth

as it is

in heaven.

Give us

this

day

our daily

bread.

And

forgive us

our trespasses,

as

we

forgive

those who

trespass

against

us.

And lead

us

not

into

temptation,

but

deliver

us

from

evil.

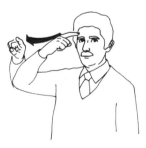

For

thine is

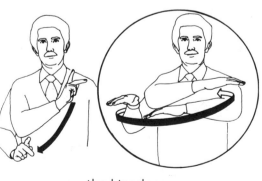

the kingdom,

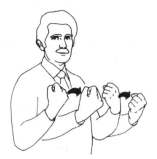  

and the power,   and the glory   forever.

Amen.

GLORIA PATRI

Glory to the Father, and to the Son, and to the Holy Spirit, as it was in the beginning, is now, and will be forever. Amen.

Glory

to the Father,

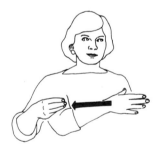

and

to the Son,

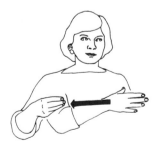

and

to the Holy Spirit,

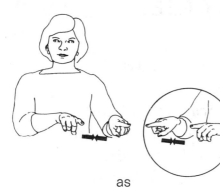

as

it was

in the beginning,

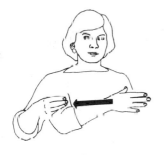

is now,

and

will be forever.

Amen.

THE APOSTLE'S CREED

*I believe in God the Father Almighty, Maker of
heaven and earth.
I believe in Jesus Christ, His only Son, our Lord, who
was conceived by the Holy Spirit, born of the Virgin Mary,
suffered under Pontius Pilate, was crucified, died,
and was buried. He descended into hell. The third day
He rose again from the dead. He ascended into heaven
and sits at the right hand of God, the Father Almighty.
From thence He will come to judge
the living and the dead.
I believe in the Holy Spirit, the holy Christian church,
the communion of saints, the forgiveness of sins,
the resurrection of the body, and the life everlasting.
Amen.*

I

believe in

God the Father

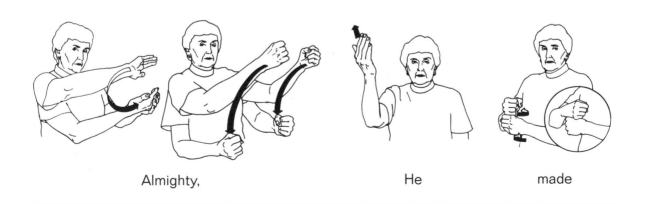

Almighty,　　　　　　　　　　　　　He　　　　made

heaven

and earth.

I

believe in

Jesus

Christ,

His only

Son,

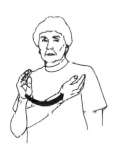

our

Lord,

who was conceived by

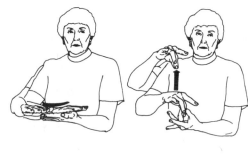

the Holy Spirit,

born

of the

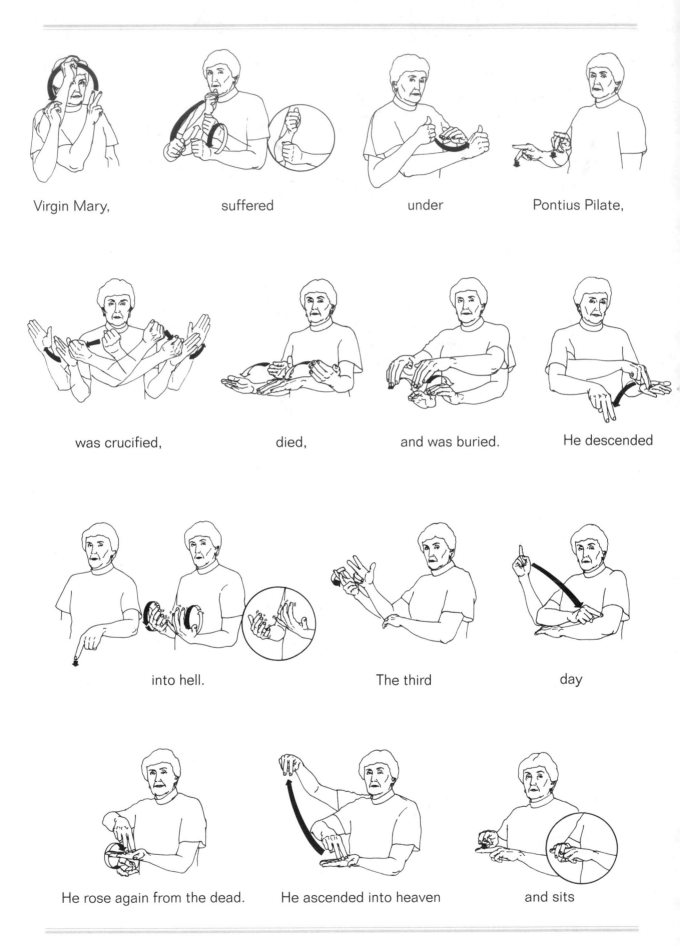

Virgin Mary,

suffered

under

Pontius Pilate,

was crucified,

died,

and was buried.

He descended

into hell.

The third

day

He rose again from the dead.

He ascended into heaven

and sits

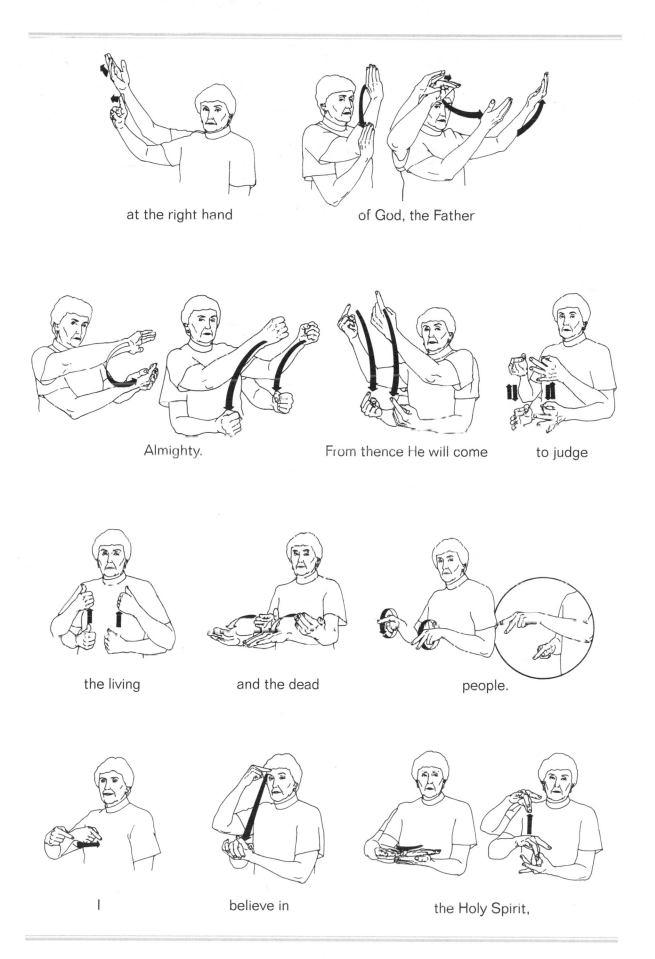

at the right hand

of God, the Father

Almighty.

From thence He will come

to judge

the living

and the dead

people.

I

believe in

the Holy Spirit,

the holy
Christian church,

the communion of saints,

the forgiveness of

sins,

the resurrection of the body,

and

the life

everlasting.

Amen.

PRAYER FOR GRACE

Let the words of my mouth and the meditation of my heart be acceptable in your sight, O Lord, my strength and my Redeemer.

Psalm 19.14

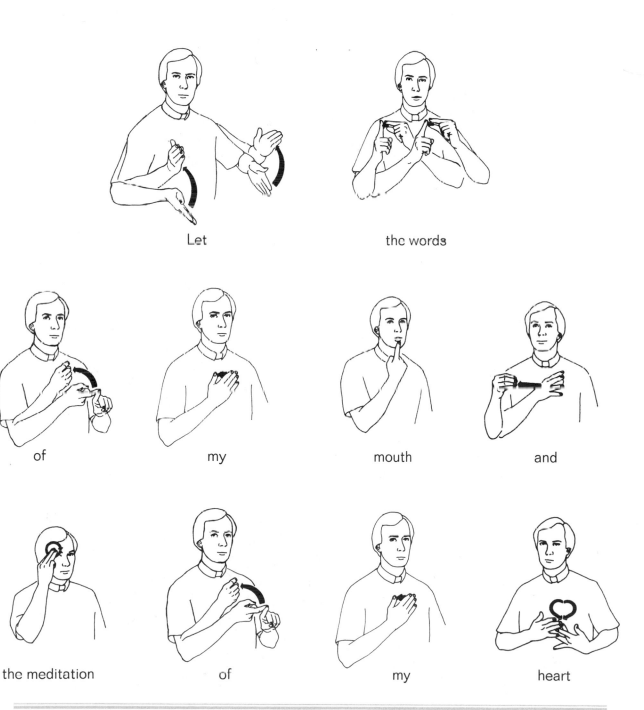

Let   the words

of   my   mouth   and

the meditation   of   my   heart

be acceptable

in

your

sight,

O

Lord,

my

strength

and

my

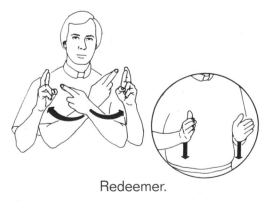

Redeemer.

GIVING OF THANKS

O give thanks unto the Lord, for He is good, for His mercy endureth forever. Amen.

Psalm 106.1

O

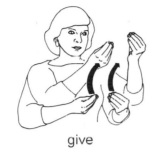

give

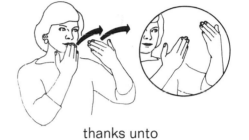

thanks unto

the Lord,

for

He

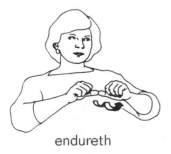

is good,

for

His mercy

endureth

forever.

Amen.

THE SHEMA

Hear, O Israel, the Lord is our God. The Lord is One.

Hear,

O Israel,

the Lord is

our

God.

The Lord is

One.

BLESSING OVER THE SABBATH CANDLES

Blessed are you, O Lord our God, King of the universe, who has sanctified us with His commandments and commanded us to kindle the Sabbath lights.

Blessed are

you,

O Lord

our

God,

King

of the universe,

who

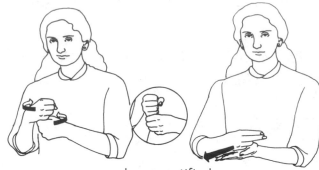

has sanctified

us

with

His

commandments

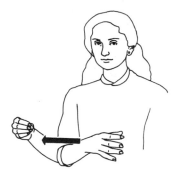

and

commanded

us

to kindle the Sabbath lights.

THE KIDDUSH

Blessed are you, O Lord our God, King of the universe, who created the fruit of the vine.

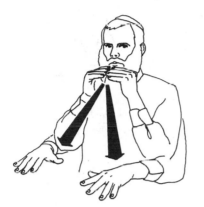

Blessed are

you,

O Lord

our

God,

King

of the universe,

who   created

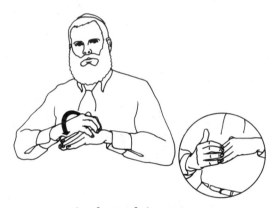

the fruit of the vine.

BLESSING OVER THE BREAD

Blessed are you, O Lord our God, King of the universe, who brings forth bread from the earth.

Blessed are

you,

O Lord

our

God,

King

of the universe,

who

brings forth

bread

from

the earth.

ABOUT THE AUTHOR

DR. ELAINE COSTELLO, author of *Signing: How to Speak With Your Hands*, has been an educator and author associated with the field of deafness for more than thirty-five years. She holds a bachelor of science degree from Washington University in St. Louis and a master of science degree from the University of Kansas, both with a major in deaf education. For ten years she was a classroom teacher and supervisor in schools for the Deaf, followed by ten years teaching and developing curriculum at Gallaudet University in Washington D.C., the world's only liberal arts university for the Deaf. For the last fifteen years before retiring, Dr. Costello founded and served as director of the Gallaudet University Press.

ABOUT THE ILLUSTRATOR

LOIS LEHMAN, who has been deaf since birth, is a native of Buffalo Center, Iowa. A graduate of the Iowas School for the Deaf in Council Bluffs, she received her bachelor of arts degree from Gallaudet University. Best known for her skill in drawing the human hand, she has illustrated many books, including *Signing: How to Speak With Your Hands*. Ms. Lehman is presently employed at the Pentagon as an illustrator in the graphics division. She is married to Robert H. Lenderman.